DATE DUE

OCT 1 9 '68			
GAYLORD			PRINTED IN U.S.A.

A
Churchill
Canvas

John George Spencer Churchill.

A
Churchill
Canvas

John Spencer Churchill

With Photographs

LITTLE, BROWN AND COMPANY   BOSTON   TORONTO

TO

MY WIFE

LULLAN

Preface

A N AUTOBIOGRAPHY is not only an opportunity but
also perhaps a necessity for revealing the whys and
wherefores of a private life and professional career.

Unfortunately, many great men cannot spare the time
to write their stories, or are reluctant to do so because of
secrets. For these people, their achievements stand as their
autobiographies — and how boring they can be when writers get to work on them! Of course there are exceptions,
and three instances come to mind of memoirs so reward-
ing as to render superfluous the work of any biographer.

Catherine the Great, in her candid account of the first
thirty tempestuous years of her life, discloses more of her
real self than all her achievements. And when Richard
Wagner took it upon himself to write *My Life* up to the
age of fifty, when his troubles diminished as a result of
meeting King Ludwig of Bavaria, he told his story to his
second wife Cosima. Even though it is clearly edited by
her, the revelations in this document do, in my opinion,
surpass all six volumes of his biography by Ernest New-
man.

A third example is the initial thirty-five years of struggle of my uncle, Sir Winston Churchill, recorded in *My Early Life*. It exposes his innermost thoughts and reactions so precious that no biographer could hope to capture them. Alas, my uncle's desire for autobiography has been lost forever, and the rest of his story must be left to someone else's pen.

To my mind, the essence of autobiography is sincerity of purpose and unadorned veracity. Accordingly I present my humble treatise on my own struggling years, telling what went on behind the scenes, as it were, without much information on the serious side of my career and profession.

This book came into being when I told it to my wife Lullan while on holiday in the South of France. It was the year of my fiftieth birthday.

I am indebted to my brother Pebin and other relatives and friends for reminiscences, and to John Harman for his editorial advice.

J.S.C.

Adam and Eve Mews, London

Contents

Preface   vii

I   Churchills, Spencers and Berties   3

II   Uncle Winston Moves In   27

III   Acrobatics at Harrow   48

IV   The Churchills Invade North America   74

V   Beret, Cloak, Riding Breeches   99

VI   Romance of a Pagan   142

VII   The Sword and the Scabbard   185

VIII   George Spencer, Interior Decorator   226

IX   Adam and Eve Mews   272

X   Today and Tomorrow   297

Illustrations

John George Spencer Churchill
Frontispiece

In special section between pages 148 and 149.

The Author's Mother, Lady Gwendoline Churchill
The Author's Father, Major John Strange Spencer Churchill
The Author with His Grandmother, Lady Randolph Churchill
The Author, Aged Four
At Blenheim, 1913
With His Brother, 1917
Fullback, Rugby
The Author and His Brother, Brighton, 1925
Harrow: Gymnastic Champion
Family Group Taken in the Admiralty, 1914
In the Admiralty Twenty-five Years Later, 1939
Lady Randolph Churchill's Funeral, 1921
In America, 1929
At Downing Street after Clarissa's Wedding
Lullan Boston and the Author
Wedding Picture of Lullan Boston, Author's Fourth Wife
Lullan and Author Playing Piano
Princess Natasha Saying Good Morning to the Author
The Author Painting

Meditation in Positano, 1952

Author Playing Piano

Decorative Painting for Lloyd George: the Bay of Tigullio, Italy

Painting of Dunkirk from Bray Dunes

Angela Culme-Seymour, First Wife

Mary Cookson, Second Wife

Kathlyn Tandy, Third Wife

Sally at Eighteen

The Anson Bomber and Wing Commander Cundell and the Author

A New Hat

The Beard, 1951

General View of Marlborough Pavilion, 1949

Presentation Portrait to Sir Winston on His Eightieth Birthday

Bust of My Uncle, 1933

Bust of Wagner, Bronzed, 1932

Bust of Author by Fiore Henriquez, 1951

Illustration of Sand Castle at Overstrand, 1914

Working on Illuminated Transparent Glass Painting

Cloak and Beret at Portofino

The Author with Spanish Group of Artists in Segovia, 1950

Sculpting Group at Slade School, 1949

Italian Group of Artists in Rome, 1952

Sir Winston Conducting Water Operations

Sally and Her Temple House, Fairlawne, 1937

Yester, Scotland

The Author and His Brother on the Land at Rushall, 1932

A
Churchill
Canvas

I

Churchills, Spencers and Berties

I WAS CHRISTENED in Westminster Cathedral plain John George. Even now my kinsman the Duke of Marlborough calls me John George — in full — and so does my cousin Randolph when he wants to be pompous.

But in life I became Johnny; and it was I who decided it should be Johnny with a *y*.

The name is said to be derived from zany, meaning a clown. Certainly I have accepted that role. Encouraged by my mother's younger brother, Jimmy Bertie, who used to tease me a lot and is a more proficient clown than myself, I have invariably played the fool. It just came naturally. He and I were the madcaps in our dignified and serious-minded family circle. My grandmother once told me that Jimmy Bertie (pronounced, for some reason, Bartie) was so odd that up to the age of five he was quite unable to find his own mouth.

"What did he do when he felt hungry and wanted an egg?" I asked.

"He always put it in his ear," was the answer.

I must say I have never put egg in my ear, but I have

become involved in some pretty extraordinary happenings one way and another, because of either my own folly or inherited destiny, or both. Some years ago I went to a fortuneteller in Battersea Pleasure Gardens. "I am a Gemini," I told her. "My birthday is the thirty-first day of May, 1909."

"Great heavens!" she exclaimed. "You are a terrible fellow! You have a dual nature. It is as if the twins Castor and Pollux were struggling against each other. You have tremendous vitality and yet you are lazy. You are faithful, yet you can be unfaithful. You are an idealist and a dreamer, but at the same time you are a man of action. You are extremely talented, and misfortune is mingled with your success. You are proud yet humble, violent but controlled. You suffer from dreadful fits of depression and are also very gay."

She paused dramatically and added: "Now let me see your palms."

I held them out across the table. She gazed in disbelief. I have three lines on each: the Heart, Head and Life lines. Nothing else.

"You are the master of your own future," she said. "You have no Fate line. You are the one who decides what happens. These are the hands of an engineer, or perhaps a surgeon."

"Wrong!" I was able to interrupt at last. "I am, amongst other things, a musician. And these are the hands of a musician — I think."

She smiled the superior smile of a woman who is never caught out. "They are sensitive, strong and capable hands.

Anyway, engineering and music have a lot in common. Both are mathematical."

She was right. In fact, most of her findings were so astoundingly correct, and such a large number of people born under my sign of the zodiac have the same capacity for a double nature, that I am prepared to believe it is the stars which give us our temperaments. However, if the possibly inevitable characteristics of a Gemini are somewhat alarming, they are nothing compared with what I have without doubt inherited from my grandparents.

On my father's side, my grandfather was Lord Randolph Churchill, son of the bewhiskered, obstinate, yet kindly seventh Duke of Marlborough. Lord Randolph had tremendous zest and self-confidence, making little headway with lessons at school but excelling at sport (just as I did in years to come). At Eton he was nicknamed Gooseberry because of his protuberant eyes, and when he went to Oxford a favorite pastime was breaking windows. Fussy about clothes, he had a reputation for being a bit of a dandy and became a heavy smoker, using a diamond-encrusted cigarette holder (I much prefer cigars; the best I can afford). He had an alert eye for a pretty woman — as an artist I do not exactly ignore feminine charm myself — and when in 1873 he went to Cowes Royal Regatta and saw the fabulously beautiful Jennie Jerome, daughter of wealthy New York stockbroker Leonard Jerome, he decided to marry her. His father was horrified. He looked down his ducal nose and remarked: "Mr. Jerome seems to be a vulgar sort of man." Nevertheless, the upkeep of Blenheim Palace was crippling the family budget, particularly after the extravagances of the fifth and sixth dukes, and when Mr. Jerome let himself be persuaded into offering a dowry of fifty thousand pounds, opposition to the marriage promptly melted.

I remember the dark-eyed Lady Randolph well. Her graciousness and domineering personality made a tremendous impression on me. Robert Rhodes James, in his biography *Lord Randolph Churchill,* records that although she was spirited and delightful company, she had a habit of making dreadful *gaffes.* For example, one afternoon when Lord Falmouth was being entertained at tea at her town house, she happened to glance through the window. A four-wheel cab had stopped in the street and an elderly woman was getting out.

"Who on earth is that old demon?" asked Lady Randolph.

Lord Falmouth replied with dignity: "It is my mother."

I cannot recall having blundered as badly as that, but I claim to have inherited Lady Randolph's vitality and musical talent. She was of course the mother of my uncle, Sir Winston Leonard Spencer-Churchill, and my father, Jack Churchill. She had two sisters, each remarkable in different ways. The eldest, Clara Jerome, married a Mr. Frewen, and her daughter Clare became the famous sculptress Clare Sheridan, who plays a great part in my life. Her next sister, Leonie Jerome, married Sir John Leslie, and her son, now the famous writer Sir Shane Leslie, very nearly comes up to the standard of the zanyism of the Berties. He maintains, incidentally, that there could very well be some Red Indian blood in the Jerome

family, through Leonard's wife. It is an honorable supposition.

The Churchills are Protestants of long standing who as
a rule find it hard to laugh at themselves. This can create
an aloof atmosphere at times. By contrast, on my mother's
side, the Berties exude an enormous sense of humor, combined with the indomitable will to survive which is essential for an active, varied life. My maternal grandpa,
Lord Abingdon, had his appendix taken out when he was
ninety, and I went for a walk with him in the snow at
Oxford only a few weeks after the operation.

Mother's mother, who was very small, elegant, reserved
and charming, did something which is rather interesting.
She left Grandpa and ran off with another man into the
middle of Europe. Grandpa chased and found her, and
gave an ultimatum, saying in effect:

"If you come back, I will forget and forgive. But if you
don't, there'll be the most awful stink."

She came back, and he kept his promise. The subject
was never mentioned again. Which is the reason why I
made an identical offer to my first wife, Angela, when she
ran away. I gave her a chance. "Return," I said, "and we
will say no more about it." She accepted the offer but
stipulated that I must wait for her to finish her affair,
which I refused to do.

My younger brother Peregrine and I were Grandpa's
favorite grandchildren, though we did not inherit anything from him except a watch which my brother still
possesses and a gold-topped walking stick which I left on
top of a bus; I am seldom lucky with inheritances. The

two of us used to stay with Grandma and Grandpa at least once a year. They invited us because they were fond of my mother, who was very beautiful, and because their own children were always away and the house seemed empty.

Peregrine and I enjoyed these visits. Allowed to do entirely what we liked, we had the run of the place. We got on well together. We understood each other and shared the same interests. Peregrine was destined to become an engineer; consequently our play was either constructive — we built bridges, dams and treehouses — or it was organized with mathematical precision. If we went for a bicycle ride, it was to a prearranged spot. We worked out a timetable beforehand, planning the journey minute by minute, and stuck to it. Peregrine in other words was a calming influence, in contrast to my Uncle Winston's son Randolph, who had completely the opposite effect. He brought out the imp in me. We could not be in the same room together without there being a frightful prank. The outcome was usually a frantic chase throughout the house, upstairs and downstairs, with cushions being snatched from chairs and sofas and hurled around as ammunition; how our parents stood it I do not know. Yet although I was a boy who thrived on company, I was independent. I could be completely happy on my own. During the last war I often wondered how I would occupy my time if I were taken prisoner. The answer is that I would not have even needed a book or pencil and paper to be content. I would have sat back and either composed music or listened to the hours of music "tape-recorded" in my head.

Grandpa, who was a Roman Catholic convert as a result of marrying a Townley as his first wife, had two main eccentricities. The first concerned breakfast. When the rest of us had come downstairs into the dining room, we would wait for him. As soon as he arrived, each of us was given a bowl of the most delicious porridge. Thick cream and salt (it had to be salt, not sugar) were added, and then, holding our bowls, we advanced to the window and ate the porridge standing up. Goodness knows why we had to eat the porridge course standing at the window; it was just one of those extraordinary things. The solemn silence of the occasion was broken from time to time by a whirring noise, caused by Grandpa's waxed mustache scraping the inside of his basin.

Grandpa's other eccentricity was changing houses. During the twenty years or so I knew him he must have moved at least twenty times — a fantastic performance. The reason, I am told, is that he had quarreled with his son, Lord Norris, who died before I was born, and was determined to wipe out the Abingdon fortune by spending as much of it as possible. Accordingly he began the most costly Grand Tour of Oxfordshire ever devised, buying enormous country mansions one after the other and selling them again, endearing himself to estate agents no doubt, and testing the patience of my poor grandmother, who had to bear the domestic brunt of perpetual upheaval. Practically every time I went to stay with Grandpa and Grandma I had to find my way to a different address. As a result, I have stayed in almost every big house around Oxford. Brackley, Great Milton, Headington End,

Bicester, Cumnor — Grandpa bought and sold them all. Grandma coped with the situation magnificently. She traveled in India for many years and had a vast collection of skin rugs, ornaments, round brass trays and similar bric-a-brac to shift at each move. But she managed to install herself firmly in each house and make it seem a permanent home, with an atmosphere that was peculiarly "Abingdon." She carefully collected the rose petals as they fell off the bushes in the garden and put them in bowls and vases, filling the place with fragrance. No milk was ever wasted. There were always muslin bags hanging in the pantry to make delicious cream cheese.

My grandparents had far more servants than people usually employ nowadays — housemaids, parlormaids, butlers and cooks — but neither of them liked ostentation. They lived quietly. Rare moments of splendor occurred when each of them died, and the Berties with the help of my father staged banquets at Abingdon with lashings of port. Banquets used to be definitely "the thing" at funerals. The Duke of Marlborough, traditionally a thoughtful, generous and most efficient organizer of family gatherings, staged an appropriate banquet at Blenheim when my father died.

It was the Bertie side of the family which started the use of the remarkable Christian name of Peregrine. In 1552 Richard Bertie married Katherine, widow of the Duke of Suffolk, whose first wife had been the sister of Henry VIII. Katherine was an ardent Protestant and therefore unpopular with Queen Mary, so she and her husband fled to the Continent, where they lived as wandering exiles. It seems that on October 12, 1555, she was visiting Cologne Cathedral when her labor pains began. She hurried towards the door but got only as far as the porch when a son was born. She called him Peregrine be-cause it means stranger in a foreign country. Thus it became a family name.

The Berties have a habit of going haywire about Chris-tian names. Grandpa's brother was called Alberic, which is reasonable, I suppose, but his sons were Arnaud and Schomberg! The latter had a daughter Dagmar, which I feel is going a bit far.

My mother was christened Gwendoline and her eldest brother Arthur. When they were very small children, neither could pronounce the other's name properly, so my mother became Goonie and my uncle was Tata. Soon after I was born I was nicknamed Toto, much to the irritation of my father. He quickly put a stop to it. Writing from Blenheim, where he happened to be staying, he ordered: *For goodness' sake don't call him that or it will stick to him for his wretched life.*

My brother's christening in Westminster Cathedral was a memorable ceremony at which Mother got terribly con-fused. She really wanted a girl — I did my best to help by praying hard for a baby sister — and she had been think-ing entirely in terms of girls' names. Whereas I'd had the Duke of Norfolk for a godfather, my brother had Uncle Winston. This fact decided one of my brother's names, and after agonizing indecision Mother agreed to call the boy Charles Winston. The priest was about to make the sign of the cross when she raised a hand.

"No!" she said. "Call him Henry Winston!"

He soon became known as Peregrine Winston, but since I was only four, Peregrine was too much of a mouthful for me. I invented the superb name of Pebin (or, as my uncle writes it, Pebbin), which he is called to this day.

My sister, ten years younger than I and now Lady Eden, had an even more unusual name-giving. She was suffering from a cold and had to be christened in the day nursery at home. Her godmother, Lady Islington, liked her own name of Ann, but Mother wanted to be more colorful. Inspiration came. Suddenly she remembered that she was currently reading the novel *Clarissa Harlowe* and the famous poem *Aucassin and Nicolette*. What could be better? My sister got the three: Ann Clarissa Nicolette.

Father's courtship of Mother had a delightful romantic touch. He used to ride on horseback the seven miles between Blenheim Palace and Whytham Abbey, the Abingdon family home just outside Oxford. Whytham was a fine house set in a lovely beech wood. How anyone could bear to sell it I could not think, but it went the way of all Grandpa's homes. The buyer was a Dutch South African named Schumacher who felt that his name sounded too foreign. He changed to, of all names, ffennell. Mr. ffennell built a gigantic stoep on the back of the abbey. The idea was to remind him of the land of his success, but it made the place look like a tea-garden restaurant. He died and left the property to Oxford University, which I cannot help feeling must have been one of his more rational acts.

In their courting days, Mother and Father had to contend with stiff opposition from their families. For one thing, there was the difference in faiths; for another, the Churchills are not nearly so firmly rooted in the past as the Berties, who tend to regard them as upstarts. Not to put too fine a point on the matter, I would say that the Berties scorn the Churchills. They have a great capacity for ruthlessness. They can break off a conversation simply by leaving the room. I cannot actually remember any of them getting up from the breakfast table and leaving for Hong Kong without another word, but it would not surprise me if one of them has. Berties do not care two hoots who anybody is. And to me, this complete independence is immensely attractive.

The Churchills are not without history, however; not by any means. My uncle in his life of Marlborough traces the family's genealogy and arms from Otho de Leon through his sons Richard and Wandrill, Lords of Courcelle, the younger of whom came to England with William the Conqueror. After a while there emerged "John, Lord of Currichill, or as tis in diverse records, Chirechile, since called Churchill in Somersetshire." Everything went swimmingly until the reign of Edward I, when the lordship of Churchill was seized by the Crown and given to some favorite. He and his successors refused to let go of it until about Henry VIII's reign, when it passed through the hands of a family named Jennings. In 1652 the lordship returned to a rightful owner, as it were, when it was bought by Sir John Churchill, formerly Master of the Rolls, but by this time the purity of descent had been tampered with and the genealogical tree, as my uncle puts it, enters a "rather shady phase." It seems that John

Churchill's great-grandfather was a mere blacksmith.

Sarah, Duchess of Marlborough, probably had the last word on this complex genealogy business when in her old age she read Lediard's history of the late duke. She commented: "This history takes a great deal of pains to make the Duke of Marlborough's extraction very ancient. That may be true for aught I know; but it is no matter whether it be true or not in my opinion. I value nobody for another's merit."

Before leaving the subject altogether I would like to mention something about the Churchills which puzzles many people. My contemporary namesake, John Churchill of the Foreign Office, who is a direct descendant of one of the first duke's brothers, has said to me that we are not really Churchills at all, but Spencers. When my correspondence gets sent to him in Chelsea by mistake he forwards it politely, adding *Spencer* on the envelope. Of course he is right in a sense; the first duke's only son died at Cambridge and the dukedom was carried through his daughter Henrietta as second duchess and then her sister Anne, who married Charles Spencer, Earl of Sunderland. Her son became the third duke, and it was not until the fifth duke that the family became Churchill again, by adding it to Spencer.

I would have thought that girls were just as capable of handing down a title as boys. In England, though, it cannot be done — unlike some Continental countries such as Spain, where indeed it has occurred in our family. The Duke of Marlborough's sister Arabella had an illegitimate son by James II of England who was created Duke of

Berwick, as was the custom in those days. He married the Duchess of Alba and so became the Duke of Alba and Berwick, the latter being his English title. Debrett and Burke, the snob reference books, do not admit it, however, which always annoyed the late Duke of Alba.

To return to the troubles Mother and Father endured when courting, they probably found the Churchill family motto "Faithful but Unfortunate" somewhat depressing, but at least the Bertie motto "Valor is Stronger than a Battering Ram" lent encouragement. Eventually their respective families saw reason and the couple were married in the Roman Catholic church of St. Aloysius, Oxford, in August, 1908. My uncle married Clementine Hozier one month later, and the two weddings were the social events of the year.

Father bought No. 10 Talbot Square as a London house and I was born in a small bedroom on the top floor. A year later the family moved to No. 41 Cromwell Road, and not long afterwards Mother made a trip to Russia with Admiral Beatty and his wife and son David on a "prestige" mission.

Mother was an extremely intelligent and attractive woman. She had terrific social talent and charm, and although untutored made up for her academic deficiencies by studying the latest reviews of books, concerts, plays and so on. This made her very knowledgeable about the contemporary scene and she was never at a loss for something worthwhile to say. The eminent men and women in the world of the arts who were her guests found her a delightful, amusing and well-informed hostess.

Father, too, had elegance and charm. He was slightly better-looking than my uncle, with a more clearly cut mouth, blue eyes, and the same distinctive cranium as all Churchills. People sought his company, but frankly he was not what I would call intelligent. Although he shared my passion for Wagner he had no real understanding of art, and his love for his first-class library hardly went deeper than admiration for the covers and bindings, especially first editions; he seldom actually read the books. We had about nine servants, including at one period an excellent cook from the French Embassy whose wages amounted to only a hundred pounds a year, so he was completely free of the domestic chores which can burden a husband's life nowadays. When not preoccupied with business affairs he sank into a brown leather armchair with *The Times* or a book by his friend A. E. W. Mason, who was a frequent visitor, and did not surface again until the next meal was ready. In the evenings he had a habit of saving electricity by walking round the house switching off lights, leaving the rest of us to grope through corridors in the dark.

He worked conscientiously as a stockbroker, Monday to Friday every week except for three weeks' holiday in August, and made a comfortable income, but although his cautiousness saved his clients from losing their money, without doubt he could have done much better for them and himself if he had shown more enterprise and dash. Boldness was constantly being urged upon him by my uncle, whom he idolized, but who, it must be acknowledged, pinched all the brains of the family.

It is often thought that because we are Churchills we

never have financial worries. The truth is that we have to work for our living the same as everyone else. There was no succulent nest egg, no vast family fortune to inherit. When my grandfather Lord Randolph died, he provided a lot of extremely complicated trusts to be divided and subdivided among his children and grandchildren. After all these years I still have my own trust, but, having been retrusted and eaten into by death duties, it does not amount to very much by today's standards; when tax has been taken off, it just about pays my gin bill. Father was able to launch into the Stock Exchange because at Harrow he befriended such pupils as Lionel Rothschild and Ernest Cassell. They stood by him in later years and loaned him money to buy his partnership which he paid off with interest. Today I am great friends with the sons of these famous and generous men.

How early can one remember? I cannot recall anything before the age of four, but I am told that when I was two I was distraught at losing my pet dog Beno. He was found on January 20, 1911, after a month, and next day the *Daily Mirror* published a half-page of pictures — I was nephew of the then Home Secretary — showing Beno proudly sitting in my pram with me. The dog was given to Grandpa and lived to the fine age of fifteen, so although I do not remember the lost-and-found episode, it lived with me for years afterwards.

One of the first incidents I do remember is being painted by that brilliant painter of children Harrington Mann when I was four. The picture turned out to be very good indeed. He also painted Mother, but it did not quite come up to the standard of the one of me, and both pictures were badly damaged when relegated to the attic for the Second World War. John Sargent, on the other hand, did a magnificent charcoal sketch of Mother and another of my grandmother, who wanted him to do one of Aunt Clemmie as well, but I do not think he ever got around to it. I have the original of the sketch of my mother, and my uncle has the original of his mother's. Both these magnificent drawings set for me at a very early age the example of the charcoal technique in portraiture. I also remember my bust being carved in marble by some woman sculptress whose name escapes me. It was a most creditable piece of work but has completely vanished, though who on earth would want the bust of a small boy with Chinese slit eyes and a button snub nose I cannot imagine.

Right from my earliest days I had a great affection for Uncle Tata. He was an austere but engaging eccentric who, it was whispered, had got himself into a difficult situation with a lady. His drastic answer to the problem was to become a monk at Downside Abbey. Nevertheless, he was definitely not cut out for the rigors and routines of monastic life. He kissed the wrong ring of a visiting cardinal and was out of the monastery pretty soon.

Uncle Winston was extremely fond of him. He had a quick brain and was most capable. He served as a staff officer in the First World War with the rank of major, but like all intelligent men was hated by the Army and had constant quarrels with the General Staff. The Foreign Office later sent him to Danzig; then he went to South

Africa, started a wattle farm, and married a divorcée named Ramsay. At the start of the next war he asked patriotically: "What can I do to help?" and was immediately put in charge of a prison camp. The laugh is that he spoke German so fluently, and looked so like a German with his brisk, upright manner, that the authorities had second thoughts. They put him inside the camp for a time as a prisoner.

When he died in 1957 he was buried in the cemetery of the Monastery of the Friars at East Bergholt, Suffolk, which is next door to Randolph's house. I was amazed to find myself taking part in an enormously long, winding procession, two deep, which included a choir. At the head were Uncle Tata's remains, pushed on an affair which I can only describe as a perambulator. Apparently it is a tradition for funeral processions at the monastery to make a tour of the grounds, for we trudged through the grass while horses peered curiously over hedges and neighed at us. Cows mooed and ducks quacked. I have never known a funeral quite like it.

When the moment of burial came we gathered round the hole and waited. Nobody seemed to know what to do. The priest in charge beckoned to my late uncle's young son Richard, who now is heir to the earldoms of Abingdon and Lindsey.

"If you want to put a flower or something in," he said, "now is the time for it."

Richard obliged, and that was the end of the ceremony.

Afterwards we adjourned to the Sun, the famous pub in Dedham next to the mill which Constable painted so often, and got gloriously tight. All in all, the event was typically Uncle Tata.

As a child, I often stayed at Blenheim. To us, the Duke of Marlborough of those days was always Uncle Sunny, and his wife, who later married a most pleasant Frenchman named Balsan and lived in New York, was Cousin Consuelo. I never made out the reason for these nicknames, since both the duke and duchess were first cousins of my father.

The total effect of their fabulous home is exceedingly fine. Given by a grateful nation to the first Duke of Marlborough for winning the battle of Blenheim, it is the biggest private house in England, except perhaps Welbeck: a British answer to Versailles in warm-colored Taynton stone. The beauty of the bridge over the great lake could not be surpassed; I give everyone responsible full marks for that. Furthermore, the basic conception of the palace is on the grandest scale, in splendid defiance of convenience. There are more than three hundred rooms to dust and clean; the state dining rooms are one hundred yards from the kitchens in the vaults, necessitating a complicated system of lifts and special hot cabinets to get food to the table before the gravy congeals, and pantry workers used to be so cut off from the rest of the world, slaving in the womb of this vast edifice, that they needed bicycles to get to their lavatories.

But despite the magnificence, Blenheim is an architectural monstrosity. Vanbrugh was not the architect to choose for an English stately home. Though Comptroller of the Works, he was a playwright — and a Dutchman,

anyway. His efforts at interpreting the Italian style in
England have produced a bastard of a building. He altogether misses the delightful classic proportions at which
the Italians excel. To take but one example, he built in
front of the balcony at one end of the gigantic Hall an
arch, wide and low, which makes me shudder whenever
I see it. Utterly unattractive, it belongs to no architectural
pedigree except perhaps the underside of a railway carriage roof. A more obvious blunder, of course, is the omis-
sion of a grand staircase. If one is going to put up with
the exhausting business of living in a palace one does, I
think, deserve the consolation of a really impressive flight
of stairs, with lots of white marble and crimson carpet,
down which to sweep aloofly whenever there is a ball or
reception. But incredible though it may seem, Vanbrugh
was so busy with his colonnades and gilded ceilings that
he forgot about such a utilitarian item as stairs. Eventually, in order to provide a means of getting from the
ground floor to the bedrooms which did not involve climbing ladders, he inserted a flight at the side of the Hall,
behind some pillars.

Four thousand or more visitors now tramp round
Blenheim daily, paying very welcome half-crowns for the
privilege. The Milk Cocktail Bar has achieved unique
success and crowds approach with due reverence the
small, heavily wallpapered bedroom with its brass bed-
stead in which my uncle was born on November 30, 1874.
The most popular exhibits in the palace, I am told, are
his baby shirt and locks of golden hair.

This atmosphere of commercialism, sadly unavoidable,

is enormously different from the Blenheim I knew as a child. In those days the palace was fully occupied and lived in. The splendor of Edwardian England was just passing its zenith. Carriages jingled up and down the gravel drives; guests, as elegant as if gowned by Cecil Beaton, moved with immense hauteur, and ladies who wanted to put in an appearance at breakfast were expected to wear jewelry and ankle-length dresses — a tiresome tradition which always made Lady Randolph protest that it was overdoing the pomp. The housekeeper, Mrs. Rymond, presided over the running of the palace and controlled every detail faultlessly. The cavernous grand salon, which today has the air of a museum, with visitors shuffling past the big banqueting table and tall chairs, was a family meeting place at mealtimes. I remember eating my bacon and eggs in there and feeling not in the least overawed by my surroundings. The gold plate, now brought out only on extra-special occasions, was used quite ordinarily, though I would say that the thrill of eating off gold is very overrated. One's knife and fork make as much clatter as if the plate were enamel, and I was always worried for fear some of the gold would chip off and get mixed with the vegetables. Of course, people who do not have their gold plate on public exhibition but like it to be known that they possess some are forced to eat off it. I remember once an old Spanish friend of mine, the Marques Santo Domingo, gave a large dinner party in Madrid, and towards the end of the meal I found a beautiful gold side plate in front of me. The food to be

eaten from it was sensible. It was a single, solitary chocolate.

I particularly recall that Blenheim had a "palace smell."
One sniffed it appreciatively on entering. It was rather
like the weighty smell of locked-in history which is still
found in English cathedrals, but with subtle domestic
hints of dusty brocade and decaying velvet. Perhaps the
windows were not opened frequently enough; perhaps
there was wood rot somewhere. Whatever the cause, it
was as thick and satisfying as the aroma of a good cigar.
These days, with the aristocracy abandoning stately homes
for cozier houses in the grounds or one wing of the building, it does not exist any more, which is a pity.

The technique of dealing with children at Blenheim
was to keep them strictly apart from the grownups. Undoubtedly child psychologists will condemn this as cruel
and harmful, but there is something to be said for it in
a home where the Brussels tapestries on the walls are
irreplaceable, where the exquisite collection of Meissen
china (which the present duchess spends three months of
every year cleaning) is priceless, and every little knick-
knack on every slender table is worth a film star's ransom.

Pebin and I and our cousins Randolph and Diana had
our own children's suite, well out of earshot of the rest of
the palace. The gun room, a completely circular room, was
allocated to us for dining purposes, and I still make a
point of looking for it when visiting Blenheim; now the
hide-out of the Duchess's private secretary, it has memories. Upstairs across the corridor opposite our bedrooms
was a door labeled W.C. — family initials which often

raised laughter. Bathtubbing arrangements, I remember, were surprisingly primitive. The baths were huge affairs and must have needed a fantastic amount of hot water to fill them. But to wallow in one was a luxurious experience. It was possible to sit up in comfort and contemplate, in the same sensible manner that the Japanese do when bathing.

One person who definitely did not like her bath at Blenheim was Isabel, our nurserymaid. She was bending over the tub, getting the water ready, when Randolph crept up and gave her bottom a shove. She toppled into the water fully dressed.

Perhaps the most fascinating item in the palace to a child's eyes was the enormous stuffed lion in the Hall. At first glance it looked exceptionally real and frightening, and when I was little chap I used to tiptoe past it warily, especially in the evenings, when shadows made the animal seem bigger. The great novelty was that you could make it roar by pulling a cord attached to, of all places, the creature's navel. Of course, as soon as we made the discovery of this, there was no stopping us. The Hall echoed and re-echoed for hours like the lion house at a zoo. During a Christmas party once, Randolph and Diana pulled the cord so often, and everyone got so heartily sick of the constant noise, that they were punished by being pushed out into the snow. They had to stand there until their voices froze and they promised to give the animal a rest.

Christmas usually included a visit to my uncle's. He adores children and used to enjoy playing with us. Charades, with their secrecy, dressing up and acting, particularly appealed to him. He was a generous uncle, and we in return always gave him the best presents we could afford, though choosing a gift for someone who already had everything he needed was a worry. I solved it by asking the advice of his butler, or his valet Walden, to whom he was so greatly attached that when in later years he wished to go abroad incognito he called himself Colonel Walden. Some of the presents, such as a pair of braces or a toothbrush, struck me as most dull, but at least I felt they were needed.

The wonderful part about it is that my uncle loved, and always has loved, receiving presents. No matter how small and humble the gift, he accepted it with surprise and pleasure.

"For me?" he would ask, his eyes lighting up. "How very kind!"

Then he would take the parcel into a quiet corner, open it carefully and examine the contents with the greatest possible interest.

To me, my uncle is exactly the same today as he was when I was a child. The chubby, pugnacious face and deep growling voice have not changed. In my early days I beheld him in fear, though not without criticism. This was because he lacked a mustache. Father had a large one and was so kind and generous to us children, and adored Mother so much, that I was convinced a mustache was the outward symbol of goodness. I assessed people by their mustaches. And I used to study Uncle's bare upper lip and wonder.

It was at Overstrand, near Cromer in Norfolk, that he

assumed his status in my mind as the supreme master builder. In the summer of 1914, our families spent an unforgettable holiday there. Five children were in the party — Diana, Randolph, myself, and the two new arrivals, Pebin and my cousin Sarah — and we rented two cottages. My father's was called Beehive Cottage; at the opposite end of the lawn was my uncle's, Pear Tree Cottage.

Excursions to the beach were organized with military thoroughness. We put on our waders, climbed down the cliffs, and were issued buckets and spades. Then Father and Uncle marked out on the smooth sand the ground plan for a fort of colossal dimensions. When finished, it was large enough for each of us to get into a turret and fight the incoming tide. As the waves swirled and creamed round the crumbling walls, my uncle was fortress commander.

"More sand for the outer defenses!" he shouted, flourishing his cigar. "Stop the moat from flooding! The inner walls are weakening. Hurry!"

Our excitement mounted. We shrieked and dug frantically while my uncle, his trouser legs rolled up to the knees, supervised our efforts with benevolent authority. Taking on impossible odds, fighting a battle he could not hope to win, intrigued him. Not until the very last moment, when all was lost and our glorious castle had vanished, were we allowed to abandon our posts and retreat.

He has always behaved like that on the sands. He was just the same with his daughter Mary Soames's children at Frinton.

II

Uncle Winston Moves In

AT THE END of August, 1914, our buckets and spades were packed away, the sand was shaken out of the picnic rugs, and we all trooped back to London. The capital was excited. In those days, the technique of war had scarcely advanced beyond cavalry charges and dressing up in splendid uniforms. It was colorful, stimulating — and victory seemed easy.

My uncle was one of the few people with enough vision to foresee the horrific struggle in store. For months past as First Lord of the Admiralty he had been busily shaking up the Royal Navy, getting it on a wartime basis and making it war-minded. His job as First Lord, which he attacked with typical enthusiasm, overflowed into our own lives to the extent that he brought his favorite senior officers to visit us. One of these was Admiral Beatty, a tough egg if ever there was one, with the unmistakable air of the sea about him. He wore his hat at a jaunty angle and walked with almost the swagger of a stage actor.

An outstanding moment in my young days was when he presented me, for my sailor suit, a hat ribbon of his flagship H.M.S. *Lion* of which I was extremely proud.

Father was called up in the Queen's Own Oxfordshire Hussars and posted abroad with the rank of major. Before he sailed, my uncle had a most remarkable photograph of the two families taken in one of the drawing rooms of the Admiralty. Seated in the middle was my grandmother, Lady Randolph, and on either side of her were my mother and Aunt Clemmie. Flanking the grownups were Father and my uncle, while the children were spread along the front. That was in October, 1914. Exactly twenty-five years later, in October, 1939, in the same Admiralty room and under the same picture, those of us who could be mustered from the original photograph were taken again in the same poses.

Christmas was spent at Blenheim. I believe it was one of those rare white Christmases, and we had the thrill of tobogganing down the Park Gate slopes and onto the ice-covered lake. The war had not yet got under way; the austerity which subdued later years was yet to come, so the duke and duchess held another of their famous fancy-dress parties. The rambling, mellowed palace came gloriously to life, with lights at every window, plenty of bright talk, laughter and, faintly from the long library, the sound of music. It must have been Mr. Perkins, whose business it was to come out from Oxford and play the long library organ from time to time to keep it in trim, who introduced me to Bach. The organ was a gigantic five-manual affair, and fifteen years elapsed before he allowed me to play it. Then I chose *The Mastersingers* overture, of all pieces! He was a bit shocked, but an orchestral effect played entirely

by ear is much more manageable on an instrument of this
kind.

Even at the age of five I was an eager party-goer. I
liked dressing up. For the Christmas 1914 celebrations at
Blenheim I wore a baggy suit and a battered bowler,
swung a cane jauntily, blackened my upper lip with burnt
cork and went as Charlie Chaplin. Imitations of Chaplin
and Lloyd George were my favorite party pieces.

The late Lord Birkenhead's family were guests at the
palace and I made firm friends with Eleanor Smith
and her brother Freddie, and my cousins Ivor and Cyn-
thia Guest. It was Eleanor who as Lady Eleanor Smith in
time ahead achieved fame as a writer on gypsy and circus
life, and introduced me to the exciting world she loved.

Randolph and I continued to terrorize Blenheim with
ferocious energy. When I think what our parents suffered,
I can only look on them as saints. Randolph kept daring
me to do dreadful things. Occasionally I refused; I was
too frightened of the wrath that would follow. But when I
set Randolph a dare he accepted it regardless. Randolph
was fearless. He still is.

The polished wood floor of the long library was scattered with polar bear rugs. We used to amuse ourselves by
playing with them, wrapping them around us and staging
bearfights. This rowdyism the duke and duchess tolerated
with boys-will-be-boys resignation. It so happened,
though, that the library was decorated with a pair of life-
size statues on pedestals. These depicted, in white marble,
two well-proportioned women having just stepped out of
the bath — or at least, so it seemed. Each was nude except

for a cloth arrangement clutched across her middle as a token gesture of modesty. It more or less hid her stomach, but only a quick glance was needed to discover that the cloth was quite inadequate at the rear. The lady's posterior was completely uncovered.

I nudged Randolph. "I dare you to wallop her one," I challenged.

"Done!" he replied, and although he was only about four, he scaled the pedestal as nimbly as a monkey. Very soon the august and dignified conversation of the duke, the duchess and their guests was rudely interrupted by loud and hearty whacks on a marble backside. The grownups were appalled. Everyone agreed that decency had been violated in a way which was quite beyond a joke. Randolph, protesting and struggling, was bundled off to bed and made to miss a party that evening.

The grownups indulged in fun of a different type. There was the terrible occasion when the duke and his friends decided to fill a kümmel bottle with ordinary water. Lord Birkenhead went and took a full glass of it in one swoop, thinking it to be kümmel, and collapsed with surprise. I am told that afterward he hated water so much he even cleaned his teeth in soda water.

During the early summer of 1915, after the failure of the Dardanelles, where Father was camp commandant, my uncle's political fortunes went under shadow. He was sacked from the Admiralty and made Chancellor of the Duchy of Lancaster. Asquith, the Prime Minister, is quoted as commenting: "I regard his future with many misgivings. I do not think he will ever get to the top in English politics."

From then on, whenever my uncle visited us, a majestic sadness hung around him. He withdrew to Hoe Farm, in Surrey, where we spent part of the summer, and was browsing around the house one sunlit afternoon, looking for a constructive means of filling in time, and suddenly saw my box of water-color paints. It was a fateful moment. There and then he decided to paint a picture. He had no idea how to go about it, but he sat down and was happily occupied for the rest of the day.

The result pleased him. And since he never does anything halfheartedly, he at once launched into painting in oils. He bought an enviable collection of equipment: an easel, palette, canvases, and tubes of every color.

What was to be his first big subject? Having long admired a Daubigny landscape owned by the Duke of Westminster, he borrowed it and made a most masterly copy which hangs in my home today.

I am pleased to think I may have played a part, if only an accidental one, in prompting my uncle to try his hand at painting. From the outset he had professional help and encouragement from that highly successful portrait painter, Sir John Lavery. Sir John, a close friend of our families, was also a talented painter of interiors. When I became old enough to analyze his work I discovered his inability to invent. He could not paint anything unless it was right there in front of him, under his nose. He was a sufficiently great man to admit that he lacked the talent for imagining details, whereas I possessed it, and when

Lloyd George asked him to do a mural at Churt, he recommended that I execute it, which I did in 1935. I admired Lavery's paintings with the same sincerity with which he admired mine. But we were quite different; his work was not at all my style. His wife Hazel, incidentally, was an extraordinarily attractive woman with green eyes and red hair. She was the "colleen" who used to appear on Irish stamps.

When not painting at the farm, my uncle used to amuse us by playing games. His specialty was "gorillas." He put on his oldest clothes, crouched behind bushes and hedges, and waited for one of us to come near. Then there was a terrifying eruption, a blood-tingling roar of "Grr! Grr!" and my uncle emerged, his arms swinging limply at his sides. He chased us and made for the nearest tree. The realism was alarming, but we squealed with delight and enjoyed this exclusive performance hugely. Few people can say they have seen an ex-First Lord of the Admiralty crouching in the branches of an oak, baring his teeth and pounding his chest with his fists.

For years my uncle had driven himself hard at his work, and the sinecure of the Duchy of Lancaster irritated him beyond endurance. He sailed for France and was given command of the 6th battalion of the Royal Scot Fusiliers early in 1916. He saw a great deal of action at dangerously close quarters, and even found time to do one or two paintings of Plugge Street, where his battalion was stationed.

As an economy measure, my mother and Aunt Clemmie decided to share our house in Cromwell Road. Fitting two families plus servants into a single tall, narrow building was in itself a squeeze, but very shortly the situation became incredible. Lloyd George assumed power as Prime Minister, and although he and my uncle had sharply disagreed on numerous previous occasions, my uncle was brought back into top-level politics as Minister of Munitions.

Instantly our cozy home became Uncle's war headquarters. The most important statesmen of the day, Lloyd George among them, knocked for admission at all hours; I recollect that dispatch boxes cluttered the hall and stairs, and we used to open doors to find the most unlikely rooms crammed with secretaries banging at typewriters. Telephones were installed at strategic points. Randolph and I had a fine time picking them up and shouting rude messages at bewildered operators.

At other times our nanny kept me quiet with painting lessons. Mostly it was a matter of carefully copying one of the birds made of silver which decorated the dining table. Also I used to study books. My father compelled me to read *The Conquest of Mexico* and *The Conquest of Peru*, a choice of literature for a small boy which strikes me as exceedingly strange.

When Pebin and I were given a box of Meccano we retreated to the one spot in the house which had escaped the invasion: the dining room. No sooner had we started work than my uncle drifted in, puffing at the inevitable cigar.

"And what are you making, eh?" he demanded.

"A cantilever crane," I told him.

"Hm." The cigar was sucked thoughtfully. "A bascule bridge would be much better, you know."

"But we haven't enough pieces!"

He waved a hand impatiently. This was a minor matter. A secretary was sent out to buy box after box of Meccano. Then, apparently forgetting he had a war on his hands, my uncle took off his coat and began preparing for the largest model bascule bridge ever. Pebin and I were enlisted as assistant builders, and much to the distress of the womenfolk, who were already upset at the chaos in the rest of the house, the dining room became our workshop. Hints were dropped about the inconvenience of half-finished girders resting across the sideboard, and of nuts and bolts littering the carpet. Protests were made. But my uncle refused to be deflected from his declared purpose. The final construction was a gigantic piece of engineering some fifteen feet long and eight feet high, with a roadway which could be lifted by means of wheels, pulleys and yards of string. The servants were forbidden to touch it, and my uncle gazed fondly at his creation during meals.

Eventually it proved to be too much of a nuisance in the dining room, stretching as it did from wall to wall across one end, and was transferred into the hall. If anything, this new site was even worse. Visitors, including members of the Cabinet, had to stoop under the raised center section of the bridge to get in and out of the door.

Two nurses and two nurserymaids were employed to look after us children. They were constantly changing because we were considered difficult. I often wonder, though,

if our naughtiness was not partly due to the punishments
we had to suffer. In a playful mood one day, Randolph
tipped his baby sister Sarah out of her cot. At this his
nurse's eyes glinted with sadistic pleasure. She pinned him
down, opened his mouth and forced a spoonful of mustard
inside. As if this was not enough, she rattled the spoon
against his upper and lower teeth as hard as she could.

Food fads used to come and go, just as they do now, but
were seldom pleasant. We were given blood pressed from
raw meat and mixed with tapioca. The result resembled
a ghastly mess of fishes' eyes, but likes and dislikes in food
were never tolerated. Our nurses stood over us and swiftly
dealt with anyone who tried to get out of eating a single
blood-red eye. I have never been able to make out why
such disgusting foods should be considered palatable, let
alone for children.

The delicious cake for tea helped to make up for the mis-
ery of lunch. Before the cake was even brought in, however,
we had to eat a fixed number of pieces of bread and dripping followed by two slices of bread and jam. And we
were not allowed much cake. Benger's Food last thing at
night was the other treat to which we all looked forward.

We fought back against this tyranny so obstinately that
in moments of crisis the nurses resorted to tricks to gain
control of the situation. For example, we had the notorious episode of the chocolate creams. Little Sarah was
especially fond of these sweets, and the larder was kept
well stocked with them. Lord Riddell, who was one of
Randolph's godfathers, and my godmother, Viscountess
Harcourt, always presented us with an enormous box at

Christmas. Nevertheless, we were strictly rationed to one each after a meal, and then only if we were considered "good."

This meager ration did not satisfy Sarah's appetite at all. She tiptoed to the larder when no one was looking and stole an extra cream for herself.

The creams must have been counted. The theft was discovered and a terrible hullabaloo arose. Anybody would have thought from the fuss that we had raided Mother's jewel case. Sarah was too frightened to own up, and naturally the rest of us preserved a loyal silence. Our lips and hands were examined for telltale smudges of chocolate, but it was impossible to name the culprit.

Then, late one evening, agonized shrieks came from the night nursery. Our nurse, her starched white apron crackling, rushed in fiendishly. There, sure enough, was Sarah sitting up in bed howling her head off. An illicit chocolate cream, half eaten, was in her hand. She had been to the larder again, not realizing that the nurse had taken out the cream fillings and replaced them with mustard.

At least once a day we were taken for a walk in Kensington Palace Gardens. Sarah and Pebin went in their prams, and we joined the stately parade of nannies. A policeman used to be on duty at the top of Queen's Gate opposite the statue of General Lord Napier. He was a bluff old fellow. Randolph regularly dashed up to him and prodded him in the stomach, and this apparently was within the law. Unfortunately one morning he followed up the prod by exclaiming: "You look like an old monkey!"

The policeman was angry. A lesson had to be taught.

He "arrested" Randolph and marched him off to the police
station. No charge was made, of course, but the shock was
enough to quieten Randolph for a while.

The amount of time we spent with our parents was but
a fraction of the day. Our nurses used to escort us into our
mother's bedroom at 9 A.M. to say a respectful good morning. Then we were hustled away and did not see our parents again except for about half an hour around four or
five in the afternoon. We were usually brought down from
the nursery and shown off when guests were present.
These were invariably famous politicians, painters and
writers. I remember seeing Sir James Barrie, who was a
surprisingly small man, sitting on our sofa with his little
legs dangling off the ground.

On such occasions I was asked to do a party piece.
Margot Asquith always wanted my Lloyd George imita-
tion. Margot, a valued friend of Mother's, was a formidable woman — more formidable even than Nancy Astor.
About thirty-five years old in those days, she was a strict
disciplinarian. Pebin dared to remain seated one afternoon
when she entered the room. Margot tried to shrivel him
with a glare.

"Get up!" she ordered. "Even guttersnipes in the street
get up when I pass by."

Little Pebin pondered this, and after reflection commented most logically: "But I am not a guttersnipe . . ."

He had a happy knack of making very sensible replies.
"What do you want to be in life?" he was once asked.

"A retired chocolate taster," he answered.

When there were no guests to be amused we romped

around and set the Steinway Welte Mignon piano playing. This was an incredible instrument, one of the first electric pianos in England, bought by my grandmother, who was very musical. Upright and lavishly embellished with decoration, it worked, like a pianola, by means of perforated rolls of paper. It was equipped for no less than sixteen variations of tone and had two important advantages: it gave exact reproductions of pieces played by such masters as Paderewski and Pachmann, who must have had the most delicate touch of all time, and while the music was being played the keys moved up and down. At a very early age I first heard the magical strains of Wagner's Fire Music from *The Valkyries,* arranged by von Bülow, and many pieces by Chopin. I used to sit and watch the rippling keyboard, fascinated. After a while, the machine was responsible for my trying my own hand at playing Chopin, Beethoven, Bach and Wagner. It was working as recently as 1950, when our only remaining D.C. electricity supply was changed to A.C. I still keep the piano part. The keyboard is the lightest I have ever touched.

In the summer of 1917 our two families went down to Lullenden, an old house in Sussex. We children were billeted out with our nurses in a barnlike place some distance from the main building.

My uncle was loaned three German prisoners to do the gardening: Nicholas, Bernheim and Rosenburg. Nicholas was rather jolly and fat and used to play with us, but Bernheim was lean and short, and Rosenburg positively evil-looking. Our nurses regarded this enemy trio with suspicion from the start, and when one of us suddenly fell ill and had to be rushed to bed, Mother was told. Rosenburg was accused of trying to poison the drinking water. Perhaps he was attempting to kill my uncle, which would have been quite a feather in his cap. So he was removed.

That summer, a boy I knew visited me and we shared a bedroom. During the long light summer evenings, in the truly golden hours of each day, when everyone else seemed to be up and about and doing interesting things, it was impossible to settle down to sleep. We used to lie awake talking. We were doing this one evening, and twilight had come, when we heard some earnest conversation in the garden under our window. My uncle and Lloyd George were standing close together, discussing the war.

The chance for a practical joke was too good to miss. Opening the window wide, we started tipping the contents of our chamber pots onto the eminent heads below. We did it slowly enough for it to seem merely a few spots of welcome rain, and thought it screamingly funny. Undoubtedly Britain's Prime Minister and Minister of Munitions had never had *that* done to them before.

As luck would have it, our nursery was farther along the wall. A maid happened to be standing in the bow window and saw us. We were quickly caught and punished.

It was at Lullenden that Randolph was given a caravan by Lord Riddell. A covered cart affair, it was big enough for all of us to sit inside at once. Pulling it around proved to be heavy work, and Randolph and I soon decided on an experiment. We dragged it to the top of a hill, loaded Pebin and Sarah into it, and gave it a push. It reached a fine speed all right. But halfway down the hill the front wheels collapsed. To our horror — and glee — the whole contraption somersaulted to the bottom.

Nurses, parents and relations started running out of the house, shouting and wringing their hands. We had a fearful ticking off as usual, but miraculously Pebin and Sarah stepped from the wreckage with nothing worse than a shaking.

The wonderful butterflies in Lullenden's garden intrigued me, and my uncle taught me how to collect and set them. To begin with, the business of killing them by squeezing their stomachs put me off, but the creatures were so attractive I forced myself to do it and begin a collection. On seeing I was genuinely keen on the subject, my uncle showed me the large box of magnificent Orange Tips and other butterflies he had caught when he visited South Africa as Under-Secretary of State for the Colonies. This privileged demonstration was accompanied by a charming butterfly lore entirely of his own.

"You see," he explained, "caterpillars can be either good or bad. The bad ones are greedy. They never stop eating and become indolent. They are punished in their next world because they become drab Meadow Browns and Common Heaths, who live miserable lives for only one day, or perhaps two. If on the other hand a caterpillar behaves himself and is not greedy, he will emerge a gorgeous Swallow Tail, or a Painted Lady, or even a Camberwell Beauty. He will live for many days and may be allowed to hibernate for the winter and enjoy the spring the following year."

Our two families became separated when Mother decided to let our house in Cromwell Road to Lady Tree, the wife of Beerbohm Tree. Diana, Randolph and I were sent for a while to a boarding school at St. Margaret's Bay, Kent. I shared a room with John Bingham, now Major General Lord Bingham, whom I was to meet again as a staff officer in France in the last war. Also at the school was his sister Margaret, now Countess Alexander.

The school made an impression on me because I got my first taste of war. John Bingham had a powerful telescope and we used to lean out the bedroom window, watching the convoys in the Channel and listening to the German guns firing. Then a dead body was washed up and we were forbidden to go on the beach. We went just the same of course.

Our family spent the rest of the war wandering from house to house. We moved from Blenheim Palace to Sutton Courtney, from which we visited Mr. and Mrs. Asquith. Next we stayed at Cumnor Hall, where my grandfather Lord Abingdon was living. He was occupying it for a second time. He first owned and sold it before my parents were married. The house was said to be haunted by the ghost of Amy Robsart, and the man who bought it from Grandfather started a legal action on the grounds that neither he nor his servants ever saw her. He demanded that the sale be annulled. My grandfather indignantly denied any intention of enhancing the value of the property by claiming the presence of a ghost, and the court decided that supernatural visitations were not obligatory. Amy Robsart, consort of Queen Elizabeth's favorite the Earl of Leicester, was killed by some of his follow-

ers to render him free to marry the Queen. Sir Richard
Varney and a fellow called Forster murdered her in Cumnor Hall. First they stifled her in bed; then they threw her
down the stairs, breaking her neck.

We ended the war at Bedford Square in the house of
Lady Ottoline Morrell, whose personality was as precious
as her name. Mother was a friend of hers and frequently
stayed at her house at Garsington. Lady Ottoline was a
Bloomsburyite in the true sense of the word: madly intellectual, intense, yet most agreeable company. She was a
patron of D. H. Lawrence's until he wrote indirectly about
her in a way she thought offensive. Breaks of this sort between artists and patrons are all too frequent. How often
we hear of a benefactor who helped an artist in his struggling days being dropped and even derided by the artist
when he has made good! There is that urge to move on —
and perhaps forget. It is not attractive.

While we were at Bedford Square we had several air
raids. Father came home on leave and I thought him awfully brave when he ventured out into the street to see
what was happening. As a matter of fact, the house suffered no damage other than an antiaircraft shell cap landing in the gents' lavatory.

Rationing dimmed the pleasure of dining out, but we
used to find some of the best food available in London,
plus lively artists' company, at the Eiffel Tower Restaurant in Charlotte Street, run by Rudolf Stulick. At other
times we went to the restaurant owned by another of
Mother's friends, Admiral Volkoff, a White Russian émigré
of czarist times. He and his enormous wife produced an

excellent meal for 1s.4½d. This included a glass of kvass, which I always thought smelt like sick. Later in the day, when the luncheon rush was over, the dignified admiral would be seen emerging in a gray topper and morning coat on his way to Ascot. The Volkoffs had a special attraction for me in view of my increasing interest in Wagner. It was in their house in Venice that the great composer was going to have tea when he died.

Before finally returning to Cromwell Road at the end of the war we moved to Ebury Street, taking the house Mozart occupied when he lived in England. Mother maintained it was haunted; unquestionably the atmosphere was eerie. Among the eminent literary men and scholars who surrounded her at this address, one stands out more clearly than the rest because of his brain and inscrutable face: the Right Honorable Harold Baker, later the Warden of Winchester College and a lifelong friend of my mother's. Ever since my mother's death he has remained on close terms with my sister Clarissa. My father once told me that Bluey Baker, as he is known, regards Clarissa as one of the few women in this world with a first-class brain. Another visitor we used to see from time to time after the First World War was a New Zealand officer named Colonel Freyburg, now General Lord Freyburg. Being a V.C. and having been wounded twenty-two times, he was quite something in our young estimations. But then he capped it all by swimming the Channel! He married the sister of my mother's great friend Mrs. Reginald McKenna.

The first postwar Christmas we spent with Freddie

Guest at his delightful home in Roehampton. In addition to ourselves there were the Birkenheads and my uncle and his family. We went riding in Richmond Park, but little time was needed to prove that it was not the sport for me. The pony and I failed to meet any measure of agreement. We simply did not understand each other. When I wanted to go in a certain direction the wretched animal had already made up its mind to go in a different one. After I had given everybody a laugh by careering around, clinging desperately to the pony's underside, I decided that walking was a much more satisfactory means of getting about.

The next boarding school I went to was Summerfields, near Oxford. I hate schools, but have quite pleasant memories of Summerfields; everyone there was most considerate. To my mind, much as I dislike the boarding school system, it is better than any other. It forces boys to develop their characters in a way which an ordinary day school does not and cannot. They are pushed around a lot and taught to be independent, so that they quickly learn to tell everyone to go to hell. There is much to be said for it.

Summerfields was a rather tough place and one had to stick up for oneself to survive. My nickname was Hedgehog because of my unruly hair. They were trying days for me in that everyone was brilliant except J.S.C. I was stupid and artistic, befriending that now famous painter, Victor Pasmore. Many of my contemporaries at Summerfields have distinguished themselves. Name any profession and as likely as not one of my former schoolfriends has made his name in it. My closest friends were Charlie and

Johnnie MaxMuller, sons of the British ambassador in Poland, and Michael and David, sons of Mr. Reginald Mc-Kenna. To me, the McKenna boys were phenomenal. Both were able not only to play but to sing Bach cantatas and fugues.

We were all elected to the school chapel choir, and this must have been the time when I started to become a "lapsed" Catholic. Summerfields was Protestant, and although I could have gone to a small Catholic chapel some distance away, I did not bother. I had inevitably got caught up with the school choir's Magnificat and Nunc Dimittis.

An important family event around this time was the birth of my sister Clarissa in 1920. It was the tremendous culmination of a dream for Mother. She had always yearned for a girl, and here she was. From then on, the boys were just "the boys." No girl could have had as much care lavished on her as Clarissa. She was everything to Mother; too much, perhaps, because as frequently happens in such situations, Mother was possessive to a degree.

As soon as Greta Garbo became famous and film fans worshiped her as the most beautiful woman in creation, Mother saw Clarissa as Garbo II. The curious thing is that Clarissa actually began to look rather like Garbo. And Garbo does not look in the least bit like Mother.

In character Clarissa inherited numerous Bertie traits, but like the rest of us she missed that distant and alluring charm which made Mother so much out of this world. She has few of the Churchill qualities and looks, and peoples are often astounded to be told she is my sister. She is everything that I am not: good-looking, silent, retiring, and with a brilliant brain — a strange intellectual character trying to find something. The more my mother possessed her, the more Clarissa struggled to get away from it all.

Around 1920 I spent many memorable hours with another friend of the family, Hilaire Belloc. Of medium height, plump and cherublike, he used to wear a three-tier cloak which impressed me as exceedingly grand. My ambition was to have one like it myself one day. He used to take me sailing. We would start early in the morning, chug down the narrow Sussex lanes in his vintage Ford, lustily singing shocking French songs, and board his boat at Arundel. It was always a gay outing. The singing continued on the boat, naturally. We would sail to the mouth of the Arun and back again, calling at Arundel Castle for lunch.

Sometimes he invited our family to lunch with him at Horsham. The house was a sort of converted mill, very old, with low timbered ceilings. There would be Mother, Father, Pebin and myself, and Belloc's conversation was unfailingly witty and philosophical. He was a devout Catholic, and undoubtedly his intellectual approach to the Catholic religion influenced my own interpretation of it in later years. At the end of a course he liked to get up from the table with an apology, leave the room and reappear in a few minutes with an enormous omelette which he had cooked himself. He was a very good cook.

When my parents rented for the summer Sir Claude Russell's home, Wappinthorne Manor, just below Chanctonbury Ring, the famous clump of trees on the South Downs, we were near enough to Belloc for him to visit us. I remember being absolutely mystified at seeing him hanging out of a top-floor window one day. He had a bottle of brandy in his hand and was carefully dripping the precious liquid into a bowl placed in the garden below.

"This," he assured me in all seriousness, "will add ten years to its age."

III

Acrobatics at Harrow

I HAVE ALWAYS been a slave to models. Nowadays, with a wife who is a public relations consultant in the fashion industry, the models with which I am concerned are those who posture and undulate gracefully in designers' salons. But in my youth the models were of the other kind: the fascinating world of replica.

It all started with soldiers. When my brother and I learned of my uncle's impressive display of model soldiers and were told about the battles he had fought with Father, we were determined to stage model battles too. In contrast to my uncle's collection of a thousand pieces or more, we could produce only a modest army of about a hundred. Nevertheless, we had modern guns and transport, and it was transport which interested us most. The difficulties in moving troops, plus equipment, from place to place over land and water intrigued us so much that we used to study every model on the subject in the Science Museum at South Kensington.

When the family returned to Cromwell Road after the war, and we were able to enjoy a permanent home again, we graduated to electric railways. Mother's back drawing room was ideal for this hobby. It was large and had plenty of carpet space. But soon we felt cramped and started looking towards the front drawing room, which was even bigger, on the far side of the hall.

"You can only lay the railway in there," said Mother, "if you take it up every night."

We promised. As often as not, though, the lines stayed firmly down and guests had to thread their way among signals and points. The inconvenience was tolerated by my parents and even encouraged by them, I suppose because it showed some sort of enterprise with the added advantage of keeping us quiet.

Next we set about making water-line-level models of famous liners and battleships. I did the *Berengaria* on a scale of a hundred feet to one inch. Models of this kind could be bought in shops, yet ours were much better than anything ready-made. Not only did they have wireless aerials but the portholes were covered with luminous paint and glowed most realistically at night.

We carved with penknives and razor blades at every cigar box we could lay our hands on. My father's and uncle's butlers co-operated to the full.

The climax of our model-making efforts was now approaching. I was keenly interested in the history of the First World War and had made a particular study of the battle of Jutland. No doubt Admiral Beatty's constant visits to our home had something to do with it. I became what is known as a Beatty-ite, as opposed to a Jellico-ite. Beatty was an up-and-coming young naval officer of fairly junior rank when my uncle, as First Lord of the Admiralty, picked him out and promoted him over the heads of his seniors to admiral in charge of the Grand Fleet's battle cruiser squadron. Jellico, meanwhile, was admiral in charge of not only the battleship squadrons, but the Grand Fleet as a whole.

At Jutland the responsibility of the battle cruisers was to get the Grand Fleet into grips with the enemy. Beatty contacted the German High Sea Fleet all right, and brought them to the Grand Fleet, during the process of which one of his cruisers, the *Queen Mary*, was lost. Jellico deployed, in a manner considered by Beatty-ites as being thoroughly stuffy and lacking in arrogance, and the Germans turned tail and steamed off. The British gave chase but could not catch them. Beatty-ites maintain that if only Jellico had acted with more boldness and aggression he could have thrashed the Germans out of the seas.

It is an absorbing point for debate which has split the Royal Navy ever since. Jellico was an officer of long experience in the service, a steady, somewhat cautious man, while Beatty was an upstart who took fantastic risks which were not always justified, but contrived to win fame and glory. In the eyes of the public he was a sort of glittering First World War counterpart of Montgomery, while Jellico was an Ironside.

Of course, with Beatty being my uncle's protégé, our home was a stronghold of Beatty-ism. I happened to spot Jellico's son at a party recently and could not resist approaching him and shaking his hand.

"As you know," I told him, "we are all Beatty-ites. How nice to meet a Jellico for once!"

When trying to re-create Jutland in miniature, we quickly realized it was virtually impossible to make a comprehensive working model function after the first phase, which ended with Beatty's battle cruisers having brought the Germans in contact with the Grand Fleet. After that the battle became too complicated, with ships sinking or losing their steering and going round in circles.

Having decided to make all the models on the scale of two hundred and fifty-four feet to one inch, we worked out the appropriate speeds. Then — shades of our wartime bascule bridge! — we commandeered the dining room and laid a big cotton sheet on the floor. The method of making the models move was ingenious. Under the bows of each ship we fixed a drawing pin, which in turn was stuck to a magnet placed under the sheet. The magnet had a string attached to it, leading to the edge of the sheet. Thus by pulling the string it was possible to make the ship move.

We even had the little Dutch coaster which caused the British and Germans to come together when both fleets sent destroyers to find out what it was.

Beatty heard about the model and asked for a demonstration, after which he congratulated us; so did Admiral Lord Keyes. Later the ships were taken down to Chartwell for inspection by my uncle.

I ended my model-making career with replicas of the beautifully streamlined Schneider Trophy seaplanes and a model of H.M.S. *Hood*, probably the most graceful battle cruiser ever designed. I was deeply affected when this beautiful ship was destroyed by the *Bismarck* in the Second World War. I did the *Hood* at the same scale as the Jutland models. All her gun turrets swiveled and she had her full radio wiring at the masts. Split silk cord, I discovered, is by far the best material for intricate work such as aerials.

Model-making on this miniature scale has made my eyes suffer greatly from strain, but I do not regret it. If I'd had a son instead of a daughter I would have the supreme excuse for still messing about with wood and glue.

In 1921 Granny Randolph died. After going to her London home in Westbourne Terrace and seeing her coffin covered with an enormous bank of flowers, I attended the funeral at Bladon Church, the family graveyard just outside Blenheim Palace.

Her death was an event which affected even us children very deeply, her personality was so powerful. Her third husband, Montague Porch, who was very much her junior in age, was extremely kind and used to give me presents. Her second husband, George Cornwallis West, was my godfather.

She had an appalling number of debts and much of her property had to be sold. Very little of her magnificent wine cellar was left, the rumor being that a member of her staff had sold most of the bottles to a restaurant. My mother was delighted when Father inherited from Granny a beautiful Louis XV red lacquered clock. Father, being musical, also inherited all her specially bound music scores. I have them today, except for four which went astray. I came across the missing four recently in the archives at Chartwell. They are superb examples of binding, and I often wonder who was supposed to play the music.

They say that my grandfather Lord Randolph hated Eton so much that he sent both his sons to Harrow. My uncle, I think, must have hated Harrow with equal intensity; that is why he sent Randolph to Eton. My father could not have objected to Harrow such a lot, however, because that is where Pebin and I found ourselves. But I loathed it, and if I had a son I would send him to Eton. My young grandson is down for there.

As far as academics are concerned, I do not think it really matters to which school any Churchill goes. The family tradition of staying bottom of the form for years has always been steadily maintained. We Churchills develop later in life. During our school years we just do not function at all. At Summerfields my brain was useless, in dismal contrast to the brilliance of my contemporaries. I caught them up afterward. It is a family characteristic. Nothing can be done about it. If a child of mine did not show any development until the age of twenty I would not worry. And this may give some consolation to those desperate parents whose sons reveal no signs of talent in any direction when seventeen.

At Harrow I was no exception to the family trait, though I did just manage to reach the upper school before I left — a feat denied my uncle because he departed from normal school routine through an early transfer to the Army Class.

When I arrived at Harrow, the only person I knew in

the whole frightening place was one of the headmaster's sons, Neville Ford, whose younger brother is now Sir Edward Ford, the Queen's secretary. Anxious to strengthen further roots, I speedily visited another friend of the family, Mr. Moriarty, who had been my uncle's Army Class master some thirty-five years previously. He had retired and lived in a little house at the far end of the Hill. I went there for a peaceful homely tea every Sunday. He would recall how "unusual" my uncle was as a pupil; how promise of his future genius was apparent despite his escapades.

"Get to know the custodians," my father had warned me in a talk before I left home for Harrow. "They are very important people. They ring the bells, and when the bells stop ringing it means you are late. Also, the custodians are the 'police' of the school, and the first to report you."

I therefore came to a pleasant and valuable understanding with Custodian Titchener, who was custodian in both my father's and my uncle's day at Harrow, and who when necessary gave the bell an extra ring or two to see me in to school by 7:30 A.M. and thus escape punishment.

Compared with some of the other boys I was fairly well behaved. I never, for instance, climbed out the dormitory window at night to go down into the town and pick up a prostitute. Nor did I use any of our special passes for the great Wembley Exhibition of 1926 as a means of getting out to visit Mrs. Merrick's night club in London, a daring adventure for which I believe some of our opposite numbers at Eton were expelled. I did of course involve myself in some deplorable pranks, such as climbing over roofs

and raiding the headmaster's apartments, but strangely I
was never caught for these. When I was punished it was
for trivial offenses such as not doing my prep.

On these occasions I became a victim for the beating
parties which were popular entertainment among the
monitors of my day. What happened was this: every Saturday night in our House was beating night. Any boy of
my lowly status who had done something wrong during
the week was called upon during the hours of darkness —
rather in the way that the Gestapo pounced on Jews before the last war — and ordered to report to the library on
the Saturday. If the criminal calendar for the week lacked
names, charges were trumped up to ensure that the monitors got their full measure of sport. On the Saturday, the
wretched little boy was ushered into the Holy of Holies to
be confronted with a semicircle of monitors, their mouths
watering for a taste of sadism. I call it sadism because I
have always supposed that the beating parties were mainly
an outlet for sex. What else can one expect when boys are
locked up with boys for nearly eight consecutive years of
their lives? Sex had to manifest itself somehow or other.

If the head monitor was feeling particularly excited he
delivered all six strokes himself; otherwise each monitor
was allowed to have a swipe. In our House we were somewhat lucky in that the victims were seldom ordered to
take off their trousers. This gave us the chance for coun-
termeasures. We found that the agony of the cane was
lessened by carefully laying banana skins over one's bottom
and holding them in place with tight underpants. Nevertheless, the monitors scored by devising some fiendish re-

finements of torture. To the end of a very thin whippy cane they fixed a blob of lead, the idea being that it carried the cane right round the thigh and hit the groin gland near the crotch — a truly excruciating experience.

The most advanced cruelty at Harrow, which makes one marvel at what the warped juvenile mind will devise, was eventually banned, no doubt because of the permanent injuries caused. The little sinner was compelled to bend over against the edge of an open door so that each of the gluteus maximus muscles of his backside was on one side of it. Then a monitor laid a squash racket flat against the edge of the door and slashed this hard unyielding instrument down on the backside as hard as he could, the effect being rather like a guillotine. Numerous coccyges must have been broken.

The masters did not beat the boys much, but when the headmaster had reason to do so, and this was once or twice a year, it was a ceremonial event carried out behind closed doors in the famous fourth form room. In the most horrifying torture chamber manner, the victim was stripped stark naked and tied to a table. Then he was birched, the method being to draw the birch across the bare flesh after each hard blow so that the knobs on the twigs left a mass of bleeding — which in turn excited the headmaster to renewed frenzy. It used to be alleged that when my headmaster, Lionel Ford, was doing a beating two custodians had to hold him back to check his anger.

Needless to say, I took enormous trouble to avoid being beaten; nor did I beat anyone at Harrow. I am completely opposed to letting children beat each other. Harrow has produced many great men but I doubt if it is due to corporal punishment administered in this way. However, such treatment does not in my opinion have detrimental effects on anyone and may even put the sufferer's mind in proper perspective for adult life. Furthermore, I do not believe that the tendency towards homosexuality, which is the other natural result of monastic existence at boarding school, has the slightest effect on a normal person. It need not interfere with the conduct of his own life or with his associations with ordinary people, except when busybodies insist on wading into matters which have really nothing to do with them. A classic example of this was of course Oscar Wilde, whose fine brain was destroyed by the Marquess of Queensberry.

It would be fair to say that in England there is probably more nonsense talked and thought about homosexuality by such learned people as eminent politicians, bishops, moralists and no doubt lords of the realm than any other subject except prostitution. In no other country in the world where I have traveled has it been considered worthy of discussion. I think the reason may well be the surprising proportion of women who are subjected to the practices of the sodomite by their husbands or lovers, and actually like or prefer it.

I had written only a couple of letters home from Harrow when my father sent me a very terse note pointing out that my handwriting was illegible. I took the criticism to heart and decided that whereas my classwork was hopeless, at least I might be able to master some decent calligraphy. Accordingly I set about imitating my father's handwriting, which impressed me as being educated and scholastic-looking. I even went to the extent of writing with my left and right hands, forward and backward. I found it difficult to write forward with my left hand, and still do, but could easily write backward with it. My perseverance had an interesting sequel many years later when I happened to send something in my own hand to my uncle.

"I see you have a very Churchillian scrawl," he remarked. Then he went on: "The most important thing is to have a signature which is legible."

Even in his old age, my uncle's handwriting is incredibly clear, and I have often admired the precision and care with which he handles his pen. He finds it a little difficult to handle a paintbrush for his initials on a canvas, though, and I have been known to help him. My own freehand brushwork as a mural painter has had some interesting results, incidentally. It led me to Italy, where in the 1920's I made a special point of mastering the linear fresco painting technique of the Pompeians and such masters as Piero della Francesca, Botticelli and Mantegna. Recently in Japan I found that signing my name with a brush and Chinese ink, as is the custom, was very easy, much to the surprise of the Japanese. And when the late Sir Alfred Munnings bet me a bottle of port that I could not paint a straight unbroken perpendicular line from a ten-foot ceiling to the floor, I won.

It soon became obvious to me at Harrow that somehow I had to try to justify all the trouble and expense my parents were lavishing on my education. Reports on my classwork continued to be terrible, so I determined to excel at the only alternative sphere of activity: athletics. My brother and I had already become quite proficient acrobats. We worked out several acts together, including a slow-motion wrestling match, and when I was about twelve we made a comedy film, shown for the private delight of parents and relations. As a result of devoting all my energies to athletics I won scarves and badges which gave me status, and my father just — only just — tolerated my classroom record. I took up swimming instead of cricket, which struck me as too inactive, and fancied myself in the gymnasium. I was gymnastic champion for four of my five years at Harrow. Also I captained my House gymnastic team and we managed to be constantly successful in competitions.

Gymnastics led me to acrobatic diving, which I enjoyed because of the birdlike exhilaration of changing direction in mid-air. I learned the hard way. Early on I tried the dive in which one has to stand right at the end of the springboard, facing outward, jump up and turn a complete backward somersault before entering the water. I must have miscalculated, or the springboard moved or something, because I caught my head a fearful crack on the board on the way down. I was fished out of the pool unconscious.

I used to specialize in swallow dives, various handstands, and backward and forward somersaults. I picked up a lot of tips by watching other people and talking to fellow competitors at interschool matches. High-diving terrified me, but I was fascinated by the challenge of it and managed to master my dread. For this I owe a debt to Mr. Unwin, the instructor at the Bath Club when it used to be in Dover Street. My father, a strong swimmer, introduced me to the Bath, and I went there as often as I could.

In acrobatic diving I was never able to get further than two and a half somersaults. And this feat, spectacular in its way, caused me to lose my nerve.

The Bath Club pool had a high platform at the shallow end. A trapeze hung from the ceiling over the middle of the pool, some twenty-five feet above the water. When I boastfully announced to Jack Beddington and another friend of mine, Robert Byron, the distinguished writer and traveler who was killed in the last war, that I was going to do two and a half somersaults, they were suitably impressed. They went up to the balcony which encircled the pool and waited there with this-I-must-see expressions on their faces.

I stood poised on the platform, my toes curled over the matting on the edge. I hauled the trapeze bar towards me by means of a rope. I gripped the bar and swung across the water with the confidence of Tarzan; out, then back again. Everything was fine. The instant for letting go of the trapeze came. But for some extraordinary reason I hesitated. I missed my chance. After that it was impossible to dive from the trapeze at all. A new situation arose at each shorter, slower swing across the pool and I could not judge the distance. So I had to swing backward and forward, ignominiously, until I reached a standstill and could safely drop into the water feet first.

Jack and Robert thought it immensely funny. I did not.

Robert Byron, by the way, was destined to revolutionize my whole approach to art. His very important book, *The Birth of Western Painting*, introduced me to the entire Byzantine field and of course the Cretan Domenico Theotocopulos (El Greco). I cannot say I agreed with everything he said in our long discussions, but he certainly succeeded in debunking some of the classics, with the result that I was able to grade in proper perspective the importance of such painters as Raphael and Michelangelo. Even the Parthenon frieze was subjected to careful and surprising dissection.

Perhaps the most alarming accident that happened at the Bath Club was when a member dived into the deep end and went straight to the bottom. His fingers caught in the grill of the main water outlet and he dangled there, trapped, swaying like a strand of seaweed. Fortunately Mr. Unwin was instantly on the spot to save him from drowning. The man was brought up with the whole grill attached to his fingers.

I myself caused a tremendous confusion in the water when I dived from the ten-foot springboard onto Lord Wodehouse, who had proposed me as a member of the club. But my most dreadful experience was in 1930, when I was twenty-one. I tried a very high dive and badly cricked my back when my legs went over too far as I plunged into the water. It was a silly, unnecessary injury which put an end to all acrobatics.

An unexpected hazard in survival at Harrow, as far as I was concerned, proved to be the clay on the playing fields.

It was so thick and tenacious that after each game I had to wash my head in the showers with immense thoroughness. The result suddenly made itself apparent. I began to lose my hair. That is my explanation for my baldness, though other people may say the whole thing is hereditary. Anyway, it had the result that when I started a dive by standing on my head, the imprint of the fiber matting at the end of the board made my near-naked cranium look like a waffle. The prospect of baldness worried me so much that I went to Nathan's the costumiers and bought a false baldpate. I put it on to see what I was going to look like in years ahead and was absolutely horrified. I saw in the mirror the apparition I see now.

I hurried at once to a place in Bond Street where exquisitely mannered gentlemen tortured me with electric shocks. But it did no good at all. My hairline continued to recede. I resigned myself to the inevitable. Anyway, I pondered, if I look like a bellhop today I may pass for a head waiter tomorrow.

The art work I did at Harrow was mostly water colors, though my contemporary Victor Pasmore went on to oils, having been introduced to the French impressionists. I stayed up late at night studying the techniques of black and white drawing and subtleties of light and shade. Most of my work was poster-type, featuring railway engines. In 1925, when I was sixteen, I sold my first piece of art. It was a picture of a train. The buyer: Great Western Railways. Proudly I took it along to the head offices at Paddington Station. Everyone said how pleased they were with it and I was paid three pounds. I never actually saw it reproduced on the billboards, though, and on reflection I fear that the sale was mainly due to my cousin Viscount Churchill being chairman of the company.

I used to play the piano a lot at Harrow. I would take one of the stuffy little practice rooms and happily hammer away at an old upright for hours. I started a course of lessons, but the emphasis on scales was insufferably tedious. I was impatient to produce recognizable music, so I got my fingers supple by playing jazz. The one aspect of music in which I found myself sadly deficient was playing direct from a musical score. Even when I knew a simple piece like Paderewski's Minuet by ear and could play it, my fingers became completely paralyzed when I was confronted with the score. This tiresome handicap remains with me today. There seems to be very little communication between my eyes and my fingers. Yet I can write music and read a full score to myself, which I often do on a train journey with great pleasure.

The everlasting memory which stays with every Harrovian is of course the school songs. Even to this day I can play almost all of them, and my uncle can sing the words. He and I often enjoyed evenings at Chartwell when we solemnly went through the songs one by one.

My uncle is not musical by any means, though some of the soldiers' songs of the Boer War and other campaigns have merited his attention. He has had a special record made of them. Generally, his liking for a piece is decided by the grandeur and emotion it contains. I remember one day when Sarah and I were listening to Brahms' Symphony No. 1 on the radio in the dining room. The solo horn's majestic passage was being played as my uncle came in to have lunch. It appealed to him at once.

"That is very fine," he said. "We must hear it again from the beginning."

I pointed out that it was a broadcast, not a gramophone record, but that the same theme would recur presently. We sat down to lunch. Whereupon as the meal proceeded, and the repetition of the passage drew nearer, an intense concentration developed at my uncle's end of the table. The music moved him very much indeed.

The tune which never fails to bring tears to his eyes is "Land of Hope and Glory," though I sometimes doubt whether he can really tell the difference between this and "God Save the King." Certainly the former is very much nobler, more original and more suitable as a national anthem. Besides, the basic melody of "God Save the King" was used by many early composers on the Continent and appears in one of Beethoven's quartets. John Bull's claim to have written "God Save the King" (or Queen) comes rather at the end of the list.

I was in my middle teens at Harrow when Father decided it was time I knew something about wine.

"Try the port," he instructed one evening after dinner. I drank a glass dutifully but it revolted me. I don't think anybody likes port at first. I found that I much preferred a light white wine. I did not take to whisky for ages; in fact, not until the last war. Father used to drink several glasses of it during a meal, which is something I could never do. Nevertheless, his appreciation of the qualities of wine was extremely well developed, and keener than that of my uncle. Father's friend Lionel Rothschild had the cellar of a connoisseur and the two men used to share their knowledge. Father bought in bulk, but was a moderate drinker. Mother too drank surprisingly little, yet was the fortunate possessor of a natural taste and became sufficiently expert to pronounce judgment on a claret without particularly liking the stuff. In the 'twenties, when cocktails became fashionable, neither my father nor uncle dreamed of having them in the house. Often my uncle did not have sherry, which meant that there was nothing before dinner. But today, probably due to the modernizing influence of Christopher Soames, Chartwell has cocktails and even my uncle drinks them. He is not the sort of person to be left out when something is being handed round to everybody else.

He is always a bit shocked when he meets someone who never touches alcohol. It was very amusing when Thomas Dewey, who is a teetotaler, came to Europe while running for the United States Presidency after the Second World War and called at Chartwell, as so many people do. My uncle was delighted to see him and offered a glass of champagne. Dewey declined. Again my uncle offered it, and again Dewey said a polite no. My uncle was astonished.

"But you *must!*" he insisted. "Come on, now. Come on."

Like everyone else before or since who has tried to refuse a drink at my uncle's, Dewey had to yield. He took the glass.

By the time I was sixteen I was a frequent visitor at Chartwell. Randolph and I used to camp out in the grounds

at night and climb over the roof. Once we were sent upstairs — out of harm's way, it was thought — but our room
turned out to be next door to one of the maids, who was
rather pretty. Her name, I distinctly remember, was Ger-
trude. She was very tolerant of some of the abominable
attentions she received from me.

My uncle cannot abide small talk, and at mealtimes we
either discussed worthwhile subjects such as literature and
art or kept quiet. If there was ever any doubt about the
meaning of a word, somebody would be sent to fetch Fow-
ler's *Modern English Usage*. Then my uncle would adjust
his spectacles and read a large number of usages to us.

He is also a stickler for correct pronunciation, though
why he calls Nazis the "Narzies" has always surprised me,
unless he does it on purpose. When I used to pronounce
"Lenin" the way it is spelled, he always corrected me, saying: "Leneen." I daresay Clare Sheridan, having been to
Russia, had enlightened him. But Randolph and I insisted
on pronouncing "Soviet" to rhyme with "diet." After all,
we argued, one does not talk about the "Dee-et" of Worms.

Many is the time I met Bernard Baruch at Chartwell.
One occasion stands out a mile. He and my uncle were
about to enter the dining room when Randolph switched
on the gramophone which was just inside the door. The
record was a popular item of nonsense of the day: "Barney
Google with the Goo Goo Googly Eyes." My uncle was so
angry at this cheeky allusion to his honored guest's name
that he snatched the record from the turntable and dashed
it to the floor. We were severely reprimanded.

Randolph and I occupied our spare time by learning

golf. We practiced our driving on the upper lawn, from which point we would hit as hard as we could across the wide valley below. Because the lawn was separated from the main house by part of the garden wall, this arrangement was ideal for the physical safety of my uncle and aunt — or so we thought.

One afternoon I sliced. Normally a rogue ball of mine simply smacked into the garden wall and bounced off harmlessly. But not this one. It went over the top. With a devastating crash of glass it shattered the drawing room window and landed on the mah-jongg table where Venetia Montague and my mother, aunt and uncle were in the middle of a game.

Randolph was in heaven. "Johnny, for once it's you in trouble!" he exulted. "You've done it at last!"

I was too frightened to know what to do. I went and hid for a while, but had to reappear eventually and the row was terrific. Yet I must say that considering the mess and inconvenience I caused my aunt, she could not have been more tolerant, kind and forgiving.

Diana, Randolph and I sometimes went and played on the Limpsfield golf course and the experience was always totally incredible. True to our family motto, "Faithful but Unfortunate," our shots landed in the wrong places. No matter how loudly we bellowed "Fore!" irate colonels were hit in the backs of their purple necks by our balls. We wasted hours threshing about with clubs in tall grass. And when we holed in one by mistake the gray-haired tweedy woman in front of us found our ball in the hole and argued it was hers.

We gave up golf fairly quickly.

The nucleus of Chartwell is a rectangular-shaped Elizabethan building of rich red brick. The walls of this were
exceptionally thick, so my uncle immediately set about
altering them. He persuaded his architect to halve the
thickness of the old walls, which could stand it, and to
make this the standard measurement for the rest of the
walls, including new extensions. In my opinion his efforts
at achieving a sensible consistency were not entirely
successful because the architect missed the chance of
functionally improving the charm of the original house,
but it marked the beginning of the changes that were to
take place as soon as my uncle moved in. Chartwell is
continually changing — I notice it every time I go — and
although at last it is now looking mature and complete, I
doubt if it will ever be finished.

Originally the valley in the garden contained a large
pond. Way back in 1923 it was perhaps as much as a
hundred feet below the level of the tiny spring which
bubbled up beside the house and fed it. The overflow
trickled away down the valley. My uncle grandly insisted
on calling the pond a lake, but it was about the size of the
Round Pond in Kensington Gardens. Furthermore it was
choked with weeds. Just as the incoming tide on holiday
beaches led to the construction of huge works, so the
pond at Chartwell provided a splendid new opportunity
for the mastery of water.

No time was wasted in producing a lake worthy of the
name. Earth-moving equipment arrived, complete with
an army of stout-armed men in overalls and gumboots.

The pond was drained and the weeds cleared. Railway lines were laid along the bottom and engines busily pulled away truckloads of mud. Of course we were all issued with boots and spades and ordered to contribute to the work. A wide dam was built with sluices to control the outflow of water, and the lake, as indeed it became, was allowed to fill up.

It was about three hundred yards long and nearly finished when my uncle made his daily tour of inspection and conceived yet another scheme. Why not have an upper lake to catch the water from the spring before it reached the main lake?

More earthworks, more railway lines and workmen. This second lake was destined for fish. But even before the dam was ready and the lake had started to fill, plans were drawn up for an upper-upper lake for swimming. In the middle of this latest operation it was decided to have an upper-upper-upper or fourth lake on the far side of the valley. This was to be fed by a siphon arrangement and a pipe leading across to it. Formidable earthworks were needed for such a project because the position was high up the valley wall. The dam had to be exceptionally strong. Again we paraded for duty with shovels, trolleys and so on — no guest, however mighty his status in the world outside, was exempt — and we set to work. Alas, Lake No. 4 was never much of a triumph, though we bathed in it for a time. The dam kept cracking.

These alterations were accompanied by tremendous activity elsewhere in the garden. Despite my uncle's literary and parliamentary duties, he found time to supervise the felling of trees to make new vistas, the planting of saplings and laying down of tennis courts. A delightful little hideaway house was built halfway up one of the trees outside the front door; this was for Sarah and my brother Pebin. It has since been taken down, but the summer-house constructed for Mary is still there.

Looking round Chartwell in the 1930's one might have thought that with four lakes, new orchards, kitchen gardens and various animals, including some polo ponies, opportunities for change had been exhausted. Not a bit of it. Four more pools were created near the spring, plus a miraculous system of waterfalls and rockeries. The pool we used for swimming had the luxury of heated water. The boilerhouse chimney was cunningly concealed in the trunk of an old oak and gigantic rhubarb leaves hid the filtering equipment.

My uncle also established a fishery. The first occupants were trout and they had a special spawning section. One of the upper pools was filled with beautiful golden orf, which used to come and talk to my uncle when he fed them, but I believe they were all stolen during the war and had to be replaced. Not long ago a special upper pool was made with rocks for smaller-sized golden fish. Monstrous lorries panted in from the depths of Wales carrying colossal chunks of mountainside. These pieces were skillfully implanted so that now they seem to be natural parts of the landscape.

In the 'twenties, when I became old enough to assess conditions at home more critically, I realized that although Mother and Father got on well enough together, there was no intellectual communication between them. Apart from a game of mah-jongg after dinner they hardly spoke to each other. My father would come downstairs to breakfast each morning, carefully shutting the windows as he descended. Then, when he had left for the City, my Mother came down and opened them again. The procedure was repeated when he returned home. On his way upstairs to his study to read the *Evening Standard,* Father would shut the windows. Mother followed and reopened them.

I was on close terms with Mother, who used to hold court most mornings in her special way. She would have "elevenses" consisting of digestive biscuits and a decanter of port in the drawing room. Erudite literary figures such as Augustin Birrell and Logan Pearsall Smith would appear, or a painter would arrive to sketch Mother and discuss art.

Our visitors also included Majorie Anglesey, the sister of Diana Cooper. She lived in the street next to us in London and our two families often met. Her eldest daughter Caroline Paget was my first love, though her mother was so attractive I cannot be sure that I wasn't in love with her as well. It was a thrill whenever we met.

Both Mother and Father helped to educate me in the social graces. When I was seventeen and being taken out by them in the evenings, they took enormous pains to brief me on the finer points of etiquette.

"When going to a ball it is particularly important to be very clean, properly shaved and powdered," Father warned. "You will be at close quarters with ladies, who will notice every detail."

Mother had an interesting tip.

"In the taxi, just before you arrive at the front door," she said, "wet the end of a finger and rub your eyebrows and eyelashes. This will make you look fresh and alert. Your eyes will sparkle."

When the family came home after a ball or party, Mother and I would stay up late in the drawing room together, discussing the people we had seen and what they had said. Mother was a most discerning judge of character and could sum up a stranger at a glance. She would sit and talk, idly poking at the fire, and then we would doze off until about four o'clock, when we went to bed. I still like sleeping on sofas.

Mother's habit of poking at fires, incidentally, was incurable. Almost daily in our home carefully laid grates refused to burn because Mother had stabbed the life out of them. She was so notorious for this habit that whenever she went visiting the hostess gave special instructions for pokers to be removed from fireplaces. Mother's other unfortunate weakness was being late for meals. Wise hostesses always rang the dinner gong half an hour early, and by this stratagem managed to get her downstairs more or less on time.

Both my parents went to the opera a great deal. They liked it, but I suspect the main attractions were social — drinks in the intervals, and so on. I was about eighteen when I saw my first opera, *The Valkyries*, at Covent Garden. Father had given me a book about Wagner to read beforehand and I was well primed. The drama, power and sheer magnificence of the performance had a lasting impact on me. I went home in a sort of drugged haze, determined to learn as much about Wagner as I possibly could.

Before I left Harrow I was studying *The Mastersingers*, *Tristan and Isolde*, plus Scarlatti and odd pieces of Beethoven by means of the electric piano. I tried to learn them by ear. If I came to a complicated chord I played the roll very slowly and watched how the famous pianist tackled it. After that it was a matter of diligent practice.

I also began to paint seriously, and to model in clay. In short, my activities as a social lion, amateur artist and musician were progressing famously. But my father pointed out that I was nearly nineteen and it would not be long before I had to start earning a living.

"What," he asked, "do you want to be?"

I wished I knew.

IV

The Churchills Invade North America

FATHER WAS AT A LOSS to know what to do with me. On my passport I had *Occupation: Student,* and the vagueness hid a multitude of sins. I did not know what I was studying, or for what purpose. My academic record at Harrow had revealed nothing and I seemed to have no ambitions. Father took me for a walk down Cromwell Road for a serious discussion on the situation.

"I think the best thing would be to organize you into Shell Mex or British Petroleum," he said. "If you behave yourself and don't play the ass, you will have a very good career."

This appeared to be a reasonable suggestion. Then came the snag.

"Of course, you will probably be sent to a remote outpost in Mesopotamia or somewhere for ten years as a junior clerk to learn the business."

I did not like the idea of that at all and said so. Exasperated, Father demanded: "What would you *like* to do?"

In my heart I wanted to answer: Music, painting and sculpture, but felt it was fatuous even to consider this.

There was really no money in it and therefore the idea would not be tolerated for a moment.

"I don't know. . . ." was my infuriating reply.

"What do you mean you 'don't know'?" We walked on in silence. "Well, I suppose if you refuse to do anything sensible you can always come into the office."

He meant the Stock Exchange. But meanwhile he considered it worth sending me to Oxford to see if I would develop in a definite direction. The problem next became one of actually getting me into the university. The only means of enlivening my brain to cope with the entrance examination seemed to be to send me to a crammer. The one chosen was probably the most extraordinary that ever existed. Near Stanway Hall, in the heart of the Cotswolds, and known to my parents because it belonged to their friends the Wemyses, it was run by a man known as "The Priest" and his wife, whom we called "The Priestess." I quickly formed the opinion that they had no sense of organization and no idea of how to teach, but the place was crowded and evidently thrived.

When, as was only to be expected, I failed in every paper, my father tried again. I was sent to a Mr. Theodosius for special coaching. With a name like that, and considering that his premises were close behind University College, there seemed to be more hope. But there was no hope whatever. My friend Lord Cherwell, or Professor Lindemann as he was in those days, and Sir Roy Harrod heard of my disastrous exam results and commiserated with me, shaking their heads and saying they saw no likelihood of getting round my deficiency in classical languages.

Luckily my failure acted as an inspiration. I became determined. I resolved to show everyone what I could do. Since my mind was uncomprehending, and I had no chance of mastering the languages on an intellectual basis, I decided to learn the textbooks by heart.

This I did — and passed. So little impression did the performance make on me that I cannot even remember what the subjects were. I have not passed an examination since and can only say that if I do in the future I will regard it as a deterioration of my powers. It is perfectly normal for my thinking processes to seize up at the prospect of sitting down and scribbling under a ticking clock.

I went to Pembroke College, where my acrobatic technique of playing Rugby football led me into trouble. When tackling another player I did not wait for him to come to me; instead I charged at him, causing him to misjudge the speed at which we approached each other. And when about to be tackled with the ball I dived over my opponent's head, landed on the nape of my neck, completed a full somersault and carried on.

These disconcerting antics earned me the nickname of Bungie, the slang for an India rubber. My swan song came when during the course of a single game I broke a player's leg and another's collarbone, winded two more and butted a fifth with my head so hard that I knocked him unconscious. After that I kept acrobatics for special occasions.

I managed to win two wagers off Freddie Smith, now

Lord Birkenhead. The first was for diving over twenty-two undergraduates kneeling in line in Tom Quad (when landing I just grazed the last man, who rolled over too); the other was for diving over Freddie's table in his rooms after dinner one evening, without touching any of the glasses, bottles or other things on it.

I dabbled in art in a rather aesthetic way, believing that being an artist meant dressing up in the outlandish clothes that artists are supposed to wear. Also I satisfied my craving for music by playing the chapel organ from time to time. The dean overheard me once and was most indignant.

"What was that irreverent music?" he asked.

Only with difficulty was I able to convince him that what I had played, though tuneful, was quite respectable. It was Wagner's Good Friday Music from *Parsifal*.

Another of my Oxford recreations was railways. Together with some fellow enthusiasts headed by John Sutro and Lord Rosse, I formed a private and exclusive club. The idea was to have a complete evening on railways twice a year. It probably seems an odd idea of pleasure to go all the way to Cardiff and back, but railway travel was far cleaner and more comfortable than it is now. The climax to our activities came when I persuaded my cousin Viscount Churchill to let us borrow King Edward VII's dining car plus kitchen car. We set out from London, hitched to an ordinary passenger train from Paddington, and made for Oxford, where the famous stationmaster, Mr. Smith, in top hat, had us shunted into the middle line for a magnificently regal dinner. He then attached us to the 7:40 P.M. back to Paddington. One could do that sort of thing in those days, and it did not cost much.

My most important distraction at Oxford, however, was my first big romance. The young lady in question became an extremely important person in my life. We met at a dance at Lord Wimborne's home, Wimborne House, behind the Ritz. It was a lavish, fabulous dance, the entire house lit by candles. And there, most delectably, with very dark eyes and an intelligent snub nose, was Sophie — the name I shall give her to spare her blushes.

I fell for her at once. Her mother did not like the look of me at all, and as much as said so, but Sophie and I started to go around together. We frequently went to the opera at Covent Garden. Then we would have dinner. I would sketch her in idealistic poses and talk about art with a capital A. It was all great fun and terribly highbrow, though I sensed danger in that she was much more mature than I. My humble talents were really no match for hers.

By the summer of 1929 our friendship had deepened into love. We had almost reached the point of getting engaged. Then her mother decided that drastic action was needed to break up the situation. Sophie was whisked off on a trip to India. Both of us were very brave about it. Before Sophie went we had a secret supper party with lots of tears and pledges of undying devotion.

I too traveled abroad. It so happened that Canadian Pacific Railways offered my uncle a holiday tour across Canada. The invitation generously included his brother and both wives, but neither Aunt Clemmie nor my mother

wanted to go. Uncle and my father took Randolph and
me instead. I was twenty, and Randolph, a sort of Nordic
or Anglo-Saxon equivalent of Rudolph Valentino, was
eighteen.

We sailed from Liverpool on the *Empress of Britain* on
August 3, 1929. The crossing to Quebec was uneventful
except when at seven o'clock one morning the captain of
the liner, Captain Latta, got us out of bed to look at an
iceberg. The captain was an entertaining host at table
and had a fund of stories. It was he who had caught Crip-
pen and his mistress when the latter was dressed as a boy.

As everyone knows, the spectacle of entering Quebec
is outstanding. Captain Latta invited us up to the bridge
to see it from the best viewpoint, but Randolph had disappeared.

"Where has he got to?" growled my uncle.

Mysteriously, Randolph was still missing when the ship
docked and we disembarked. He could not be found anywhere. Eventually he turned up at our hotel in a taxi with
some wonderful excuse about being locked in a bathroom,
and was thoroughly ticked off.

Next morning our hosts and local notables appeared,
offering their services to my uncle. "Where would you
like to go and what do you want to see?" they asked.

My uncle's first request amazed everyone. "The Heights
of Abraham," he said.

"But that's a golf course!" one of the officials protested.

"I want to see the battlefield," said my uncle stubbornly.

"What battlefield?"

My uncle was getting impatient. "What do you mean,

what battlefield? I refer to the Heights of Abraham which Wolfe scaled to defeat Montcalm."

Wolfe? Montcalm? Nobody seemed to have heard of them. Amidst confusion we descended into a fleet of cars and set off. My uncle wanted to begin the tour at the bottom of the Heights, to see exactly the situation that faced Wolfe and his men on the night they made the attack. None of our guides knew which road led down there, so maps had to be sent for. Eventually we found ourselves staring up at a rugged, sandy, grass-covered cliff about a hundred feet high. What was so extraordinary was that my uncle gazed at it, brandished his walking cane, and exclaimed: "Ha, why yes!" He seemed to recognize the place.

Randolph and I had already guessed what would happen, and we were right. "You two," said my uncle, pointing, "are General Wolfe's army. Climb the Heights and the rest of us will engage you at the top."

The climb was exhausting enough in shirtsleeves in daylight; it must have been dreadfully difficult at night, carrying guns and equipment. When at last Randolph and I scrambled over the rim of the cliff we were faced with the unique sight of Quebec's top citizens scattered over the golf course and advancing towards us, representing various enemy units. My uncle, who elected to be Montcalm, then ordered us all back to the cars. He had seen what he wanted to see. He was satisfied.

Our hosts arranged a fishing trip near the great falls of Montmorency. My father was pleased because he adored fishing, but no one else in our family has ever understood the joy of this patient pastime, which we feel is ill-rewarded unless one is hunting something big such as whale or shark. So while Father was contentedly occupied with rod and line, my uncle and I got out our sketchbooks and canvases.

Each of us was presented with a Stetson, which my uncle adopted at once as a welcome addition to his hattery, and we soon became known as the Churchill Troupe. The rest of our time in Quebec was spent in visiting distinguished people, among them Sir Robert Borden, the Prime Minister during the First World War. He was a most impressive-looking man and he and my uncle had a great deal to discuss, but naturally Randolph and I had little interest in the talk of long ago. Sir Robert kept us occupied by giving us a large collection of the speeches he had made and pamphlets he had issued during his political career.

In Ottawa the Prime Minister of the day, Mr. Mackenzie King, looked after us. I remember a very unusual incident on the steps of the House of Parliament. We had been shown round the chambers and were leaving the House. As my uncle reached the foot of the steps, a thickset little man came up.

"Mr. Churchill," he said, "I would like to give you this box of cigars in admiration of your achievements."

My uncle accepted the gift gratefully. "Thank you so much," he said. "We have met before, I think. It was in India in 1897, when I was with the Fourth Hussars."

"Yes," agreed the man in surprise. "I was the regimental trumpeter."

"I remember you well," my uncle assured him. "How very kind!"

It was a supreme example of my uncle's memory for faces.

On arrival in Calgary we went to see the oil wells. Two very important gentlemen who either owned or managed them took charge of us and we were taken to a typical well to be shown how it worked. Before long, though, my uncle's questions became so detailed and searching that neither of our hosts could answer them. A scientist had to be summoned from the laboratory, and he looked astounded at my uncle's grasp of the subject. The managers trailed behind my uncle, rather humble at not knowing how their own plant operated.

After dinner in our hotel that evening my uncle declared: "I think I now understand how oil is produced and refined." He gave us boys a summary of what he had learned and finished by saying: "Tonight I propose writing a short treatise on the matter."

He did.

At this stage of the trip Canadian Pacific Railways suggested we would enjoy the Rockies more if we went through them by open car. My uncle sat in front with the chauffeur. Randolph, my father and I sat behind. The day was warm, the sky clear, and the scenery incredibly magnificent. After a couple of miles my uncle let out an almighty yell followed by a rich stream of abuse.

"Stop the car!" he shouted. "A 'wapse' is up my sleeve!"

His left arm had been resting along the top of the car door and the insect was swept into his jacket. After the

sleeve of his shirt had been rolled up and the sting examined, he quietened down. To take his mind off the pain we
went for a stroll. The perfume of the pine trees was terrific, but spoilt by the stronger smell of our parents' cigars.

We stopped at Lake Louise for a while in a private
chalet. On our first evening the beauty of the lake, the
scent of the trees and the surrounding silence, so heavy
that one could almost hear it, were disturbed only by
Randolph quoting from memory the long definition of
prostitution from Lecky's *History of European Morals*.

At ten the next morning my uncle loaded his painting
gear aboard a rowboat and asked me to take him to where
he could paint the lake and the mountains behind it.

"Leave me now, Johnny," he instructed when we had
found a suitable spot, "and come back at one o'clock."

Vicious wild bears were said to inhabit the forest but he
insisted on being left. I became boatman-in-chief on that
lake and rowed him to numerous lonely points for different paintings. It was always rather a relief to go and collect
him at the appointed time and find him safe. He would be
sitting on his little stool hard at work at a picture, wearing his Stetson, with his nose covered with one of the
special Churchillian nose shields. Like the rest of us, my
uncle has a very fine, sensitive skin, and he protected the
top of his nose from the hot sun by means of a piece of
gauze tied round his nose with tapes. It looked somewhat
peculiar and of course he took it off when photographers
were around. His delicate skin is probably the reason why
he never grew a mustache and why he wears a hat even
when only going out into the garden.

When we reached Banff, Randolph and I spent most of the day in the sulphur swimming bath where the water was about ninety-five degrees. Once again he showed his bravery and daring.

"How about a double acrobatic dive from the top board?" I asked.

To my utter astonishment he accepted. Anyone can dive from a height of as much as ten feet without being an expert, but an acrobatic dive from thirty feet when you do not know how to do it is, to my mind, more frightening than a parachute jump from an airplane. When jumping by parachute one's chief responsibility ends with pulling the ripcord, whereas in diving it is essential to leave the board correctly and control one's balance through the air all the time.

I chose a fairly simple dive. I lay on my back with my head at the end of the board and raised my legs at right angles. Randolph then placed his stomach on the soles of my feet. Viewed from this face-downward position the bottom of the pool some forty-five feet below looked a long way off. He asked for a bit of encouragement.

"If you don't panic you will make it," I told him. "Just keep your body straight and I will see that you enter the water all right."

I did a backward roll over the end of the board. Randolph left me and sailed down head first while I followed him feet first.

Loud applause from parents.

From Vancouver we went by boat to Seattle. My uncle had a special letter of authority from the American ambassador in London so that customs formalities could be waived. This was not to allow us to beat Prohibition and smuggle in a crate of Scotch but simply to eliminate the delay and inconvenience of baggage examination. Actually we had nothing at all to declare except my father's 16-millimeter cine-camera and the rolls of film belonging to it. Nevertheless, the head customs officer insisted on closely examining every single item of luggage. The contents were pulled out, studied and thrust back in again. My uncle got so angry I thought he would explode. He had some pretty direct things to say.

"What are you looking for?" he shouted. "I have already told you we have nothing to declare. The point of this letter from the ambassador is to assure you of my integrity."

"We are looking for guns and ammunition," replied the officer.

Guns and ammunition! Did we look like gangsters?

It was no good. We just had to sit and wait. My father had practically to swear on the Bible that his camera was purely for private use and not for photographing military secrets.

"Monstrous! Absolutely monstrous!" fumed my uncle around his cigar.

But when our suitcases had been shut and locked again, an extraordinary change came over the customs man. His tough face relaxed. "Mr. Churchill," he said, "I apologize for this inconvenience. May I invite you and your party into my office for a drink?"

Well, in view of the appalling treatment we had suffered, our parents thought that a drink might calm them down. They accepted. No sooner had we entered the man's office and made sure that the door was shut behind us than he opened a cupboard and produced two bottles of really excellent champagne. We gulped it gratefully.

Of all the lunatic experiments carried out by any government of English-speaking people, Prohibition probably deserves first place, not because of the intention — it was well meant — but because of inevitably disastrous consequences. The hooch and other illegal concoctions which the nation drank instead of ordinary healthy wines, beers and spirits must have caused an enormous amount of drunkenness, illness and death. And that was all Prohibition achieved. My father and uncle, being perfectly normal, natural men, liked the simple habit of drinking to quench their thirst and supplement the enjoyment of food; furthermore, they had every intention of doing so despite Prohibition.

It was impossible to organize bottles of wine for meals, almost all of which were official or semiofficial functions, but Randolph and I cunningly managed to supply our parents with something worth drinking before the speeches. Although we looked (we hoped) innocent youths, each of us had a long thin metal flask of best brandy hidden in an inside pocket of his jacket. When the coffee had been poured out, we drank ours quickly and tipped our parents' into our cups. Then we refilled their cups from our flasks — a tricky business which meant absorbing the attention of the nearest dignitaries with lively conversation.

Our host in the American West was William Randolph

Hearst. At that time he was conducting a fierce anti-British campaign throughout his vast newspaper empire and we were not by any means sure how he and my uncle were going to get on together. However, a fleet of cars picked us up for the long but beautiful journey through the giant redwood forests to Hearst's ranch at San Simeon. On the way we stopped at a restaurant, where the owner came up against my uncle's insistence for accuracy in facts.

"Now this fireplace, Mr. Churchill," said the owner, "is the largest in the world."

Randolph, my father and I, having learned that the giant redwoods were the largest trees in the world, were quite prepared to accept the man's claim. It was one of those monster Jacobean fireplaces with niches in which one could sit right close to the blaze.

"That is very interesting," commented my uncle after some cogitation. "But how do you know it is the world's largest fireplace?"

"Well," drawled the owner, "many people come here, and so far no one has said that it isn't."

This reasoning seemed to satisfy my uncle.

Our entry into Hearst's ranch was the sort of fantastic experience which could happen only in America. When we still had several miles to go our cavalcade was met by private uniformed policemen who led the way as out-riders. The main entrance to the grounds resembled that of a medieval castle. The colossal gates slowly rose into the air like a portcullis and we passed underneath. A wide cattle grid made the road bumpy, the reason for the grid

quickly becoming obvious. The moment we were through
the gates we were surrounded by a zoo of wild animals:
buffalo, giraffe, elephant — the lot. The grounds were in
fact a kind of private big game preserve. In the distance
on top of a pyramidlike mountain stood the house, for
which we made at speed.

Hearst treated our visit as a state occasion. Although
he had been separated from his wife for some time he
decided — for form's sake, I suppose — to summon her
from New York to act as official hostess. His very close
friend, the blonde, blue-eyed and fabulously attractive
film star Marion Davies, was temporarily banished to her
house at Santa Monica near Hollywood.

The house itself was unbelievable. Hardly a single thing
in it was wholly American. The basic design of the main
building was copied from a Spanish church and the façade was an original wooden structure lifted bodily from,
I should think, Morocco. I made a drawing of it. Inside
the building were copies of the tapestries at Blenheim, a
refectory table which originally belonged to a European
monastery, and faithful copies of Greek and Roman statues. The garden, laid out in open patio style, was surrounded by intriguing little paths that led amidst trees
with every now and then more marble statuary. Strangely
enough, it was in Hearst's garden that I first saw the
famous Greek statue of the Venus of Cyrene, the original
of which is in the Neopolitan Museum in Rome. Hearst's
swimming pool was the only item which did not seem to
be copied from anything. It was probably original.

At mealtimes in the main hall an enormous crowd of

people gathered at the long refectory table, but Hearst evidently favored the rather bewildering tradition, practiced at Blenheim, of not introducing anyone to anybody else. It was quite impossible for my neighbors to tell me the names of the other guests, who appeared to be friends of the Hearst family or journalists calling on business.

Butterflies abounded at San Simeon. When two or three large brown striped ones, known I believe as Milkweeds, settled on my arm, my uncle wanted me to collect all the species in sight, but I refused. Randolph and I were already butterfly-chasing in the sense that we were paying court to several of the charming women guests. My uncle observed our progress in this direction with great good humor and laughed when one of Randolph's young ladies, after I had successfully plied her with romantic conversation under the stars, deserted Randolph and paid her attentions to me.

"You know," my uncle remarked to his son, "I think it is just as well we are leaving soon because Johnny seems to be making unexpected progress!"

His benevolent attitude changed, however, when Randolph and I decided to make an expedition in the night. Hearst accommodated his guests in two-bedroom villas in the grounds. Randolph forced his way into one of them but made an awful error. It was his father's bedroom. Uncle Winston woke up at once and was exceedingly annoyed. Blasted by a withering reprimand, we both retired feeling very sheepish and fed up.

Much to our surprise, considering Hearst's campaign against England, he and my uncle got along together most cordially. After four days we climbed into another large fleet of cars and were taken to Los Angeles. Hearst and my uncle occupied the leading car, my father and some dignitary sat in the second one, and Randolph and I were in the third. The policemen on motorcycles escorted us through the game preserve and down the valleys to the coast road.

In Los Angeles our hostess became Marion Davies. We were given bedrooms in a plush hotel but for entertainment were taken to her villa at Santa Monica. As exotic as one would expect a villa in Hollywood to be, it had black marble bathrooms. A huge swimming pool separated the house from the beach.

Hearst said to Randolph and me: "Draw up a list of all the film stars you would like to meet and I'll get them to come along for a banquet."

Luckily it so happened that when I was cramming at Stanway Hall before going to Oxford, one of my friends, David Herbert, was a great expert on film stars. As a result of this friendship, and the fact that I was practicing drawing by sketching stars' faces from photographs, I was easily able to draw up a long and impressive list to which Randolph readily agreed.

Hearst was as good as his word. The first night on which he was our host and Marion Davies our hostess, we entered the villa to find an enormous line-up of stars. Except for Greta Garbo, whose disinclination for company is well known, the cream of Hollywood was there. All four of us walked down the line shaking hands. We felt rather privileged, because usually meeting a film star is a matter

of being presented; on this occasion the stars were presented to us.

The evening went well. Charlie Chaplin and Marion
Davies danced a *pas de deux,* the interesting thing being
that Charlie's feet were so small he was actually able to
step into Marion's shoes. Hearst, plump, rotund and hospi-
table, was in very good form. He contributed to the
entertainment with a solo act in which he let his legs go
wobbly and lurched his enormous frame across the room to
the rhythm of the band. It was so funny that it has been
part of my own parlor trick repertoire ever since.

The star I liked the most was a sweet black-haired girl
of about seventeen named Mary Brian. But I could make
very little progress with her because a handsome young
actor seemed to be catching her attention the whole time.
So I found very agreeable company with Billy Dove,
Bessie Love (what extraordinary names) and Bebe Daniels,
whom I met in London recently — we reminisced about
our frivolities of thirty years ago. Randolph and I both
discovered that our tastes in these beautiful creatures
coincided when we met Dorothy Mackail.

I formed an attachment to tough guy Wallace Beery,
but Harold Lloyd seemed rather too disappointingly ordinary off screen.

Marion Davies was wonderful to us boys, but very
cautious in her flirtations. And no wonder, for a certain
guest on the Hearst yacht who paid a lot of attention to
her had died in unexplained circumstances. This unhappy
event made us wary.

Louis B. Mayer, head of Metro-Goldwyn-Mayer, invited us to lunch, and after a lengthy tour of his studios it was announced that we boys would spend the evening at a cinema while our parents were entertained by some chorus girls. Naturally Randolph and I did not approve of this arrangement and we switched programs.

Next day an expedition to catch swordfish was organized. Father went on it with my uncle, who promptly caught a wonderful hundred-and-eighty-eight-pound specimen, which struck me as smart work on the part of their hosts. Randolph and I meanwhile amused ourselves by looking round Twentieth-Century-Fox.

Sight-seeing round studios can become dreadfully boring. They are all the same. The frantic confusion is uniform; only the sets and actors are different. Unless one knows somebody in the film there is not much point in going. In Japan recently when I was asked to see some local studios, it was the first invitation I skipped. I had no doubt that inside they would be exactly like Elstree, Pinewood or Hollywood. Twentieth-Century-Fox ensured our keenest interest by parading a mass of lovely girls for our benefit. Then, when Charlie Chaplin showed us round his own studios, where he was making *City Lights* at the time, he treated us to a special showing of his unpublishable archives. These were sequences which could not be used because they were too embarrassing. One of them concerned the harnessing of a horse-drawn fire engine.

"I wanted it done extremely rapidly," Charlie explained. "Putting the harness on horses always takes a long while, so we thought we would film the harness being taken off, which is much quicker, and reverse the film."

Everything went famously while the scene was being shot. Unfortunately, as the archives proved only too clearly, no one noticed that the excitement had caused one horse to relieve itself. When the film was reversed, the result of this relief leaped off the ground and all disappeared inside the animal with breath-taking exactitude.

An interesting social development concerning my uncle took place in Hollywood before we left. Randolph and I, in order to make speedy headway with the various women film stars we met, adopted the rather foreign custom of kissing their hands on meeting and leaving them. It was flattering and dashing, but not altogether too eccentric in a film capital. We were surprised and delighted when the time came to say good-by to Marion Davies. Each of us gave her a very warm kiss on the hand — whereupon my uncle raised his hat, bowed and did likewise.

We crossed America as the guests of Mr. Charles M. Schwab, head of the Bethlehem Steel Company. He put at my uncle's disposal his private railroad car, an elaborate affair containing bedrooms, bathrooms, a kitchen, drawing rooms and an open observation platform. It was hitched to the end of a train and shunted off when necessary so that we could visit famous spots such as the Grand Canyon.

Having seen the Yosemite Valley, which was the broadest, longest, deepest and most remarkable valley in the world, it was not surprising to find that the Grand Canyon was the longest, deepest, widest, etc. Perhaps because of this surfeit of statistics and out of sheer devilry, Randolph and I stood on our heads on the canyon's edge. Our parents always seemed to suffer from some kind of vertigo at seeing other people doing dangerous things. They reacted to our daring with a violent shout of alarm. Actually it was not very perilous because we were some distance from the edge, but I admit it looked frightening.

I have two very clear recollections of Chicago. The first is the building of the Chicago *Tribune*, where we visited its president, Colonel Robert McCormick. The vast, plain façade had a strange accumulation of lumps projecting around the front door. On closer inspection they turned out to be pieces of stone let into the building, each with an inscription underneath. These inscriptions showed that there was a piece from the Great Wall of China, another from the Taj Mahal, from the Coliseum, St. Paul's Cathedral, the Houses of Parliament, and so on. Only an American mind, surely, would think of making such a collection and displaying it in this way.

The other interesting spectacle in Chicago was the huge Armour canning factory. It is laid out with conveyer belts for dealing with pigs, sheep and bullocks with terrifying efficiency.

"What you are about to see," announced our guide proudly, "are the processes by which animals come to the factory alive and in a short space of time leave in the form of sausages or tins of meat."

Whether we wanted to see it or not, we were stood in the middle of the place and shown the animals coming in: the pigs squealing, as they always do on such occasions, and the sheep in deathly silence, like city workers trooping to their offices on a Monday morning. In a matter of seconds each animal was strung up by its hind legs on a moving hook to be slaughtered by one man, bled by the next, skinned by another and so on until the carcass was lowered on a conveyer belt in sections and meat was squirted like toothpaste out of a nozzle into an enormously long sausage skin. This gruesome spectacle, fascinating though it might be for people who like that sort of thing, was definitely not for me. It was days before I enjoyed eating meat again.

Even more fantastic was the presentation box given to my uncle at the end of our visit. Our guide explained: "These items are made from parts of the animals which are not edible." The box was filled with luxurious soaps, creams, lipsticks and other aids to feminine beauty.

I never ceased to be amazed at the number of swimming pools in the States. Even the smallest town seemed to have one, with the result that Americans are first-class swimmers. When one meets a stockbroker, for example, or any other type of sedentary-looking executive, he invariably turns out to be an expert diver.

As soon as we stopped at a hotel during our American tour, I found the piano and amused myself by playing Wagner, Strauss waltzes and Chopin; I was still not able to master any Bach at that time. Also in spare moments I wrote reams and reams to Sophie in India. I remember writing in one of my letters: *It seems to me extraordinary that the Lord Almighty, or Nature, has devised the means whereby the result of a union of the souls and bodies of lovers is the creation of another person who is an entirely independent and different individual.* I suppose that I myself am a case in point. My parents, who were very much in love with each other, produced what could be described as a "love child" — i.e., J.S.C. What could their feelings have been when as the outcome of their liaison they found a peculiar little boy who grew up with a mind so rebellious and unconventional as to seem to have nothing to do with their union?

The Condé Nasts threw a lavish dance for us in New York. I can only dance well with a good partner, and that night I danced superbly. My partner was Adele Astaire. She attracted me so much that next morning I followed up our meeting with a visit to her home. She received me very politely.

"Let's sit on the sofa," she said.

The situation began to get somewhat interesting, and I was making some pressing attentions when the door from the kitchen burst open and in came an enormous Negro. I suppose he was her method of coping with amorous young men. Certainly it worked. I fled.

From New York my father and uncle went down to Washington and to Gettysburg for an on-the-spot reconnaissance of the battlefield, but Randolph and I were due back at Oxford in a fortnight so we were sent home on the *Berengaria*. The late Lord Birkenhead and Sir Harry McGowan, both of whom were guests at the Condé Nast dance, were making the crossing too and agreed to look after us.

In the dining room we sat at Lord Birkenhead's table. He looked forbidding, but had twinkly eyes. Seated at the table in addition to Sir Harry, who had the typical face of a shrewd Scotsman, were half a dozen men who appeared to be hangers-on. Their main function seemed to be to say yes and provide entertainment by playing cards. In return for this effort they were able to enjoy the unique company and wit of people such as Lord Birkenhead and share the cigars and drink in which great men indulge.

A popular way of keeping the ravages of good living in check is a Turkish bath, and Lord Birkenhead and Sir Harry would have one every day while Randolph and I swam in the ship's pool. I had always thought a Turkish bath to be a rather desperate affair. Imagine my surprise when I went to have one myself and passed their cubicle. His Lordship and Sir Harry were sitting stark naked steaming their guts out, but each was smoking a fat cigar and each had a double whisky and soda in his hand.

After dinner each evening Randolph and I used to retire from the table, ostensibly to go to bed, but of course we wandered round the lounges and tried to have as much fun as we could. Towards the end of the voyage Randolph formed a friendship with a very young Dutch girl — she was fifteen — who was returning to Holland with her parents. Somehow news of this reached Lord Birkenhead. I do not think he was unduly concerned, but the situation gave him the chance for one of his unique observations. On the final night of the voyage, when Randolph and I got up to leave as usual, he gravely called to us in front of everyone to sit down again.

"Your parents have put you in my charge," he said. "Therefore I feel it is my duty to give you all the advice I can. It has come to my notice, Randolph, that you have been seen in the company of a charming lady on this ship whose parents are Dutch, and I believe they are not a little concerned as to what it is all about. Now if you wish to indulge in this sort of pastime you must do it in such a way that it does not cause offense to anyone."

We fidgeted in our chairs, tapped our cigars on our ash trays and wondered what was coming next.

"Only the other day," continued Lord Birkenhead, "I found myself in a similar situation. It was at the Condé Nasts' party was it not, Harry?" Sir Harry nodded. Lord Birkenhead went on: "I found a delightful young lady and wished to converse with her. It was very crowded. There seemed to be nowhere to sit in privacy, so we went to the ladies' cloakroom, which did not seem to be permanently engaged. I had reached the middle of some very ordinary amorous talk when a man appeared at the door. It occurred to me that he was the lady's husband. So before he had time to say anything or cause trouble I got rid of him. I simply said most politely, but firmly: 'Excuse me, sir, but obviously you have made a dreadful mistake. I think you have failed to observe that this is the *ladies'* cloakroom.'"

Randolph did not, I hope, emulate his temporary guardian's example.

My father and uncle got back to England early in November. It was a somber time for the Western world; Wall Street had crashed.

V

Beret, Cloak, Riding Breeches

B ACK AT OXFORD I had a premonition. I felt convinced that whatever my Father might plan for me in commerce, eventually my career would be something to do with art. Accordingly I concentrated on music, I painted pictures and did sculpture. For expert help I joined the Ruskin School of Art and studied under Rutherston, Sir William Rothenstein's brother.

Of course I also had my share of the bright life which is a chief reason for being an undergraduate. I developed two special party tricks. The first was to sit in an ordinary wooden chair, grasping the seat with my left hand and the back with my right, and without touching the floor, slowly twist my body until I was standing on my hands. It was quite an acrobatic feat which I stopped doing only when I injured my back.

The other trick, which I still do today, was a favorite of mine at Middleton Park, where my host was my contemporary Lord Jersey, known in the best English custom of dukes, marquesses and earls as Grandy, short for Grandison, his second title as son of the earl when he was born. We went to Middleton Park for week-end parties. I found a length of balustrade in a really high place — at the top of the main stairs, for example — and stood very close to it. Then, in the middle of a deep conversation with someone, I suddenly toppled right over the balustrade backward. This is absolutely guaranteed to raise a scream of horror from the rest of the guests. Every dowager in the house instantly succumbs to the vapors. It looks terrifyingly dangerous. The secret is that at the instant of actually sitting on the balustrade I grasp the inner edge. After toppling over I can haul myself back again.

The night when it was I who thought my end had come was during a car trip back to Oxford from a riot of a party at Cheltenham. It was very late. My friend who was driving was extremely rich and crazy about speed. We were scorching along at ninety miles an hour and smashed into an enormous Buick coming in the opposite direction. This enemy vehicle sliced off the whole of one side of our car. We skidded for I don't know how many yards and stopped in a field. Why we weren't killed or seriously hurt is a mystery. I decided then and there that I would never drive a car — and never have, though I can make the machine move.

A longer but no less madcap expedition in which I involved myself was a fortnight's trip to Rome with James Lees Milne, two girls and another boy. (Thirty years later, by a strange coincidence, Colin Crewe, a half brother of one of these girls, who was the sister of Lord O'Neil, became my son-in-law.) Our respective parents thought the whole thing most unorthodox and arranged for the British

Embassy to keep an eye on us. The Embassy found this difficult. We stayed at the Hotel Ambasciatori, sampling the pleasures of a foreign capital in a slightly irresponsible way. One of our eccentricities was that after a heavy day of sight-seeing, which we did separately, we would foregather for a meal and then siesta with our legs resting perpendicularly up a wall, discussing our experiences. Like most young people I had a very sweet tooth, and in consequence we sampled that delicious but dangerous muscat grape champagne, Asti Spumante. I still love it today, but it can give one the biggest head of all.

Sophie wrote from India, listing the art galleries and churches I ought to visit, and this gave me a momentous introduction to the world of classical painting. At once I sensed that it had a parallel in the music I had been hearing. Tracing the development of classical painters to the climax of Raphael was to me very similar to going through the Gregorian chants, Bach and so on up to Wagner, and on to Debussy and Stravinsky.

I appeared to attract attention by wearing a large green hat and a black cloak lined with scarlet, an outfit which I considered to be very practical and aesthetic. The hat was attached to the collar of my cloak by a strand of elastic. When I paused at a monument or canvas and wanted to look at my guidebook, I simply threw the hat into the air, knowing it would be dangling at the end of the elastic when I wanted it again. The girls were thoroughly impressed by this theatrical behavior.

Our entire trip to Rome and back, including hotel bills, cost only thirty pounds each. That was 1929.

On returning to London I realized for the first time that quite a few Churchills exist on both sides of the Atlantic. One of Randolph's girl friends came to England on a short visit, and the friend introduced me to a female companion. I was flattered when this woman declared that she was dying to meet me. I went to her flat in Down Street. She was large and very American.

"Aw gee," she began, "so *you* are the nephew of the great Winston! Let me tell you right now how pleased I am to see you. I sure will give him a full description of you when I get back to the States."

This was rather puzzling. My uncle had not mentioned he was going to America.

"You know, I haven't seen Winston for some time," she went on. "When did you last see him?"

It was hard to imagine how such an enormous woman could have fitted into my uncle's life, but my uncle has always been amazing. I presumed it possible. "I saw him only a few days ago," I said. "I had lunch down at Chartwell. He is in very good health, thank you."

"Chartwell?" she queried. "What's that?"

"His place in the country."

She frowned. "I know Winston's place in the country very well, and I am sure it is called something quite different."

After a lot of perplexing references to so-called relations who were totally unknown to me, at last I realized what had happened. The woman was confusing my uncle with Winston Churchill the famous American novelist. She was extremely disappointed to learn that I had no connections with her hero, but was merely a relative of the English Winston. After a while she cheered up sufficiently to mention that this muddle had occurred before, and my uncle had even gone so far as to send his American namesake a most amusing letter in the third person, the gist of which was that in future he would call himself Winston Spencer Churchill.

The sun seemed to shine much brighter and the autumn days were as heady as spring when Sophie returned from India. Bright-eyed, she described the Indian sculpture she had seen and the temples she had visited. I had little money to spend on her; I could not afford any orchids or champagne. But our talk of art kept us high in the clouds.

If her mother had known we were meeting each other again she would probably have had a fit. She was busy with important marriage plans and had contrived to get various minor Continental royals interested in her daughter. Once more Sophie was sent off on a cultural trip abroad. Heavily chaperoned, and with a girl friend, she was to go to Italy to study painting and then to Germany for music.

I went along too, strictly unofficially, by the easy method of trailing her like a detective. I wore a false mustache, which completely changed my looks. It was all a true-life farce which led to hilarious situations. I kept arriving at the same art galleries they visited, and by extraordinary coincidences called at the same restaurants and shops. By the time we reached Florence the chaperone twigged that something most odd was happening, but fortunately Sophie explained that she had met me in London and I was allowed to join their party. I studied museums and churches with them. At the end, the chaperone said firmly:

"This is where we must leave you. Now we are going to Assisi."

I went to the station to bid them good-by, and having done this, jumped into the guards' van as the train moved out. To their utter astonishment when they reached Assisi they found me booking in at the same hotel.

The rather extraordinary love chase reached a complicated phase when it took us through northern Italy to Lake Maggiore. Sophie stayed at Pallanza, in the castle of the Marquesa Casanova, which is on one side of the lake. I stayed at Baveno on the opposite side, because it was there that Wagner wrote his prelude to *The Rhinegold.*

In the evening I rowed across the lake, climbed the castle wall and got into the grounds. Sophie met me in the woods, wearing her nightdress. Life is an awful bore if one doesn't have a spot of fun. We were young. The setting was superb — typical Italian woodland, shadowy with moonlight — and the whole adventure appealed to us as extremely romantic. We fully believed that nobody else knew about it, but the Marquesa Casanova, a very distinguished lady, has since told me many times how she remembers closing her eyes to our secret rendezvous.

Then came the question of going to Germany. Sophie was attending the Wagner Festival at Bayreuth, whereas I favored the one in Munich. Accordingly we arranged that I would go to Munich for a few days and meet her in the woods at Bayreuth after the first act of *Tristan and Isolde.*

For a while I had company in Munich. I met a Harrovian friend of mine, Charles Vereker, the son of Field Marshal Lord Gort, who was also a great Wagner lover. In addition, I found Caroline Paget, daughter of the Marquess of Anglesey, to share my Wagnerian interests. We went about on bicycles, the cheapest and easiest means of getting around the town, and landed up appropriately enough in the beautiful Englischergarten. She was heavily chaperoned, which was just as well in such romantic surroundings.

When Charles left I had a worrying and unlucky experience. I decided to go to the Opera House for *The Mastersingers,* which was due to begin around six o'clock in the evening. On arrival I looked for a place to chain my bicycle. Several of my friends had had theirs stolen and it was a wise precaution to padlock one's machine to something solid. As everybody who went to prewar Munich will know, a little theater called the Residenz, now destroyed by bombs, was squeezed between the Opera House and the Residenz Palace. It had very stout ornamental railings. The theater itself was heavily shuttered and appeared to be temporarily out of use, and I thought I would be exceptionally clever. I chained my cycle at front and rear, right across the closed main gates.

After the first act of *The Mastersingers* I strolled out into the street for a breather. To my absolute horror I saw a scene of pandemonium. The Residenz was in use that night, very much so. A Mozart opera was beginning at eight. The audience had not been able to get in because of my bicycle. Five hefty policemen had been called, and lifted the gates, plus cycle, entirely off their hinges in one piece! These policemen were now strutting up and down, thirsting for the culprit.

I did not dare look too closely. I pretended I had nothing to do with the matter. Anxiously I dashed back into the Opera House for the second act, wondering what would happen. At the next interval I came out again. The policemen were still there. I returned to Wagner more worried than ever. I could see myself spending the night in jail.

The Mastersingers did not end until 11:30, by which time the Mozart next door was over. I came out of the Opera House warily and found the Residenz shut and barred again. The gates had been lifted back in position. And the five policemen were still prowling around, waiting. With elaborate nonchalance I walked across the square to a café for some bacon and eggs. When I had finished, the policemen were looking decidedly impatient. I hurried away in the opposite direction for a walk through the town. I came back again at half-past twelve and peered round a corner at the Residenz. The square was quiet. To my relief, it was empty. The police had given up and gone away. With immense care, and looking over my shoulder, fearing a trap, I tiptoed to my bicycle, unlocked it and furiously pedaled off down the bumpy, cobbled street as if the entire police force of Germany were after me.

In the train on the way to Bayreuth to rejoin Sophie, I

suddenly remembered that I was not wearing my false mustache. It was a difficult item to adjust without a mirror, so I went along to the lavatory. I wondered what the rest of my traveling companions would think when they saw the transformation, but luckily when I returned to the compartment the train had arrived at Nuremberg. Everyone was too busy getting in and out to take any notice. I had to change trains myself, and at once went off to see the Church of St. Catherine, in which the whole first act of *The Mastersingers* is laid. Comparing the original church with the set I had just seen at Munich, it was obvious that the stage designer had worked with great accuracy.

At Bayreuth, Wagner's son Siegfried was taking an active hand in the festival. It was a thrill to see him. For *Tristan and Isolde* I occupied a seat in the stalls three rows in front of Sophie, and was appalled to glance up at the man sitting next to me. It was someone I knew very well: my friend Christopher Sykes, the writer and traveler. At once I buried my face in my program. But worse was to happen. Christopher turned to me.

"May I borrow your program?" he asked.

"Pliz?" I replied, hoping I sounded very foreign and stupid. "I no understand."

Christopher apologized and said: "It doesn't matter." Twenty years later I asked whether he recalled this incident and he did, but he confessed he had no idea it was me. So my disguise must have been fairly convincing.

While at Oxford for the next term I tried my hand at my first mural. It was a church interior, based on the

Upper Church at Assisi, and had several Giotto frescoes in deep perspective. The entire mural, done in water color and chalk on a wall in my rooms, was really a perspective stunt. The choice of subject was significant. I had no architectural training, but was fascinated by the problems of size, proportion and so on which are elements of architecture. The knowledge I gained subsequently molded my whole approach to designing murals.

The dean and bursar were sufficiently impressed by my effort to point it out to the master, who was then vice-chancellor of the university. Between them they decided to preserve it. I hardly think it deserved such a compliment, but it remained there for some eighteen years before it became impossible to clean. I imagine that liberal splashings of beer had given it an antique glaze.

My minor triumph in one direction was followed by tragedy in another. Sophie went off to India again and there met a much older man, very intellectual, who was a world-famous expert on the Indian culture she adored. Overwhelmed by admiration for him, she came back to England and saw me as very small fry by comparison, youthful and immature.

She dropped me. It was like the end of a marriage, or a death. I had to face up to the fact that all was over; I played music for hours to purge my soul — Wagner mostly, the sad and mournful bits, and some of the wonderful études of Chopin.

As far as my studies at Oxford were concerned, I pulled myself together and soon realized I had no hope of passing the preliminary examination, which an undergraduate has

to take after two years. If he fails to pass he is sent down
because it is assumed that he has not been working. Certainly I had not worked. So rather than be sent down, I
resigned, and reluctantly agreed to my father's suggestion
of going into the Stock Exchange. Although I had been
foolish in my academic studies at Oxford, at least I had
enriched my knowledge of people, made hundreds of
friends, and absorbed important influences which were to
affect my life.

I bought a bowler hat and a neat City suit and became
a sort of clerk in his firm, Vickers da Costa, at a nominal
salary of fifty pounds a year plus half commission, which
meant that I received half of the firm's commission on
work I produced.

Thus I embarked on a City career against my better
judgment. When I tried to waver and protest that I
wished I could be a professional artist, my father refused
to listen. He could be very dogged about things and was
known by my cousins as Uncle Well-I-Know-But. Whatever proposition was put to him, he always had an ob-
structive answer beginning with: "Well, I know, but . . ."
Because I was regarded as the dunce of the family, I came
in for a lot of well-I-know-buts, my activities in painting
and the arts being dismissed as "playing the ass." Even my
personal and emotional affairs were criticized. If I disappeared into the woods with a young lady for an amorous conversation it was "playing the ass in the bulrushes."
A career in professional art was "playing the ass in the
gutter."

"Why slave for a few pence," Father argued, "when for

doing nothing except sign a few documents you can drink champagne and smoke cigars for the rest of your life?"

"I don't particularly want champagne and cigars day and night," I replied. "I would rather live the life of an artist than be a stockbroker."

However, I tried to persevere with the City and became a Blue Button. I was allowed on the Stock Exchange floor but could not deal. The Stock Exchange as a whole struck me as a very bewildering place. My father refused to explain the difference between a stock and a share, saying that I ought to have known such an elementary fact long ago. The result was that I never understood what was happening. No money of my own was at stake, and if Amalgamated Lard went up 6s.4d. or the bottom fell out of Consolidated Buckets, it meant nothing to me. When I used to be up in the gallery of the house, standing at the telephone and watching the signals of our man on the floor so that I could pass on the latest prices, I must have made mistakes which cost the firm hundreds. What I liked doing, though, was going round the various banks to collect business. Often it meant a long wait in some vast marble mausoleum of a banking hall. People used to look at me rather oddly because I sat there twiddling my bowler hat, happily studying the classical "orders" of the columns. If I felt inclined I took out a pencil and paper and made sketches.

A great friend of the family, Mr. Reginald McKenna, who was head of the Midland Bank, was sympathetic and organized a large order for me to handle. It was for stock worth something like two hundred thousand pounds. Cer-

tainly it was very exciting to get my two-hundred-and-
fifty-pound commission — very exciting indeed — but I was
not blind to the fact that this was more a gesture than a
reward for acumen and hard drive.

It took me twelve months to decide that sooner or later
I would have to leave the Stock Exchange and take the
plunge as an artist without money behind me. This was
the result of meeting Clare Sheridan.

She is a big woman physically, rather Wagnerian, with
an intense face and penetrating eyes. We met at a party
and discovered we were cousins. Clare is a first cousin of
my father because her mother was the eldest of the three
Jerome sisters of New York. She must have been exceedingly attractive as a young woman. When I met her she was
about forty, but still very vital and bombastic. I fell under
her spell at once. My uncle has always been attracted by
her strong personality. My father was fond of her too, but
Mother could not stand her, the reason being that she is
a revolutionary, a disrupter, with a stimulating habit of
urging people to follow their own inclinations.

Undoubtedly she had an extremely disrupting influence
on me. At the time of meeting her I was working at the
Stock Exchange during the day, painting a mural in Hyde
Park Gardens by the light of one lamp in the evenings for
Lord and Lady Islington, and spending the rest of the
night on a vast scheme in my poor tolerant mother's drawing room. The design covered all the walls and the ceiling
in a most complicated perspective decoration of architecture and landscape, spread into the half-landing and
eventually worked its way up the stairs. It included fake

marbling and fake mahogany and pine, the latter executed
with beer and sprayed with a special pine scent. My
sprawling masterpiece was destroyed by the National
Women's Teachers' Union when they bought the house
from my father in 1938 because, as they told me recently,
they felt they might have been distracted by such scenes.
I must admit there was a very racy Leda and the Swan in
one panel.

Clare used to come and watch me at work. If she caught
me at Hyde Park Gardens she brought food and wine for
a picnic. Her two children, Margaret and Dick, came
along too sometimes. Margaret, who looked like a Fra
Angelico angel, was exquisite. I spent hours painting her
and — yes — kissing her. I do not think Clare would have
approved had she known. After all, we were cousins.

Clare gave me hearty encouragement, urging me not to
waste my energies at the Stock Exchange but to turn to
art full-time. She presented me with her autobiography to
date. It was called *Nuda Veritas*. If veritas, it was certainly nuda. She had upset my uncle, Lord Birkenhead
and others by visiting Russia and sculpting Lenin and
many other members of the Soviet government at a time
when they were not friendly towards us. She confided in
me a great deal which was far too libelous to publish in
the book.

When she took me along to her studio, where she always wore a smock, I was shown her latest work. Obviously she had tremendous talent, but strangely enough,
as can happen in portrait sculpture, it was her limitation.
Her work was inspired not only by the power of the head

of her subject but by the character and brain as well. The more powerful the subject, the larger the bust. Lenin, therefore, was executed in two and a half times life size, my uncle twice life size. This in my opinion is a fault in sculpture, particularly with busts, but is usually the result of immaturity and inexperience. In Clare's case it was the outcome of relying entirely on her talent and creating without knowing why, despite her maturity.

Further encouragement for my efforts came from Sir John Lavery.

"The boy will definitely go far," he predicted. He came to view the mural in my mother's drawing room and brought with him his wife, Lady Lavery — who, by the way, kept having trouble when arriving at receptions where there was an announcer at the door. Asked for her name, she would discreetly whisper "Lady Lavery," at which the reply was invariably: "First door on the left, madam."

Sir Edwin Lutyens also showed keen if reserved enthusiasm for my mural when he came to dinner. During the meal he usually made about ten puns, which were capped by my father's favorite toast: "Champagne for our real friends and real pain for our sham friends."

Knowing that I now hovered on the brink of turning professional, I gave the situation careful thought and pondered on the perils of art as a means of earning bread and butter. I came to the conclusion that there must be a large number of people born with talent, which enables them to pursue their art with a flourish in youth, giving a false impression of genius. The test comes later. It comes with most artists and composers between the ages of thirty and forty. What happens is that reason begins to take over, and the artist discovers he cannot simply do a thing without wondering why, and find that it comes off. He realizes that the mature, considered approach to the problem calls for more than just flair. And this is the stage at which so many — in fact, most — people in the arts fail and fade. To succeed requires that extra bit of specialized knowledge and controlled discipline which not everyone possesses. Acquiring it calls for hard work and study. Even then one has to fight depression and adversity, and rely on luck and opportunity, neither of which can be inherited. And how many important artists have died in poverty, their genius unknown or discovered posthumously? This business of opportunity applies in other spheres too, of course. It is possible that if the opportunity of 1939 had not arisen for my uncle, he would have been forced to slide and waste his genius on lesser affairs. Napoleon had a similar turning point.

The adulation and encouragement which came my way was regarded by my father with some suspicion. He knew it was urging his son to "play the ass in the gutter." My mother on the other hand was secretly very pleased and happy about it, and I think my uncle was kept informed of the situation. He even began to refer to my father as Well-I-Know-But-Jack.

Then suddenly an incident happened which decided the matter. I asked Freddie Birkenhead round to our house one afternoon. It was unusual for him to say anything sensible about me, but he looked at my mural and stroked his chin thoughtfully.

"You really are a talented madcap," he commented. "Why don't you do this professionally?"

"I will," I said, "if you find me a commission!"

That evening he and I dined with Neville Ford. Now Neville was absolutely unique at imitating Freddie's father, Lord Birkenhead. I, for my part, have long made a study of my uncle and claim that I am probably the only person in the world who can actually imitate him in speech and gesture so that, if I were properly made up, it would be difficult to spot the deception. In fact, a film company has already approached me about playing this role. Freddie knew of our imitations and made an offer.

"If you will imitate your uncle," he said, "and you, Neville, will imitate my father, I will organize Johnny a commission."

We protested, but agreed on condition that we both had enormous cigars and lots of brandy. The evening was a memorable success. At the end of our performance Freddie told me: "I know a man who is probably mad enough to commission you to paint his flat."

Next day he called at Cromwell Road with Chipps Channon, the late Sir Henry Channon, M.P., who declared himself to be impressed by my efforts. He promised me a hundred pounds to paint a Benozzo Gozzoli–like fresco round his dining room in Gloucester Place.

"I want it to depict my friends arriving at a fabulous party," he said. "Make it an Italian setting."

My first commission!

The following morning I went to the office in the City and asked to see Mr. Cecil Vickers, the senior partner. He rose from his desk and paced up and down. "Well, what have you got to say?" he demanded.

"I want you to help me," I said timidly. "I do not think I am cut out for this sort of business, but it is no good telling my father. He refuses to take any notice."

Mr. Vickers continued his pacing and inquired: "Have you any idea what you would do instead?"

Rather sheepishly I told him: "I think I can paint walls with frescoes."

"But do you know how?"

"Of course I do." I hoped the lie sounded convincing.

Mr. Vickers considered the matter in weighty silence for a moment, then said briskly: "Right, I will tell you what to do. Go to your father and tell him that you are leaving the firm on January first, 1932, in order to take up a career of painting. I will support you. But you must be honest with yourself and if — only if — you fail, come to me here in this office and I will take you back."

These were generous words. It was twenty-three years later when I went back, and then it was because Cecil Vickers' son Ralph, the present head of Vickers da Costa, invited me to decorate the new boardroom in King William Street.

From time to time in life there are occasions when one has to take a deep breath, put one's head down and press on regardless. This was one of those occasions for me. I threw myself into Chipps's commission with everything I had.

I must admit that I did not possess very much as far as technique was concerned; my experience was negligible. Nevertheless my basic architectural and landscape design was good, and the rest seemed to come naturally. The mural contained about one hundred figures and faces, all of which had to be portraits. It was necessary to copy from photographs the few of Chipps's friends who were in America, but the remainder I was able to study from life. They surged in and out of the house, constantly interrupting me. Regularly at about eleven o'clock every evening a crowd of them used to arrive in high spirits. I would be hard at work in the blue woolen boiler suit I wore for murals (and which later I like to think became the model for my uncle's famous siren suit), and after inspecting what I was doing they started playing rather idiotic games. One of these was to go through the telephone directory, find an odd name and ring the victim up, whatever the hour. I recall that one poor man, the Reverend Mr. Busfun, was so pestered by inquiries as to whether he had been enjoying himself on London Transport that he asked for his name to be taken out of the book.

I was fascinated to overhear how Chipps organized his luncheon parties. He would ring Emerald Cunard, for example, and say he was giving a party at Claridge's. If Emerald showed signs of declining, Chipps promptly told her: "Well, Prince Paul of Yugoslavia will be awfully upset not to see you." At this, of course, Emerald accepted, whereupon Chipps immediately rang to invite Prince Paul, warning him that if he did not come Emerald would be disappointed. In a very short time he managed to draw up a glittering guest list of twenty or more. I was always invited too.

"But I can't possibly come to lunch and work on this painting!" I would protest. But I was dragged off, and yielded to Chipps's persuasion with pleasure.

When the mural was finished, and Chipps had said he was pleased with it, he went away for a while. Freddie Birkenhead, a sound sleeper, occupied the flat for a night and accidentally left a cigarette end burning in a drawing room chair. The flat caught fire. The firemen burst in with hoses and roused Belton, the butler, who in turn knocked respectfully on Freddie's bedroom door. The place was rapidly filling with smoke.

"My lord," shouted Belton, "the flat is on fire!"

"On what?" asked Freddie sleepily.

"On fire!"

"Oh, don't worry. Everything is insured." He turned over and went back to sleep.

The flat was badly damaged and when Chipps married he disposed of the lease to some member of the Willoughby family, who told me he thought my mural so frightful that he had it destroyed.

In this way some three months' work was obliterated with a few slaps of a house painter's brush. Although the mural was indeed immature, it was not as bad as all that. However, I knew its shortcomings and realized how much I had to learn if I was going to settle down to a career as an artist. Being twenty-three, I felt too old to go to an art school. Anyway, art schools can be a waste of time in that one has to forget all one's training before it is possible to create. Consequently I decided on a really intensive course of self-tuition. I would learn my trade by trial and error. My father was giving me an allowance of ten pounds a month. With that I could just about survive without the need to earn.

First, though, I deserved a short holiday. I went to Portofino in Italy to stay in the magnificent villa of my mother's friend Mrs. Audrey Herbert. An interesting crowd had gathered there, including Hilaire Belloc. It was good to see him again. I was anxious to show off some of my high-diving from a rock in the gardens overhanging the sea, and when I said I had forgotten my bathing trunks, Belloc kindly offered to lend me a pair of his ordinary underpants.

The guests collected to watch my dive. I decided to enchant the ladies with a lot of the preliminary palaver — arm-swinging, standing on tiptoe, etc. — which is not essential for diving but makes sure that everybody is watching.

Then I leaped into the air. Unfortunately, Belloc's waist measurement was very much larger than mine. The instant I left the rock, the underpants and I parted company, amidst shrieks of laughter from everyone.

Back in England for my self-imposed retreat, I rented a remote farmhouse in the depths of Wiltshire near Upavon. I lived there alone for eighteen months. It was hot in summer, desperately cold in winter, and the house was supposed to be haunted; at night the creepiness terrified me. I lived on baked beans and sausages. My only domestic help was Florence, who lived in the village and used to venture in every morning to tidy the wreckage and cope with the washing up.

Yet I was able to fill my time with uninterrupted work which would have been impossible in London. I had masses of textbooks and artist's materials. I covered acres of canvas with painting. I sculpted figures and heads, one of which was a magnificent bust of Wagner, and cast them myself. I composed music and studied harmony. Also I decorated the house with murals, which were very much disliked by the owner at the time, though the present one tells me that one of the rooms, in which I painted curtains round the walls, is still as I left it.

During those eighteen months of learning my profession the hard and in my opinion the best way, by actually doing it, I formulated what I call my principles or maxims. A deep impression had been made upon me by Wagner's once saying that an artist needs to make certain rules for himself and stick to them. I suppose my "discoveries" ranked as glimpses of the obvious to established artists, but at least I came across them myself. And obvious though they may be, a surprising number of artists who ought to know better forget them.

The first maxim I evolved is that the mind must work the hands, and not the other way round, or the result will be merely doodling. Work on a blank canvas must be preceded by careful thought and planning. The second maxim is that each type of work, whether it be a mural, frieze or portrait, has its own set of laws regarding what can and cannot be done. When an artist busy on a carved frieze, for instance, is faced with the problem of putting three objects one behind the other, a definite technique of carving has to be developed.

During my study of portraits I discovered, as many artists had already discovered, that one of the biggest difficulties is to know when to leave off. The artist can go on adding and adding until the picture is overloaded with detail. Years later, when I painted Tilly Losch, she urged me to leave the canvas in a state which I called half finished. I had to admit she was absolutely right. Further painting would only have spoilt the effect of spontaneity, perhaps lost it altogether.

The association between architecture and murals, I realized, is very close. The size and technique of a picture is dictated by its surroundings. Different types of architecture therefore require different types of painting, and this explains why today, having executed some sixty murals, I have no individual style. Anybody who commissions work by, say, Henry Moore, has a pretty shrewd idea what the final result is going to be like. But not with me. It is no use deciding "Let's have a Churchill!" because I evolve a style suited to the opportunities and limitations of each commission.

Limitations, I might add, do not worry me. On the contrary, I delight in the challenge they present. I do not think much of stunts such as mobiles, which are simply cases of art being "different" for the sake of it, without much inspiration. To my mind there is much more achievement in thinking up something new within rigidly fixed limits. A quartet is one of the highest forms of art in my opinion because the whole of the composer's inspiration has to be expressed within an extremely tight pattern. Yet wonderful results can be created.

There was, however, one aspect which gave me great worry: the difference between invention and the borrowing of ideas or themes for the purpose of invention. It produced many difficulties for me because I felt I was not a stylist and that therefore when I used other people's inventions or themes they would not appear as my own inventions. This situation can very well lead to eclectism in art, or in other words, copying.

When Bach borrowed somebody else's themes or ideas they were so transformed by his personal treatment as to be totally different from the original. Sometimes, however, the themes are recognizable though treated differently. The plaintive theme of the ballet *Giselle* by Adolfe Adam, produced in 1841, has an extraordinary feeling of the love motif of Eva which predominates in the second act of *The Mastersingers*. And we know from Wagner's *My Life* that he was greatly inspired by Adam and composed *The Mastersingers* later.

Even the most famous composers, I found, resorted to variations of their own works. With Wagner I also discovered that the melodic theme of the quintet in *The Mastersingers* is identical with that of the "Siegfried Idyll," but written differently. Then I found that the chord sequence of the "Liebstodt" from *Tristan and Isolde* is the same as that rather common number from *Tannhäuser*, "O Star of Eve." In this respect it took me twenty-five years to realize that a charming étude in F sharp I wrote in Portofino is in fact a distant relation of the Fascist anthem "Giovanezza"! And similarly, a delightful sardana, a Spanish peasant dance form which I once heard outside my bedroom window in Barcelona, was actually very close to one of the variations that Rachmaninoff wrote on Paganini's theme.

One of the most extraordinary cases of "lifting" ideas and detail gave me food for thought. I found on having examined *Venus Sleeping* by Giorgone in the Royal Gallery at Dresden that Titian used the material in two different paintings, in *Venus Reclining* in the Uffizi Gallery in Florence and in the background of *Noli Me Tangere* in the National Gallery, London. Furthermore, Titian went to the extent of cutting off the end of the farm in Giorgone's background and yet left the shadow which that end had cast. Nor were the styles of the two Venetian painters very different, so that it was a case of the younger borrowing the inventions of the elder. Even with this encouraging precedent, I still felt that it was most important to develop my powers of absolute invention.

All this appeared to me to be fairly straightforward, but far more complicated becomes the problem when one examines, for instance, the difference between the architectural principles of St. Peter's in Rome and St. Paul's in London. The problem that faces the student is that while the principles of architecture appear the same, the result is quite different. What makes St. Paul's such an English creation when it is so closely based on St. Peter's?

I soon decided, however, that it is the inspiration and presentation which bring about the most satisfying feeling of originality, from wherever they emanate.

The degree to which music was going to feature in my career was still uncertain, so I was pleased when Madame Dahrenburg, a pupil of Clara Schumann, gave me an introduction to Sir Hugh Allen, principal of the Royal College of Music. I presented the college with the bust of Wagner I had made and proudly embarked on a course there, but my hopes were shattered when my friends and tutors at the College, Herbert Howells and Gordon Jacob, decided that, at twenty-three, I had started too late.

A musical experience I enjoyed was hiring the Albert Hall for one hour in order to play *The Mastersingers* overture on the gigantic organ. The caretakers were amazed when I let the instrument have it fortissimo at the end. It was thrilling. Also I frequently practiced on the organ in Steinway Hall.

I attended the Royal College of Art under Gilbert Spencer, the brother of Stanley Spencer, who announced that he could not teach me any more painting technique, so I left. Then I went to the Central School of Arts and Crafts, where Bernard Meninsky kindly and privately took me under his wing for drawing and line technique. Although he was an artist with a tremendous sense of form and space, he did not, in my opinion, have a very good color sense, so for the technique of color I sought out Hesketh Hubbard. He put me through a rigid course. For architectural study I spent a great deal of time with Sir Edwin Lutyens and Robert Byron. Their condemnation of Sir Herbert Baker's secretariats of the Government House in New Delhi and praise of Sir Edwin's main building and dome formed to a considerable extent my taste and critical judgment in architecture. And for sculpture study I mostly relied on Clare Sheridan, who had learned her technique for modeling under Epstein. Later, for frieze work, I went to the British Museum and studied the various techniques of Egyptian incised relief, Assyrian bas-relief and Greek high relief.

Having broken with the City and swung into artistic life, I was determined to be independent of convention. I wore exactly the clothes I wanted, in defiance of what people thought. I had a black velvet beret and two black Spanish cloaks, one lined with blue, the other with red. Both were fastened by elaborate gold chains across the front. Instead of trousers I wore my father's leather riding breeches: bright orange with lots of buttons. My somewhat startling Wagnerian outfit was completed by a walking stick, which I carried with a relaxed air. This getup, however, was no more unusual than that of a very distinguished neighbor, G. M. Young the famous historian, who lived about five miles away and was introduced to me by Robert Byron. About twice my age, he dressed in late Victorian knickerbockers with an extraordinary hat which made him look like Beckmesser, the Town Clerk in *The Mastersingers*. We became close friends and often lunched together at the Garrick Club.

When Squadron Leader Elliot, now Air Chief Marshal Sir William Elliot, brought some friends to my farmhouse to see "this weird eccentric making busts," I asked if I could go and inspect his local aerodrome. At that time everyone was tremendously interested in the building up of the Royal Air Force. Elliot kindly agreed, and I arrived in full splendor, my cloak swirling in the breeze. He received me without so much as a movement of an eyelid, though he has since mentioned that my appearance caused a sensation.

My family did not say much about these eccentricities. My mother ticked me off now and again, but accepted them as behavior to be expected from me. She'd had an extremely strict upbringing herself and was determined to allow her own children freedom. My father gave me no advice on clothes at all. What is so extraordinary is that it was only a couple of years before he died that I managed to find out the name of his tailor; even then, he was very cagey about it. My father's clothes always struck me as most distinguished, and his anxiety to keep the secret was I suppose understandable.

However, I noticed very carefully the points which made his clothes and therefore his presence most distinguished. I soon realized the awful cult of Harrovians to have their suits too tightly fitting and even waisted. I observed the ghastly line of "Oxford bags" with their twenty-two-inch bottoms popular at the time and suitable only for battleship decks. But then I found the tight Edwardian drainpipe cut of trousers too exaggerated in the other direction. It was clear that whatever my father wore, it was so moderate and unostentatious that it was quite difficult to see why it looked so well. That is the height of good taste and elegance. Even in the matter of a haircut, I found it takes quite a talented barber to cut one's sideburns in such a way that they do not look as though they have just been cut.

It is very difficult to find a really good tailor. There are subtleties about cutting coats and trousers which many of them simply do not understand. Since I design my own clothes and have them cut as I want, my personal problem has been finding a tailor on whom I can rely to carry out my ideas. So many tailors insist on dictating to the customer. I do not follow contemporary fashion, but modestly claim to have started fashions. Around 1946 I began using a single high-placed button to fasten my jacket, and it has since caught on by degrees.

At the end of 1933, by which time I was beginning to feel more competent as an artist, my uncle gave me my first big chance to prove myself. He asked me to decorate his loggia in the garden at Chartwell.

My arrival at the house with my paints, brushes and blue boiler suit was quite an event, for I came in a new capacity, as an artist. Very generously, my uncle immediately threw open his studio and offered me easels, canvases and anything else I needed. For my part I was filled with apprehension and despondency when I reflected that I was undertaking my first major work at the age of twenty-four. My artist friend and contemporary Rex Whistler had been successfully working as a professional since he was seventeen. Clearly I had plenty to catch up. I mentioned this to my uncle, who offered encouragement.

"The exciting years," he said, "are from twenty to twenty-five." At that particular phase in his life he had been with the Fourth Hussars in India. When not playing polo and other agreeable pastimes with his brother officers, he locked himself up to study academic subjects he had not been able to master at school and which equipped him for his political and literary career to come.

The loggia, in the northeast corner of the garden, is fifteen feet square with a shallow vaulted ceiling thirteen feet high at its apex. Two sides of the building are open to the weather, and this was to cause trouble and necessitate an almost annual visit for repairs.

My uncle was in the middle of writing Volume II of his life of Marlborough, so we decided on our common ancestor as the subject for the mural. Having a definite assignment from the start pleased me. I have always liked a patron to state a preference. Nothing is more unsettling than to be told: "Oh, choose any subject you like!" One can be sure that eventually it will lead to disagreement.

I made preliminary sketches for the loggia and my uncle accepted them. The design consisted of four niches painted in *trompe-l'oeil* (or 3—D, I suppose it could be called) showing busts of the four principal characters in the drama: Marlborough, Prince Eugene of Savoy, Queen Anne and Sarah Duchess. Midway up the vaulted ceiling, at the corners, were four plaques of figures in a warm stone color representing the rivers on which Marlborough fought his battles — the Rhine, Meuse, Moselle and Danube — and in between these were lunettes depicting the four battles: Blenheim, Ramillies, Oudenarde and Malplaquet. Surmounting it all was a balustrade with my cousins Diana and Sarah looking down, and a "hole" of bright blue sky in the ceiling.

I already knew quite a lot about Marlborough and his times, but anything I did not know I was soon to learn. Every detail of my design was minutely examined, criticized, and if necessary corrected by my uncle. But I strongly resisted his attempts to interfere with aesthetic matters, and it was here that we met aspects of painting on which we differed. For although my uncle appreciated the direct approach to painting — that is, to have something before you and paint it — and although he was curious to see how I solved the problem of telling the story of Marlborough on four blank walls and a ceiling, he was a little unsympathetic with regard to imagination, which is the essence of wall painting. When I came to execute the four lunettes of the battles, extra men had to be added here and there.

"What are all those people supposed to be doing?" he asked.

"Well," I replied timidly, "they are the column of infantry moving around at that point at that time according to your book." (I always added "according to your book" to cover myself.)

"But they didn't move like that."

"I know, but they have to be fitted into the design of the whole," I argued. "Artistic license . . ."

I obtained useful support from Sir William Nicholson, the distinguished Edwardian painter who was staying at Chartwell to paint my uncle and aunt having breakfast in the dining room; the picture was to be presented to them on behalf of some organization. Sir William backed me up on all aesthetic points and often came out to the loggia to give advice. He was a great artist in his way and I quickly grew to like him. He refused to teach professionally but took me under his wing and taught me many secrets. His touch was delicate, his forte being tone and color control. Most of my knowledge about these sections of my trade I owe to him. Unlike Augustus John, he allowed me to watch him paint his pictures — one of the most important forms of instruction.

In a very short while I realized that unless I followed the same work timetable as my uncle I would not be able to show the efficiency he expected. Therefore I studied his daily routine and determined to keep to it myself. When in later years I have reminded him that what modest measure of success I have been able to achieve in my career has been due to the example he set me at Chartwell, he has always been flattered.

His timetable was certainly terrific. Even in those days he maintained that he needed only six hours' sleep at the most. That put me at a disadvantage for a start; I definitely required eight hours. At 7 A.M. he used to wake up and study all the newspapers. Breakfast was at about 8 A.M., with a menu that often included beef. Then came work on *Marlborough* until lunch at 1:15, with a break around eleven for an inspection of my work to see what progress had been made. Progress there had to be, for as anyone who has worked for my uncle knows, the consequences are serious if no results can be produced. On the way back indoors from the loggia he visited the goldfish.

Lunch was accompanied by champagne and followed by port, brandy and a cigar until 3 or 4 P.M., when he re-

sumed *Marlborough* or some other writing until five-o'clock
tea, which was improved by a whisky and soda. Further
work was done until dinner at 8:15. Dinner lasted, with
more champagne, port, brandy and cigars, until 10 or 11
P.M., at which hour he retired for more dictating, plus
whiskies and soda, until two or three o'clock in the morning.

This was a formidable timetable to follow if only because it was January and February. I found it very cold at
nights working in the garden. However, I dutifully got up
in time to be at work at 7 A.M. When I came in to breakfast at about nine, I found in the dining room Sarah or
some of the family, William Nicholson and often Bill
Deakin (later Lieutenant Colonel William Deakin, now
Warden of St. Antony's College, Oxford), whom the
"Prof" (Professor Lindemann) had produced as a brilliant
history scholar to help in the research on Marlborough,
and who told me that my uncle had examined the great
general's battlefields with the same thoroughness with
which he examined the Heights of Abraham.

I immediately resumed work in the loggia until my
uncle's daily inspection at eleven, the strain of which was
eased by alcoholic refreshment. Occasionally the progress
seemed to him to be less than on other days, though it was
really the same, and I would have to explain what I had
done.

"Can't we get rid of this vast white space?" he asked,
pointing his cigar at the lower part of the ceiling.

"I will work on that bit next, if you particularly want
me to," I told him, "but it is not necessary because my

method is to start at the top and work downward, thus avoiding any danger of messing up the bottom part."

He digested this for a moment, then commented: "I always survey the whole scene with greater clarity if I attack the white areas first and afterwards concentrate on the pockets of resistance."

Now this is a very reasonable if bellicose approach when confronted with a subject which is to be painted on a white canvas. In fact, many artists start on a tinted-down canvas and work to the darkest and lightest shades. But when a mural is being started, everything has been, or should have been, decided beforehand, so that it is mainly a matter of correct execution in the proper places.

I never ceased to marvel, though, at how my uncle gave my efforts undivided attention. One of the most important and interesting things I learned from him in those days was the emphasis he put on being able to switch his mind from one subject to another. He would suddenly stop work on the Marlborough book and go out to lay bricks for a new wall or paint a picture or feed the fish or write a political article. And whatever he was doing absorbed his attention so completely that obviously he had forgotten his previous task. I admit that as an artist I find this a tall order. When I am inspired to a high degree it is extremely difficult to switch off and turn to another totally different subject.

My uncle, having given his secretaries a good morning's dictation which had to be typed out and presented to him in the afternoon, met us in the drawing room for a glass of sherry before lunch. Sarah would be there with older members of the family, William Nicholson or perhaps Major General Packenham-Walsh, the War Office's historical expert on the Marlborough period, whom I was to meet in the war.

As often as not, lunch was devoted to unrelieved gloom about the international situation. Even in those early days of German military renaissance my uncle was convinced that war was inevitable. Being slightly fatalistic myself, I believed it too. The depressing conversation used to make William Nicholson quite sick. More than once he whispered to me: "Johnny, I'm going to leave the table on an excuse. I cannot stand it any more." I did not like it either, but always remained transfixed by what my uncle said.

The awful thing was to be asked what one thought. Any answer was fatuous because my uncle had thought it already and drawn his own conclusions. In any case, in my opinion it is pointless and almost rude for a nonprofessional to try to talk shop with a politician. Charlie Chaplin once came down to lunch at Chartwell and proceeded to fire an enormous pacifist Communistic soliloquy at the whole table. It was made in good faith and from the bottom of his heart. My uncle, who held him in great admiration, said nothing, for there was nothing to say. My own heart bled for Charlie.

I never discussed politics with my uncle, knowing perfectly well that his reaction would be as devastating as during one of his intense silences. At such times he has a way of looking straight through you. It is so embarrassing that only if one knows him very well indeed is it possible to wonder objectively what can be going on in his mind. He has looked at me in this way often enough, and I have learned that the one thing *not* to do is to try to alleviate the crisis by stirring up some sort of conversation. If one does, the situation is only made worse by "What?", "Speak up!" and "I can't hear what you say." Then, having repeated your statement, you get a terse reply such as "I don't know what you mean or what you are talking about."

My uncle fixed me with one of these terrifying gazes at the end of lunch one day. After a while I ventured: "Who, Uncle Winston, was responsible for the idiotic drink laws in this country?" By this I meant the strange confusion of opening and closing times and the club memberships which allow people to drink all day and night if they want.

My uncle continued his inscrutable stare and said nothing. "The French," I went on, after a long pause, "have a much more sensible law."

At last my uncle showed signs of coming to life. "What is this you are discussing?" he demanded.

"The English drinking laws, Uncle Winston. I am wondering who made them."

Instantly he snapped: "The Government," and relapsed into his former gloom. Which put me in my place pretty neatly.

Between the glooms we were treated to astounding snatches of thought about the Marlborough campaigns which clarified his brain for the afternoon session with Bill Deakin. Once, after the ladies had withdrawn, Bill Deakin, Major General Packenham-Walsh and I were about to sip our glasses of brandy when my uncle suddenly exclaimed: "There can be no doubt at all. Absolutely no doubt."

We were completely in the dark, but were given a clue when he continued: "With the vast forces of Marlborough's cavalry charging across the plain, what hope could the wretched French have had? The slaughter must have been terrific."

We had another careful sip of brandy. My uncle then described the entire battle of Blenheim to General Walsh and asked him if he considered it correct. It was, so we rose from the table. My uncle had mastered the battle and went off to write the brilliant description of it which appears in his book.

After tea there might be a game of six-pack bezique, but usually I missed tea altogether because it meant too much of a break in the afternoon. A whisky and soda was always brought out to keep me warm. I found that in mural painting an uninterrupted stretch of six hours was the ideal to be aimed at. If I had only one or two hours ahead of me it was hardly worth while beginning a session. I used to go to my uncle's studio in the garden, where I had a large block of clay which I was making into a bust of him. I would study him very carefully at lunch and, remembering a particular feature, go and model it in. It was a good exercise in developing my powers of observation, and by the time I had finished the loggia I had also finished the bust, though I fell into the trap of making it just a bit larger than life size. I noticed with great interest my uncle's hands, which are the most expressive and beautiful that have ever adorned a man, but alas they did not come into the bust. When painting a portrait, exquisite hands are a very tricky problem. In fact, hands in general are difficult; it is so easy, as El Greco used to say, to make them look like radishes.

William Nicholson and I used to fill in other spare moments by drawing Mr. Cat, the ginger tom of the house, or painting a scene outdoors. If my uncle felt inclined he joined us, and we competed to see who would notice what, and leave out which, in the process of elimination in our paintings. Afterward we debated which canvas was the best. Nicholson, having great artistry, delicate charm and persuasion, began to influence my uncle's painting, but the result was rather like taking horns from a bull, and I do not think the influence was a good one. If my uncle felt he was failing to make progress with the subject we were doing, he would get up and go.

We always changed for dinner. Stimulating conversation about painting alternated with further gloomy thoughts on the political situation. However, our spirits were sustained by the excellent champagne.

My uncle was like my father in that he could not stand thick soup; in fact, my father did not really enjoy soup at all because he said it interfered with his drinking. But no matter what anyone else had, my uncle always insisted on clear soup. One night the cook made a slip. When a large party had sat down to dinner, the guests were served with clear soup and my uncle with thick.

"What is this white creamy-looking stuff?" he growled, as though an attempt were being made to poison him.

During some dinners there were long periods of silence and thought, which were bearable when two or three of us were present because we could talk in undertones. On one occasion I was alone with Sarah, my uncle and Mr. Cat. The table was very long and narrow. My uncle sat at the head, and Sarah and I were opposite each other at the middle. Right at the far end facing my uncle was Mr. Cat, sitting on a cushion which had been placed on a chair.

For this particular meal Mr. Cat was given a slice of pheasant and some cream, which he ate very cleverly from a plate on the table without making a mess. We were so fascinated by the smooth way he achieved this, and Mr. Cat was so interested in doing it, that he got hiccoughs. At exactly the same moment my uncle got hiccoughs as well, with the result that the two of them seemed to be gravely bowing to each other. The spectacle was so extraordinary that Sarah and I felt on the verge of hiccoughs too. When Sarah giggled we both had to stuff our table napkins in our mouths in case we laughed. Then of course my uncle noticed and was very displeased.

"What on earth do you think you are doing?" he asked crossly. "I do not see anything funny at all."

By this time we were in agony from suppressed laughter.

Some of Mr. Cat's other habits were less attractive. One evening the Prof, Randolph, Nicholson, Brendan Bracken, Bob Boothby, my uncle and I were left in the dining room after the ladies had gone when the curtains moved and Mr. Cat appeared.

"Oh, look," said my uncle brightly. "Cat has mouse."

Although I adore cats, the manner in which they toy with their prey is cruel and unnecessary. But my uncle was not in the least put out by the life-and-death drama being played in front of him. He commented: "How interesting to see him exercise control over his victim."

William Nicholson and I felt a bit green at the sight. The Prof, who was shocked because he was a vegetarian, watched with cold scientific scrutiny. Randolph and Bob Boothby had not noticed what was happening, but Brendan Bracken, that big tough politician who had helped me throw hecklers down the stairs at my uncle's meetings, looked quite ill.

After a tense moment or two my uncle declared: "Now is the time." And indeed, quite suddenly, with no fuss, the entire mouse disappeared down Mr. Cat's throat, head first. There was no chewing. Then he cleaned his whiskers and silently stepped over to the fire for a nap.

The stricken silence that followed was broken by my uncle proudly observing: "You see, a whole army destroyed in one move!"

Even when there were no visitors, we often sat around the dining table until about 10 P.M. I was a bit alarmed when left entirely alone because I would be cross-examined about my opinion of my uncle's book on Marlborough, or about some aspect of painting. A mere answer was never enough; an explanation of why one thought as one did was necessary as well. Sometimes one's reasoning would be criticized and one's views seriously questioned. William Nicholson and I once extolled the great wall paintings of the Ajanta Caves in India, but my uncle seemed to doubt their greatness. Perhaps this was because he had not studied the business of wall painting, Oriental types in particular.

Memory was one of the subjects I used to discuss with my uncle and Randolph at this time. My uncle's ability to remember names, people, facts and passages of writing is phenomenal, and I think he attributes it to a certain extent to his father, who was said to be able to read a page of Gibbon's *Decline and Fall of the Roman Empire* and then quote it word for word. My uncle could do much the same with Macaulay, and Randolph wasn't bad either. As for myself, I am absolutely vacant where words are concerned. On the other hand I can reel off miles and miles of musical notation on the piano without any trouble.

The question of spiritual life was also talked about and my uncle always appeared to be intrigued by the fact that my brother, sister and I are fundamentally Roman Catholic in consequence of my mother's being Catholic. It seemed that he wished he could understand our inner thoughts but could not, and there was an end to the matter. My uncle, like Napoleon, has always appreciated the importance of religion for the general public even if he himself did not or could not get interested in it. He admits that he prayed very earnestly when escaping from prison in South Africa, but has never mentioned to me any other occasion of prayer.

Informative contributions to after-dinner conversation at Chartwell became easier when he asked his favorite question: "What do people say?" He was anxious to keep abreast of public opinion and used me as a private informant. Moving about as I did through a wide and varied cross section of society, I was in a good position to tell him. I made it my business to talk to anyone I met in pubs, clubs, trains and buses. I questioned my brother artists, actors, models, tramps, businessmen, musicians, sculptors and architects. On the whole, from 1934 onward, everyone was most alarmed by the Hitler situation and by the terrible Baldwin regime. But there were some unexpected views.

I had a girl friend who introduced me to her grandfather and grandmother. They were very well-to-do and lived in an enormous house in Chelsea with masses of servants. It was thought that I might make a good impression, but the grandfather's attitude was far from friendly.

"So you're a nephew of Winston Churchill!" he exclaimed. "Well, let me tell you this: whether there is a war or not, Britain will be absolutely finished if Winston Churchill gets into power again. Our only hope is for him to be put in prison and kept there."

This was a view I did not repeat to my uncle. I thought it might cause even greater despondency.

After dinner we spent only a short time in the drawing room, and at about 10:30 P.M. my uncle retired with Bill Deakin for further work. The typists were ready to sit at their machines all night to produce the draft for him to read at breakfast. Meanwhile I donned my boiler suit, jerseys, mufflers and woolen stockings, and by means of an electric light on a cable run from the house, worked in the loggia. Usually at around 1 A.M. I noticed the drawing room lights go on again. That meant Bill Deakin had come downstairs for a break with whisky and soda. I joined him and we discussed various topics of the moment, soothed by the strange, heavy stillness that settled in the house at night.

After two months the loggia was finished and a general inspection was made. It was decided to call it from then on the Marlborough Pavilion.

I took my leave of Chartwell and embarked on the perilous journeys of professional art and marriage.

VI

Romance of a Pagan

M Y NEXT COMMISSION after the Marlborough Pavilion was to decorate the enormous Hall of Mrs.
Aubrey Herbert's villa in Portofino. A luxurious ten-bed-
room affair with terraces and a private rock bathing cove,
the villa stands in a superb position looking down on the
harbor over the tops of olive, cypress and orange trees.
The architecture, though, is undistinguished. The villa is
just like one of the ordinary-looking homes that rich men
build in well-to-do suburbs of London. The famous Car-
rara marble quarries are not far down the coast at Spezia,
yet wondrously, the villa is constructed of Portland stone
brought all the way out from England.

Mrs. Herbert was to pay me one hundred pounds, plus
free board and lodging. With my check for the Marlborough Pavilion in my pocket, and my father's allowance of
ten pounds a month, my spirits soared; I had an exhilarating sense of freedom and determined to indulge in it. My
hours of work were of first importance of course, ranking
above all else, but where leisure was concerned I failed to
see why I should not do precisely what I liked and to hell
with what people thought.

My parents watched this display of obstinacy with resigned tolerance, but there was one aspect of it which
made them thoroughly apprehensive. Following my unfortunate romance with Sophie, I had abandoned myself to
Bohemian life and began courting a very beautiful and
talented girl named Angela Culme-Seymour. She had long
black hair and was natural, extremely gay, and clever. She
could paint, write novels, and play any musical instrument
she wished to study. Usually she carried a guitar around
with her.

In contrast to the wild artistic existence she liked to lead,
she could, when she wished, move with dignity in the
highest circles. She was eminently wellborn. The huge
Seymour family was ranged on her father's side and the
Orr-Ewings on her mother's. Her mother, I thought, looked
like a witch and dressed like one. She wore a huge black
witch-type hat and a black cape. Even her teeth stuck out
as if she were a character in an Arthur Rackham drawing.
Nevertheless, she produced four outstandingly good-looking children, two of whom were by her second husband,
the Reverend Mr. Woolley, V.C., chaplain of Harrow
School. The strict Protestant upbringing Angela suffered
from her stepfather proved to be her undoing. It made her
prepared to do anything as long as it was the opposite to
what he taught. The result was a most attractive personality with no scruples and no sense of responsibility at all.
And she was very good company for an artist.

"Company" was the word, for if I had doubts as to
whether she might make a wife for me some day, my parents had already decided she was quite unsuitable. My

mother felt that any wife of mine ought to be a steadying influence, which Angela certainly was not. Her family background was far from encouraging on this score. There was the famous story of her Grandmother Trixie on the Orr-Ewing side, who, on a train journey from London to Southampton with her two children and a nurse, suddenly got out at Winchester and never saw them again. One of the deserted offspring was Angela's mother.

I was too busy thinking about my new commission, and how lonely it was going to be working in an empty villa, to concern myself with Angela's faults. "Why not come out to Portofino?" I asked her.

"First I am going to Spain," she said, "but will probably be in Italy after about eight weeks."

That would be May. In the meantime I went to Italy. I had a lot of work ahead of me. My painting was to cover the walls and ceiling of a room thirty-five feet long, twenty feet wide and thirteen feet high, and I planned to finish the whole area singlehanded in about four months. For my theme I took the story of St. George. He is the patron saint of the village; furthermore, the theme offered splendid opportunities for introducing interesting architecture. I always incorporated plenty of architecture in my paintings as an exercise in combining the arts. In this I was following the example set by Wagner, who combined the arts by not only composing the music for his operas but also writing the librettos, designing the costumes and scenery, and so on. I had shown my preliminary sketches to Sir Edwin Lutyens, who pronounced the architecture to be correct and in good taste.

My routine at Portofino was to work in the villa and go
down to the town, to the Nazionale Restaurant on the
quay, for my meals. The villa had a piano, and in the evenings I amused myself by pounding through Wagner.
Lord and Lady Esher were living on the opposite side of
the valley in the famous Castello Brown at the time and
mentioned that they heard me distinctly, but politely re-
frained from comment. I suspect they became heartily
bored with my constant repetitions of *The Mastersingers*.

No sooner had I settled down to serious painting than
Mrs. Herbert wrote to tell me that an important Italian
banker, Signor Gualino, had arranged to rent the villa for
the summer and would be taking possession "some time in
May." This was a blow. It allowed me only two months for
the mural instead of four. I quickly rearranged my timetable and worked at night as well as throughout each day.
On one occasion the exhaustion caused me to fall off the
rickety Italian scaffolding onto the marble floor, which
was a painful experience. Then at the end of six weeks
came a series of distractions.

The first was Helena, a charming but voluble Polish actress, a naturalized Italian, with whom I had struck up an
acquaintance in the piazza. She was a large type of woman
in her mid-thirties, rather a heavyweight but elegant, with
a rich voice. She did not speak English very well and was
furious with me because I could not, and would not, speak
Italian. I agreed with her that I ought to learn Italian,
which is easy to master if one indulges in amorous pursuits, but like so many Englishmen I simply cannot cope
with other countries' languages. My method is to bluff my

way through by making a series of what I hope are appropriate noises. Even the Japanese have seemed to get my messages.

Helena's great pride was that she had declaimed poetry before Mussolini; therefore she insisted she must declaim to me in the great Hall where I was painting. She did — not that I understood a word — and in the evenings we strolled through the scented pines down to the sea in the moonlight. They were walks which she encouraged because she said she had quarreled with her engineer lover in Rome.

This interlude — and it was no more than an interlude, with lots of mutual admiration, artistic appreciation and approval in every direction — was interrupted by the arrival of Signor Gualino and his redheaded wife from Milan to inspect the villa. When I next heard that Angela, complete with guitar, was on her way from Spain, I pushed Helena off to San Remo. On her way back to Rome she called at the villa and I had the embarrassing job of introducing the two women to each other. The atmosphere turned distinctly frigid, and I wondered what Helena thought when she left her promising young "d'Annunzio" of painting and music, who was so romantically sympathetic towards her deep emotional feelings for poetry and recitation, to the whims of a casual, lighthearted English girl. I was relieved to see her go. I don't like tensions.

Meanwhile I was having trouble with Signor Gualino. He was the proud owner of a collection of so-called modern Italian paintings by Modigliani and Co. and detested anything based on the classics, such as my story of St.

George. To be honest, I was beginning to feel that the Hall was not really big enough for the grand conception of my design; the fantastic perspective vaulting in the ceiling seemed to sit on one's head. But evidently Signor Gualino enjoyed being blunt.

"I do not like your painting," he said tersely. "Please leave. My wife and I are moving in at once."

I thought this rather highhanded, considering it was not his house, so when I came to paint the fourth scene, St. George being condemned to death by the Emperor Diocletian, what better model for the emperor could I have than Signor Gualino? I have not been back to the villa since, but there is a rumor that he was so annoyed he had the face scratched out.

When I left the villa I rented a flat in one of the fishermen's houses that are tightly packed, like a shelf of books, along the quay overlooking Portofino harbor. I argued with myself that since I was already deep in "playing the ass in the gutter" I might just as well "play the ass in the bulrushes" too.

I said to Angela: "How about setting up house together? We are both artists."

Goethe had done the same sort of thing, marrying only years afterward, and I could see no point at all in going to the bother of a wedding ceremony. I believe that when two intelligent people wish to live in partnership they do so because they love each other. This means that they are united in body and soul and do not need to abide by civil or religious ties. I know of several couples today who live as though they were married; some of the ladies have not even troubled to change their names. Because of the views which I hold, the reader might think it contradictory that I have had four wives. But we must never overlook human frailty, and as will be seen, my reasons for having had more than one marriage have been completely out of my control.

Angela accepted my offer at Portofino and moved in with me. We got on fine together. We laughed and danced, and everyone in the village was our friend. She became known as the Girl with the Beautiful Eyes. When H.M.S. *Barham,* the flagship of the Mediterranean Fleet, was anchored off nearby Rapallo, her captain, Admiral Sir Roger Backhouse, Commander-in-Chief Mediterranean, who knew my family well, invited us to see his ship. We were taken out in a launch. I climbed aboard in my black velvet beret and red silk-lined cloak, and cannot imagine what comments must have been made below decks, but as far as the admiral was concerned I believe I was acceptable. Having built a model of H.M.S. *Barham* some ten years previously, I was able to tell him exactly what changes had been made to the masts of his ship before he took over. We celebrated with a great deal of Plymouth Gin!

Our domestic bliss at Portofino continued, but I noticed that Angela was dissatisfied. Feeling the need for security, she surprised me by saying: "Don't you think we ought to get married?"

It seemed rather unnecessary, but on second thought I conceded that marriage has certain advantages. It is far more difficult for youngsters to live together in what is

Lady Gwendoline Churchill,
author's mother.
Charcoal drawing by John Sargent. 1912

Major John Strange Spencer Churchill,
author's father. 1940.

Author with his grandmother,

Lady Randolph Churchill.

1917.

The author, aged four,
painted by Harrington Mann. 1913.

Author and his brother, 1917,
Bedford Square, when living in
Lady Ottoline Morrell's house.

Author at Blenheim. 1913.
Hatband is H.M.S. *Lion.*

The author, fullback Rugby,
Summerfields. 1921.

Harrow, gymnastic champion.

Author and brother, Brighton. 1925.
Peregrine's hatband is H.M.S. *Temeraire*.

Family group, taken in the Admiralty, 1914. *Left to right:* Uncle Winston, Diana, Aunt Clemmie, Sarah on her lap, Randolph, Granny Randolph, brother Peregrine, mother, author, and father.

Family group, taken in the Admiralty twenty-five years later (1939). *Left to right:* Author, mother, Uncle Winston, Randolph, Aunt Clemmie, and father.

Lady Randolph Churchill's funeral, 1921, at Bladon Churchyard near Blenheim Palace.
On the left: Uncle Winston, the author and his father.
On the right: Lady Randolph's sisters, Mrs. Frewen and Lady Leslie, author's mother in foreground and Aunt Clemmie and Sir John Leslie.

Group in America. 1929.
Randolph, author,
Uncle Winston and father.

Group at Downing Street after Clarissa's wedding.
Left to right: Sister Clarissa, author, Uncle Winston, cousin, Mrs. Diana Sandys, and brother-in-law Anthony Eden.

Lullan and author.

Wedding picture of Lullan Boston,
fourth wife, with daughter Sally. 1958.

Lullan and author playing piano — a Stodart oblong grand.

rincess Natasha saying good morning
to the author.

The author painting in Adam and Eve
Mews, London, W.8.

Meditation in Positano. 1952.

Author playing piano.
Background St. James's Park mural.

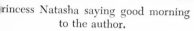

The decoration for Lloyd George of the Bay of Tigullio, Italy. *On left:*
Angela holding a map of the area. *Left distant:* Portofino — *center,*
Santa Margherita; *right,* Rapallo. 15 by 7½ feet.

Painting of Dunkirk from Bray dunes, now in the Institute of Army Education.

Angela Culme-Seymour, first wife.

Mary Cookson, second wife.

Kathlyn Tandy, third wife.

Sally, aged eighteen.

The Anson bomber and Wing Commander Cundell and the author
with air camera. 1941.

A new hat. Adapted from an
"Anthony Eden" hat. 1938.

The beard. 1951.

General view of the Marlborough Pavilion. 1949.

Presentation portrait to Sir Winston on his eightieth birthday.

Bust of my uncle. 1933.

Bust of Wagner, bronzed. 1932.

Bust of author by Fiore Henriquez. 1951.

Illustration of sand castle at Overstrand, 1914. Diana, Randolph, and author,
Mr. Winston Churchill and the author's father.

Working on illuminated transparent glass painting *Megalopolis* for P. & O. liner *Arcadia*

Cloak and beret at Portofino.

Alfresco attire. 1934.

The author with Spanish group
of artists in Segovia, 1950,
after a very good lunch. On the
ground under the author,
Zuluaga the painter and sculptor

Sculpting group at Slade School. 1949. *Left to right*
The author, Currie, Pasco, Brackachi and Blasiak

Italian group of artists in Rome, 1952, after a very good lunch. Author with beard.
Extreme right: Elena la Cava, the Italian painter.

Sir Winston conducting water operations in the upper upper upper
golden orf pool. In the pool Colonel Deakin. 1950.

Sally and her Temple house, Fairlawne.
1937. Author made this out of plywood
and painted in Parthenon colors.

Yester, Scotland. Instruction for Lady
Tweeddale's grandson on standing on his
head. 1939.

Author and brother on the land at Rushall, near Upavon, Wiltshire. 1932. Author with oil can

called "sin" than for an older couple. For example, there is
the awful business of signing hotel registers and getting
black looks from managers. And then there is the *wagon-
lits* situation.

So I wrote to my parents and broke to them the news
that Angela and I were getting married on May 13, 1934.
The local podesta, or mayor, conducted the ceremony in
the Portofino town hall with the writer Louis Wilkinson
and his fourth wife as witnesses. No marriage, I suppose,
could have been more madcap. It was a reflection of the
irresponsible and rebellious mood that both of us were in.
I was somewhat pantheistic at the time and Angela was
atheistic. When we were asked to take the oath on the
Bible we refused.

"But you must!" the mayor insisted.

"We wish to make the oath in our own way," I told him.
"Will you accept that?"

"What do you propose?" he asked doubtfully.

"Break a plate on the floor."

At this he looked even more shocked, but eventually he
shrugged his shoulders and agreed that if we refused to
act like civilized Christians there was nothing he could
do about it. The only china lying around the town hall
was valuable and eventually the poor podesta had to send
down to the Nazionale Restaurant for one of their dinner
plates. Angela and I received it from his hands and
dropped it on the floor, where it smashed instantly, and
thus became man and wife according to Italian civil law.

We embarked on the most elaborate and romantic
festivities imaginable. The fisherfolk and musicians of the

town were so pleased and excited that they staged a sort of banquet-cum-ball in a little open-air café. We danced and were toasted until the early hours of the morning. Then as soon as we reached our flat and began fading away in a haze of Chianti fumes, strains of more music reached us. Opening the windows, we saw on the quayside below guitar players and singers serenading the newly married couple.

Truly it was a pagan wedding.

A short while later we moved to a delightful villa on one of the pyramidical hills of the promontory. Angela was very lazy in those days and did little about the house. We hired an Italian cook-housekeeper who shopped and looked after the domestic side of things generally. The time passed in an ecstasy of pleasure; our evenings were spent drinking in bars with the locals. The only blight on this idyl was when Angela revealed to me her conditions for our future life.

"You must realize," she said, "that I could never possibly *belong* to anyone." I was a bit taken aback, having given her the marriage ceremony she wanted, but she continued: "We can be man and wife. But my independence must stay."

It was all extremely puzzling and feminine, but I was feeling relaxed, contented and easygoing. I did a lot of excellent painting. A view from the villa across the bay I sold for twenty guineas. Dudley Tooth negotiated the sale and paid me, but said that unfortunately his client had never paid him.

We visited Max Beerbohm in his villa about two kilometers outside Rapallo, high above the road. It looked out across the huge Tigullian Gulf and was quiet and peaceful, a perfect setting for writing and contemplation. I made a sketch of the gulf, with Portofino in the distance, which came in very useful later for a mural for Lloyd George.

Max Beerbohm was just as I imagined he would be, dapper and precious. We joined him on his terrace, where he invited us to take wine with him. His wife busied herself around us, fetching the decanter and glasses and making us comfortable while we talked about the many famous people, including friends of our families, Max had caricatured.

That eccentric writer Ezra Pound was a near neighbor, but we gathered he did not fit in with the rest of the local artistic community. He was very left wing, with a great red beard, a revolutionary type — a mixture of Hemingway and Bernard Shaw with a Red tinge; in short, a powerful fusion of violence of every kind. Max couldn't stand him.

Since I had told my relatives and friends in England about my marriage, some very generous wedding presents in the form of checks started rolling in. Angela and I decided to take advantage of this welcome windfall by seeing more of Italy. We went to Pisa, Florence, and then Rome, where we found a flat in the Via Calabria and ate in all sorts of restaurants: trattoria, rosticheria and pizzaria. Usually we gravitated towards the artistic-looking customers in these places and made numerous friends. One night we got extremely gay with a gang of artists and foolishly I mixed the white wines. Inevitably, this indiscriminate drinking spelled disaster. Returning home sitting on the bonnet of their car, with all of us singing "Giovanezza," I began to feel ill. On arrival I was most definitely ill. My bed seemed to rock as savagely as a ship's bunk in a gale, but I crawled into it, utterly wretched.

Angela was so disgusted with me that she locked herself in her room for three days. I tapped on her door and tried to reason with her, but in vain.

"You were drunk!" she said.

She amused herself in this self-imposed seclusion by writing page after page in her diary, a lengthy day-to-day chronicle which she kept all through our life together. It was a frank and unashamed assessment of her intimate, innermost feelings about everything, including her disillusionment over me. If I asked for a look she always tried to hide it away, and when I did manage to see it I understood the reason. The candor was quite astonishing. It was a shock to see my faults paraded in black and white. I felt I was reading about somebody else. There was a lot of unpleasant stuff about this not working out, and that not working out, which upset me. Being an idealist, I am unhappy when things fail.

My hopes for our marriage brightened when Angela announced that she was pregnant. The child, I thought, would anchor her to me for domestic reasons, despite her yearning for independence.

We went on up to Venice. Our hotel near the railway station was revoltingly dirty, but the city's great Tiepolo frescoes in the nearby Palazzo Labia and the pictures in the Academia more than compensated for the discomfort.

"Now let's go to Salzburg for the Mozart Festival," I said. "I have never been to Austria. We might even get to Vienna."

Angela agreed, though the pregnancy was making her dreadfully sick in the mornings, and we got off the train at a charming little Austrian place called Zell am See. The village was clustered on the shores of a peaceful lake. I rented a villa and set up my canvases in a nearby barn to paint. Also I composed a considerable amount of music, Angela taking up some of the melodies and singing them to me. One of my compositions was my Grand March in A Major, played for my daughter's wedding twenty-three years later.

We had not been in Zell am See a matter of hours before Angela was strumming at the zithers and guitars in the beerhouses and we were dancing at the water's edge by moonlight. She craved further excitement, so a curious situation developed whereby I rented a room in a castle on the far side of the lake. I slept there. Then, in the morning, I rowed back across the lake for a dramatic, exciting meeting. Thus our days and nights became a succession of heartbreaking farewells and wonderful reunions. It was not my idea at all; the castle was full of bats and I hated the place. But Angela derived intense pleasure from the emotional ups and downs. I must admit that in a way it was quite fun, and a mild form of love expression compared with some of the extraordinary things that other people do. I know a man who, when he wants to make love to his wife, sends her out for a walk in the street. Then he goes and picks her up as if she were a common prostitute. That, apparently, makes her desirable.

The landlord of our villa seemed to us to be rather arrogant and almost Nazi. Perhaps the village was a hotbed of Nazism, for we woke up one morning to find that a gigantic swastika had been marked in the snow on a mountainside. Next day Chancellor Dollfuss was shot. I do not particularly care for revolutions, and with a name such as mine I thought that the sooner we went the better. We packed our bags and left.

We halted our journey just south of Bolzano, after a distressing scene with the Italian customs. While the vast majority of customs officials are most courteous and efficient, I suspect that some of them like their work merely because it satisfies a lust for power. It was our luck to come across one of these at the Italian frontier. He was tall, slim and mean-looking, with the terrible defect of eyebrows that met in the middle. A thin bony nose drooped from beneath them. His eyes were deep-set, penetrating, and close together, and his teeth were yellow. Being a representative of Fascism, he had the right to say and do as he wished, and he relished it.

"What are these?" he asked in Italian, pointing at my bundle of canvases. "We will have to impound them."

On such occasions I cannot understand a single word of any language. I referred the man back to Angela. She explained to him that we had been through the same set of customs on our way up to Austria only a fortnight previously, carrying all the same paraphernalia, and that I

was a painter. But it was no use. He insisted on seeing the
paintings. So, with my cloak swinging, and watched by
an interested crowd who had never seen anything like it,
I rolled out the canvases along the platform for inspection.
They included an enormous collection of murals, each
about six by four feet. The officer then started being rude
to Angela and pushed her. This was more than I could
stand. I let fly with all the rude Italian I could muster and
braced myself for delivering a terrific blow to the man's
jaw. Luckily, when Angela saw what was going to happen,
she gave a shriek. I controlled my anger and missed by
seconds a jail sentence of several months.

From Bolzano, Angela went on ahead to Stresa, on Lake
Maggiore, to see her mother, and I followed two days
later, making another of my separating-only-to-meet-with-
joy excursions. There on the shores of the beautiful lake
which had been the scene of so many of my romantic
escapades in the past, I bought a colossal umbrella which
enabled half a dozen of us to shelter underneath when it
rained. It was the kind of brightly striped contraption that
is fixed over a table in an outdoor restaurant, most sensible
as regards size but rather odd to look at when carried in
the street.

Together with my canvases, plus umbrella, we went
straight back to Cromwell Road to see my parents. Our
arrival was greeted with mixed reactions, particularly
when Angela said that she thought she'd had a miscarriage. Everyone wondered whether we had started our
child before we married and were trying to avoid a birth
which would be officially premature. However, the local

doctor — not our regular doctor, but his young son — was called and declared that without doubt it was indeed a miscarriage. Naturally we believed him, and the situation was followed by tears and psychological upsets. My patroness, Mrs. Aubrey Herbert, kindly invited us to Pixton Park, her house in Somerset, for a recovery spree.

Mrs. Herbert, apart from her charms and amusing disposition, had a disease which was very catching. I refer to her adding of "What?" to the end of every sentence. Ever since I first went to Pixton at the age of eight I have been afflicted by this abominable if harmless habit. We children would be sitting down to breakfast and tucking into bacon and eggs when Mrs. Herbert would burst in gaily.

"Good morning, everybody, what? Have you got everything you want, what, what, what?"

Even at her villa at Portofino it was the same. *"Buon giorno, buon giorno,* what, what, what?"

I am now hopelessly addicted to the habit, the same as hundreds of other friends of Mrs. Herbert's. Another of my verbal oddities, I might add, is a word I invented with my roommate at Harrow, Brigadier Peter Barclay, who won what I believe was the first M.C. of the Second World War. We needed a means of giving vent to our feelings in moments of crisis without infringing decency. Accordingly we decided on: "Firch!" I always like to test and tease people by using this imaginary word as an expletive. Anyone prim and proper is instantly certain it is dreadful and unspeakably rude. But of what it is onomatopoeic, if anything, I cannot think.

Directly we reached Pixton Park, Angela climbed on a horse and went for a long ride. She was a bit exhausted afterward, and no wonder. She was still pregnant.

Towards the end of the year I happened to be at my mother's house when Sir John Lavery called to see me.

"I have been asked to do a mural at Churt but feel too old for the task," he said. "Not only that, I doubt if I have the powers of imagination necessary for a mural. Would you like to take it on?"

It was a marvelous surprise which I accepted at once. Lavery then gave me a piece of excellent advice which I have never forgotten.

"Remember," he said, "that Lloyd George is getting old, and when people get old their world becomes darker. So make your painting light and bright."

I went off to Churt for lunch. The visit was organized by Lloyd George's secretary, Miss Frances Stephenson as she then was, who later married the great man. He was fully occupied writing his memoirs, yet was most courteous and seemed to have limitless time to spend on entertaining me. This is something I have often noticed when meeting busy and important men. I would even go so far as to say that if a man has no time or only a short time for seeing people, you can be fairly sure that he is neither very important nor very busy. Indeed, I remember a letter my mother once sent from Naples to a friend in London. *Little has been happening here,* she wrote. *The Sutherlands rushed into the harbor in their yacht and rushed off again like people who have nothing to do.*

Lavery had warned me that at Churt it was advisable

to keep on the right side of Miss Stephenson, who ran the household. This was not difficult. She was both gracious and efficient. As usual, I felt out of my depth in the presence of a distinguished politician, but the atmosphere was made charming and informal by a little girl, an adopted daughter named Jennifer, who became the center of attention at lunch.

After the meal Lloyd George and I discussed the subject for the mural. There were three possibilities: the Versailles Conference, the Welsh mountains around Criccieth, or Rapallo, where Lloyd George had been for a war conference. Eventually we decided in favor of Rapallo, which I had sketched from Max Beerbohm's villa. The view was to be of the whole Tigullian Gulf, including Rapallo, Santa Margherita and Portofino. When this had been settled, I had to turn to politics for conversation, and as always when a nonprofessional tries to be intelligent about that complex subject, my questions were moronic. One of them, however, interested him.

"Please tell me, as a young man," I asked, "how it was possible for so many astute leaders of their respective countries in 1914 not to have solved their problems without going to war?" Aggressively, I continued: "Surely, men who have the greatness and wisdom to lead must also have the wisdom to settle their differences in a way which avoids the massacre of four and a half million men!"

This was a really meaty question for the old man, and he embarked on a discourse on the workings of the whole political situation from his point of view. It lasted for about an hour. I did a little sketch of his garden for him and left.

It took me two months to work out the details of the mural, which was rather tricky technically. Not only was it to be in a semicircle, but it was to be placed ten feet above the floor at one end of Lloyd George's library, which had an arched ceiling. Considerable imagination was needed to fit in the whole gulf in a manner that retained the local characteristics, which to my surprise Lloyd George knew very well. I was pleased when I thought of painting a full-length portrait of Angela standing at the left-hand side of the picture, holding a map of the gulf to show the cartography.

By the time I was ready to start the actual painting it was early March, 1935, and Angela was due to have her baby. My father maintained that where doctors are concerned there are two maxims: first, always go to the best (which means the most expensive); and second, pay their bills promptly. The prompt payment of bills is often difficult for an artist, who relies on checks from his patrons which are seldom punctual. Nevertheless, I accepted parental guidance for once and called in a society doctor whose list of patients came straight from Debrett. He recommended a fashionable nursing home in Sloane Street. When Angela had been safely installed there, I rented a large room on the opposite side of the road and stretched out my canvas for the mural.

It measured fifteen by seven and a half feet, but my preliminary work had been so detailed that I was able to execute the painting in fourteen days. When I took it to

Churt to show Lloyd George, he was thoroughly pleased and his comments were constructive. Adjusting his famous monocle, attached to the wide black silk band draped round his neck, he studied my canvas critically.

"Your wife's dress is not Italian enough," he said. "And I think some more houses and buildings would improve the peninsula."

I changed Angela's dress to a peasant fiesta costume and added several villas. When I had fixed up the canvas with adhesive, making it part of the wall, Miss Stephenson passed on to me the message that the final verdict was satisfactory. Before saying good-by to Lloyd George, I took a photograph of him in his blue felt hat and monocle. Altogether, the commission was a pleasant interlude.

It seemed that our infant would never arrive. I hung around the nursing home for days, until the baby was a fortnight late. Angela just flopped about, waiting to explode, as it were. On March 26 I was so tired of the delay that I went and had a bath. That, apparently, did the trick. The moment I started to soak the phone rang. The baby had arrived. A girl.

Within twenty-four hours came a most extraordinary personal call from the local registrar.

"And what is the baby's name?" he asked.

I was too surprised, and too worked up by recent events, to give a serious reply. "I haven't the faintest idea," I said. Then, thinking of the more amazing names in the family and remembering one of Lord Randolph Churchill's sisters who became Viscountess Wimborne, I added: "I expect it will be something peculiar like Cornelia."

To my astonishment I afterward discovered that my
daughter was officially registered as Cornelia. It is not a
name that I consider very pretty, but the Guest family
have thought it appropriate for me to call my daughter
after their grandmother. Cornelia was later christened
Sarah in Westminster Cathedral and became affectionately
known as Sally.

The folly of choosing a doctor merely because of the
titles, orders and honors among the rest of his patients
was proved when Angela failed to get well. Our doctor
had been so busy rushing round to duchesses that he
failed to clear her properly of her afterbirth. She had to
go into hospital for an operation. I must say that he
admitted his error and reduced his fee proportionately,
but the episode taught me that when choosing a doctor
or, for that matter, an artist, an architect, a soldier in war
or a politician even, he must be chosen for sincerity of
purpose and not for his titled success or ambitions in that
sphere.

My parents invited us to accompany them on a trip
to Sweden they were making in July. We accepted the
offer greedily; my wife needed a holiday after her indis-
position. In the meantime we rented a lodge-gate cottage
on the estate of Mr. Tipping, the agent of my grandfather,
Lord Abingdon. Relatives who visited us there have described our living conditions as "squalid." I do not think
they were quite as bad as that; it was just that things got
rather chaotic. We pleased ourselves. The washing up
tended to be ignored, and congestion collected in every
direction. We were very happy in those months. Angela

turned out to be a very reasonable cook when she tried, and I executed some of my loveliest paintings. A sensitive canvas of Pisa was bought by Nigel Birch, M.P., and one of Venice by Mrs. Taffy Rodd.

Our chief problem was our nurse. She was a Dutch girl who wanted to learn English, which meant the advantage that her wages were low, but she was a Nazi, having been trained at Ulm University, and her technique of rearing a baby was decidedly unorthodox. In order to let Sally sleep with a weak light on, she tied a vest round the electric bulb. This had the result that in the middle of the night the room caught fire, and I found myself holding a bucket of water up to the bulb to douse the remnants of blazing vest clinging there — a stupid thing to do. It is a wonder that I was not electrocuted.

We went down to Chartwell, where my uncle pronounced judgment on the first of the next generation of our two families. He studied Sally for a few moments in silence.

"That one looks all right," he said. "I should carry on."

The visit was spoilt by our nurse. It was a fine warm day and we sat out in the garden. When my uncle and aunt appeared she remained sprawled on the grass, despite my disapproving glares. With their usual impeccable manners they asked her about her studies and her future. As far as her future was concerned, Angela and I decided it there and then. She would have to be sacked the instant we returned home. Before dismissing her I asked why she had stayed on the ground.

"It would have been normal politeness to get up, who-ever our host and hostess were," I said.

"I am as good as anyone," she retorted. "Especially your uncle and aunt."

When she had gone we parked Sally with my mother-in-law, Mrs. Woolley, and set off on the trip to Sweden. It was the perfect example of what not to do in the way of an excursion *en famille*. My twenty-two-year-old brother Pebin and sixteen-year-old sister Clarissa were both equally gauche at this time. Pebin, who because of my mother's thwarted ambition for a daughter had been made to wear long curls and girls' dresses when a tot, had only one friend of his own age in the world, and that with reluctance. He was not the slightest bit interested in other people. My mother used to tell me he was so impossible she was almost alarmed.

"I cannot get him to go to the cinema," she said, "let alone meet anyone. He appears for dinner, after which he collapses on the sofa, reading some book or other in deathly silence night after night after night."

The war changed all that, but 1939 was still a way off. My sister was also bottling up her emotions on account of my mother's excessive fussing over her, which finally be-came so overwhelming that even Clarissa could not take it and she became more and more aloof, breaking away from home. I was rebellious myself, and sometimes wore my beret and black cloak, to the helpless amazement of my parents. And to add to our difficulties, Angela was actively asserting her independence after being possessed.

Pebin and I particularly enjoyed the stay at Tylosand

on the west coast of Sweden, where we amused ourselves by damming up a river which ran down across the beach into the sea. It was about twenty feet wide, and the flow was sufficiently gentle for sand to halt it. The enterprise had a typically Churchillian flavor, reminiscent of prewar days at Cromer. Even my father lent a hand in digging the main dam, and the successive reserve dams which eased the pressure. In the end of course the dam burst, with a tremendous outrush of water, but it was well constructed and created a sizable lake.

At night the family retired to bed quietly, but Angela wanted to enjoy herself, to be gay and have fun. She dragged me off to the nearest dance hall. She was so attractive that many of the Swedes wanted to dance with her, the customary procedure being for them to ask for my permission first, which I had the right to refuse.

"I bet you haven't the courage to ask for a dance with the most beautiful girl in the room!" Angela said.

I took up the challenge rather reluctantly and went across and spoke to the woman's escort. He gave me permission, but to my utter humiliation the woman refused. I was thoroughly put out by this rebuff.

The journey to Stockholm was made by canal. We visited the famous studio of Carl Millais, the sculptor, and I was interested to see the concert house and twin-spired church built by Tengbom. But the biggest impression was made on me by the city's town hall. It dictated much of my subsequent work. What appealed to me was that the architect, Östberg, had toured the major town halls of Europe before designing Stockholm's. His creation is a sublime epitome of all that a town hall ought to be; more than that, he carried through the entire project with the conception of an artist. He even controlled the interior furnishing, down to the smallest detail. I have heard architects condemn the town hall as an anthology of bits and pieces gathered from here and there, but to an artist such as myself it is an immensely satisfying, complete achievement. I can name no architect today who has the mind or imagination to look further than his set square.

On our return to London, Angela and I took a flat in Sussex Gardens, W.2. Giving our daughter an airing meant putting her out on the second-floor window ledge. At the height of the summer we decided that we could not face an English winter. On the recommendation of our writer friend Gerald Brenan, we decided to emigrate to southern Spain. Gerald lived near Malaga in a small village called Churriana, with his American schoolteacher wife and five-year-old daughter Miranda. Accordingly, we booked one-way tickets for Gibraltar on a Japanese liner. Our idea was to make our headquarters at Torremolinos, three kilometers from Churriana, and come back to England every summer to sell our work. We had no idea where we were going to live in Torremolinos, and the Brenans were the only people we knew in that part of Spain, but we set off cheerfully with our child, miles of canvas, china, linen, gramophones, books and so on. We also had a Scottish nurse, a large, buxom blonde of about twenty-one.

I happened to be standing on deck next to a Japanese steward as we entered Gibraltar harbor. The *Hood*, huge and magnificent, was among the ships of the Royal Navy lying at anchor.

"That battle cruiser," I remarked with pride, "is probably the finest in the world today."

The Japanese smiled enigmatically. "You think so?" he said. "We will see."

Ominous words. Within ten years the *Hood* was blown up and an even larger battleship, H.M.S. *Prince of Wales*, was sunk by suicide torpedo planes of the Japanese Navy.

At Gibraltar I hired a lorry and loaded our gear into it. We set off for Churriana. Crouching amidst a mountain of swaying, rocking luggage, we had a very uncomfortable ride, but our nurse did not mind in the least. She had only accepted the job because she thought it would be fun to join our menagerie.

When we halted at the Spanish customs at La Linea, I tried to make an impression with my beret, my cloak and my name; after all, were not Churchills something to do with English politics, etc.? My announcement of my identity, though, was greeted by hoots of laughter. I could not understand a word of Spanish, so I made a lot of what I hoped were impressive noises and kept repeating: "Churchill! Churchill!" It made the customs men practically collapse with mirth, which was most puzzling until an English-speaking Spaniard appeared. He broke to me the news that "Churchill" or the phonetic equivalent in Spanish slang means something exceptionally rude and completely unprintable. At this we all had a colossal laugh, masses of handshakes all round and a dopla of Manzanilla sherry. We were shown through the customs with V.I.P. treatment, and as we roared off in the lorry we saw the Spaniards still laughing and exclaiming to each other: "The mad English!"

We passed through Marbella, which was then a small fishing village, and paused in Torremolinos at the bus stop next to the Bar Mañana, where we immediately celebrated our arrival with a dopla of Manzanilla. It is the best sherry in Andalusia: it is not overdry and has traveled only a short distance. In those days Torremolinos was considered a minor, undeveloped seaside place where Spaniards could go and relax. A few foreigners, including some English, were doing the same, and mostly they stayed at the Santa Clara, which had about the only hotel accommodation available.

When we got to Churriana, Gerald and his wife greeted us warmly. They escorted us back to Torremolinos and found us a delightful villa. It was called El Rosario and had a blue gate and door, and was sandwiched between the great tower — the *torre* — and the church. Our nearest neighbor was the miller, a short, swarthy man who lived in his *molinos* on the far side of the tower. El Rosario belonged to an old relation of the Larios family and the rent was about three pounds a month. We employed a servant named Anna who cleaned the whole house and cooked our meals. Her wages were only one pound a month, but as is customary in Mediterranean countries, we found ourselves feeding not only Anna but about ten of her relations as well. We would have for lunch an enormous chicken from which there was more than enough surplus for dinner. Yet when dinnertime came, and we asked about the chicken, Anna would open her eyes wide and say with complete sincerity: "There is nothing left."

I took up my work again with inspired zest. I decorated the entire house with murals in different styles and painted large allegorical and mythological subjects. In a very short time we made friends of the entire village. A local lad, Raphael Montes Sanchez, his ten brothers and sister Carmen used to come in and do odd jobs for us. At the end of a few months we had created a sizable English-speaking community. Lady Anne Gathorne-Hardy, a friend and cousin of Angela's, came out to join us. Angela's mother and half sister Janetta Woolley took a house opposite ours. Geoffrey Household, the writer, moved into one built in the cliff below us, and the American journalist Jay Allen and his wife established themselves further along the street.

But despite this company, Angela had another of her restless phases coming on. She strummed at mournful melodies on her guitar and wrote elaborate entries in her diary, none of which I was allowed to see. I was working at high pressure to get my paintings ready for an exhibition I planned to give in London the following summer and had little time for frivolities. We made one or two excursions to Malaga with the Brenans, who, knowing Spain so well, introduced us to some of the seamier sides of life in that big town, but it was not enough for Angela. She craved continual dancing and gaiety.

Before we left England she had visited a fortuneteller who predicted: "A great upheaval will be caused in your life by a dark man."

"My husband?" Angela asked.

"No, not your husband."

Sure enough, the man arrived, a dark-haired French count, le Comte de Chatellus, driving a fast two-seater car. Nobody knows — not even he — why he should have been in such a remote corner of Spain at that time. But there he was. And thus, in 1936, the year of the Spanish Revolution, the scene was set for a private revolution of our own.

The count quickly struck up a friendship with us on the beach. He came to dinner at our house and I treated him as a welcome guest. When Angela said she wished she could go dancing, and he offered to take her to Malaga while I made progress with my work, I agreed. I considered it weakness on my part for any hint of jealousy to be roused within me; I put it down to youth. It is not in my nature to be jealous. I let Angela go — and was wrong to trust her.

Other developments were taking place elsewhere. My mother-in-law evidently saw fit to encourage the liaison. I can only suppose that she felt a French count would be a more suitable husband for her daughter than a poor struggling artist. Unknown to our friend Anne Gathorne-Hardy or me, she put a private room of her own house at the count's disposal.

When the domestic situation became strained and tense I suggested a diversion in the form of a trip to Granada. It was February. The mountain roads were covered with snow, making it advisable to travel by train. The buses were regarded as risky; recently one had skidded and plunged over a cliff, killing the passengers. We had our third-class carriage to ourselves for half the journey, and played the guitar and sang. Then a gypsy got in with her infant child. It being feeding time, she opened her dress and pulled out a breast. But before allowing the child to begin suckling, she turned and politely offered us a drink first. Perhaps she was hoping for some of our red wine.

At Granada I visited the Alhambra and the cathedral, but Angela let me go to these places alone. She preferred to sit in cafés writing, unknown to me, letters to her count.

On our return to Torremolinos the climax was swift. To the immense relief of me and my friends, the count announced he was leaving for Paris. Next, Angela said she would like to go and stay with the Brenans in Churriana for a while. I took her over there, innocently believing that the tension would die and we could settle down again. When we arrived she hunted through her luggage.

"Oh, dear," she said. "My jersey. I must have left it at home."

I went to Torremolinos to fetch it. I got back to find Gerald standing at the door. Simply and matter-of-factly he said: "Angela has gone."

"Gone?" Impossible. She had mentioned nothing about it to me. It was the sort of dramatic desertion which happened in novels, or to other people; never to oneself.

"It seems she had no money," Gerald went on. "She organized this visit as a means of getting some."

"And you gave it to her?"

"Yes."

"But why?"

Gerald shrugged. "It was pointless to refuse. She was determined to go. She has taken the bus to join the count in Malaga."

The date was March 26 — our daughter's first birthday. So this was the beginning of the end of my pagan marriage!

It was for me, furthermore, the start of a deeply spiritual period. I had never really been an atheist, or even an agnostic. As Father Ronnie Knox said to me at Oxford, it would appear that my disposition was more pantheistic and my spiritual life was found for me in my art. But fundamentally I have always been a Catholic, and once a Catholic always a Catholic. I regard the Church as a kind of spiritual "hospital" where the "doctors" and "surgeons" are its ministers. Their job is to keep your spiritual life healthy, and they help in this by doing your thinking for you. What happens if you venture to think on your own? Well, luckily for the Church, most people do not trouble, and it is for them that religion is chiefly intended. When a Catholic has children they are automatically brought up in the Faith, and confirmed at an early age when they do not really understand anything. On looking back, I feel that my mother, who was more a philosophical or intellectual Catholic, considered I should be given the opportunity to think about and appreciate the great philosophy of Christianity as a whole, including the Greek Orthodox and Dissenting sections of thought. I was never confirmed.

In the eyes of the Catholic Church I was not married to Angela, but a tremendous surge of emotion possessed me.

I had a grand passion, a terrific fit of jealousy. I wrapped my black cloak round me, stuffed a couple of sharp knives in my pockets, and set off for Malaga, bent on revenge.

Anne Gathorne-Hardy accompanied me. We descended on the town with the speed and ferocity of a commando attack and searched every flat and room where Angela and the count might be staying. But it was no use. They had gone — to Almeria, further along the coast, as I learned from a letter she sent. She implored me to be patient, to wait until she had consumed her desire, when she would return. This request made me writhe with fury.

I decided to return to England, via Madrid and Lisbon, to get away from it all. Suppressing the anger that boiled within me, I replied to Angela's letter with an offer to start our marriage afresh. If she would come back to me I would forget and forgive, and we would live happily ever after. I suggested a meeting in Madrid.

I will come, she replied, *on condition that you let me go back to the count.*

I consented (what else could I do?) and set off for Madrid with Anne as company. Jay Allen, the American journalist living in Torremolinos, was already in the Spanish capital, where he had gone to try to sound out the restless political situation. I have always thought Americans very good at taking one round strange places, and Jay excelled himself. He had his ear close to the ground and knew exactly which gypsy performances were being given where and when. He took us to a fantastically low night club where the shows were usually in the nude. Then in came a troupe of Gitano gypsy dancers, who performed magnificently with their natural violence. Tourists never see exhibitions of this kind. Details of the movements of such small, expert troupes are never published; the news is simply passed around by word of mouth. The reward for discovering one of their shows is Spanish dancing at its very best, in a dirty, crowded, smoky cellar with wine everywhere and a friendly, intimate atmosphere. Transferred to the stage of a big theater it is but a pale shadow of the original.

Angela arrived from Almeria looking obstinate and willful, and the three of us — Angela, Anne and I — booked rooms at the same hotel. We spent three very pleasant if strained days together. At the end Angela was still defiant. She insisted on going back to her count. It then became my turn to make conditions. Remembering the precedent set by my grandfather, Lord Abingdon, in similar circumstances, I told her:

"If you leave me, I will take on the responsibility of bringing up Sally. And if I do that, you will have absolutely no say in the matter whatsoever. But if you stay, I will forgive and forget and never refer to the subject again."

It was a moment for deep thought, but infatuation triumphed over maternal responsibilities. I went to the railway station with her for a cold and unemotional goodby. A few people have since said to me I was wrong to insist on bringing up Sally myself. Others feel I was right — including, I am glad to say, Sally.

My mother-in-law was looking after Sally in Torremolinos. The baby was in capable hands, and I considered

I could return to England at once. Anne and I took the
train to Lisbon, where we had a day or two of frivolity
and night club investigation. Then we boarded a British
liner which was on the South American run, calling at
Lisbon on her way back to Southampton.

The third-class accommodation was practically empty
and our steward was embarrassingly helpful. Although
we had booked single cabins, he offered to let us change
them for a double one. He was most surprised when I
declared that Anne and I were "good friends" in the
strictest sense of the term, and nothing more. We were
intrigued to find that outside our cabins a large area about
twenty by fifteen feet was surrounded by tall vertical bars,
forming a cage.

"What is it for?" I asked the steward.

"Oh," he said casually, "that's where we put the girls on
the way out to Rio."

"Which girls?"

The steward gave us a look which made us feel like innocent babes. "We usually pick up about a hundred of
them in Lisbon," he said. "Down-and-outs mostly. They
are collected from all over Europe. Then they are pushed
in there with two male escorts."

"Escorts?" asked Anne.

"Yes, they sleep in the cage and — well, sort of have
the lot in turn."

Think of it. A reputable British liner of a well-estab-
lished shipping company helping in the white slave traffic! We were to learn more.

"Actually," said the steward, "we deal with three classes

of girls. In addition to this grade — the "cage" grade — we have the "ballerina" or "tennis party" grade. These come in groups of twenty or thirty and have been told that when they get to Rio they will dance in a night club or take part in tennis tournaments. What happens is that they are met at the docks by a madame who whisks them off to a brothel and they are never heard of again."

"Where do they live on board?" I asked.

"They have free run of the second class, but two or three managers see to it that they don't sleep with anyone else."

Apparently the luxury of the first-class decks was reserved for the No. 1 grade, the private or really superior prostitute being sent across by an international organization. Once, through my friend the traveler and writer Eleanor Smith, I met a key man in this evil conspiracy, a Roumanian. His wife, whom he loved very much, had died from cancer despite his efforts to save her. In consequence he bore a grudge against the world and determined to avenge his grief with the worst reprisal he could imagine: the setting up of brothels to degrade as many as possible of the women still living.

When I reached London I felt utterly crushed by the failure of my marriage. Anne was the only person in England who shared the dreadful secret. We put up at the Eiffel Tower with Rudolf Stulick and his wife, who by that time were both somewhat eccentric. The rows and arguments which they staged at night were appalling, but the food was as good as ever. In Bloomsbury again I lapsed back gratefully into the Bohemian way of life. I spent hours over dinner talking with Louise and Isabel, the famous models of Augustus John and Epstein. Artists, critics, and shady characters whose hair drooped over their foreheads were also welcome to share my wine. Iris Tree was one of them. With the co-operation of the Stulicks, I arranged an exhibition of my paintings in the restaurant. Some of the canvases had been done in Spain, others in Italy. I sold an encouragingly large number.

I went to see my parents in their new house in Regent's Park, but did not mention my personal troubles. They invited me to decorate their hall and staircase for a fee, gladly accepted. I did the spires of Oxford, supported by a *trompe-l'oeil* of a tapestry of Blenheim and Whytham. Very family.

Then I went to a party given by Clare Sheridan and could not resist telling her of my plight.

"Well," she commented, "what a fool you are! I am not the least surprised that this has happened. What could a girl like Angela hope to get out of you? You cannot offer her money, and you are much too busy for perpetual gaiety. Besides, what else is to be expected if you marry your mistress? It simply can't be done."

Remembering the various lessons of life in her book *Nuda Veritas,* I found these observations rather confusing.

At the party I met Yvonne Rodd, the exotic wife of Taffy, one of the Rodd brothers. She commissioned me to paint a mural of Venice in her bedroom. This, my Opus 12, was a very delicate and subtle work in controlled and high colors inspired principally by the fabulous character of my patroness. Her bedroom was floored with black marble and had one wall covered in squares of Venetian glass with a terra-cotta Madonna and Child in the center. The head of the bed was elaborately carved wood painted silver, and the bedspread a beautiful red and yellow damask. My picture, a view of the lagoon from the Dogana with gondolas in the foreground, measured eighteen by ten feet. I had to finish it in ten days because my ticket back to Spain was for June 1.

Yvonne threw a memorable party to celebrate the mural's completion. After dinner a yogi appeared and started to swallow yards and yards of cord. Then, while we were still feeling rather peculiar with our meal inside us, he twisted himself into extraordinary shapes and pulled the whole lot out again, hand over fist. It seemed an odd idea of entertainment.

Let us now see what had happened to Angela. It appears that when the brave French count heard I was after his blood, he crept out of their apartment in Almeria early one morning, at an hour when Angela was asleep, and fled to Paris. Angela, undaunted, set off for Paris too, via Torremolinos, where she was able to borrow some money from her mother. She set herself up in the Rue Colisée.

On my way to Spain I called to see her, imagining that a reconciliation was possible, but she was surrounded by French and Italian noblemen, quite apart from various people of lower orders, and I had to give up the attempt.

I arrived in Torremolinos to find complications. My mother-in-law and Janetta had left for England, leaving baby Sally with the nurse. Unfortunately, the nurse had discovered that life in Spain was far more fun than the

Highlands of Scotland. She was walking out with a young Spaniard, a distraction which caused her to neglect her duties so much that I had no alternative but to give her the sack. As a substitute I managed to get hold of a German girl who was staying at the Santa Clara hotel on holiday. She had been drawn to Torremolinos by a crush on an Englishman living in the village, but the tense political situation was making her anxious to get back to her homeland. She agreed to work for me because she thought I might help her.

It was now about July 10. The atmosphere was electric, as always before a storm. Jay Allen did his best to keep me up to date with news of political developments, but anyone who knows Spain and the Spanish will understand that it was impossible to learn much of importance. On July 15 came an urgent knock at my door. Gerald Brenan had walked the three miles of wild countryside from Churriana with a warning.

"Things are going to happen all at once," he said. "You must get out with your daughter as soon as you can. The revolution probably won't last long. Give it a fortnight. I suggest you pack everything and go to Tangier."

A fortnight! It was twenty years to the day before I returned to Torremolinos. But, as Gerald predicted, the revolution burst upon us very suddenly. Early on July 17 Jay Allen came up the street.

"Johnny, we've a wonderful chance to see some action," he said keenly. "The revolutionaries have crossed with Moors to the frontier town of La Linea. A tremendous battle is going to be fought near Gibraltar. Come in my car and we'll have a look."

"But what about my little girl?" I protested. "I cannot possibly leave Sally here with a German nurse."

"Oh, yes, you can. It will all be over quite quickly. The Spaniards will never stand for Moors being used in their country against themselves."

In my view the golden rule when faced with a war in a foreign country is to leave hastily. I had already started to act on Gerald's advice. My luggage was packed. I might have been persuaded into going to Gibraltar had I not suffered a very full dose of war from my uncle; I failed to see anything glamorous in it. Jay went, and told me in England afterward the harrowing tale of how he was nearly killed when the Moors opened fire with machine guns at the Spanish crowd, including himself, facing them at the frontier.

Meanwhile, Torremolinos and Malaga were still under Government control. By "Government" I mean of course the left-wing Socialistic elements of Spanish politics which were in power, as opposed to the right-wing Fascist and Catholic elements who were the revolutionaries. As far as I was concerned, it did not matter who the elements were, so long as I could get away from them. But this was to prove very difficult, especially with a tiny infant of fifteen months.

The first nights were terrifying. There was the deepest of silences, broken only by the crackle of flames burning the effigy of a nun in the church plaza and the crash and thud of the church belfry being demolished. I did several pen-and-wash drawings of the various scenes, which were subsequently published in the *Illustrated London News*. At dusk at the end of each uneasy day we heard a dull ripple of rifle shots from a nearby quarry where political prisoners were being executed. The dreadful thing about the whole situation was that one had no idea who was on which side, and whether one's friends and servants were going to be shot or spared. The entire village dreaded the knock that used to come in the middle of the night, followed by the demand to know who was in.

One of my first precautions was to paint a large Union Jack on a piece of canvas and fix it prominently outside my front window. Then, because my larder was getting empty, I made a smaller Union to stick in my coat lapel, and taking off my tie (anyone with a tie was liable to be shot on the spot as a revolutionary), I ventured out into the street.

A commune had been set up in the Bar Jerez. The chaos inside was unbelievable. Everybody was armed to the teeth with guns and pistols like brigands in a comic opera. Even the children brandished pistols, some of which were so ancient they must have come from museums. The crowd was talking loudly, with lots of pushing, shoving and frantic gesticulation, and I was able to slip back a large number of safety catches without their owners noticing. But I could get no sense from anyone. No buses were running to Malaga; there was no food; nothing.

Outside the bar I met one of my local helpers, Raphael Montes Sanchez. He was exuberant. "Have you seen the bonfire?" he asked. "And we're pulling down the church!"

"Why?" I asked pleadingly.

"It is like a fiesta," he said. "An excuse to have fun."

Some fun . . .

I went to the edge of the cliff and watched Malaga burning eight miles away. The great dense clouds of smoke drifted up and hung sullenly round the mountains behind the town.

The weather was exceedingly hot, and all the foreigners in Torremolinos were getting more and more alarmed. They had reason to be; nobody knew what would happen next. In view of the confusion I considered it my duty to take command and try to establish order. I realized I was sticking out my neck. I was acutely aware of the importance of not meddling in another country's politics. On the other hand, helpless foreigners were in a state of near-panic.

The nearest telephone was in the miller's house. He had barricaded his front door; he was earmarked for execution, I had heard at the commune. After a lot of agitated hesitation he let me in, and I demanded to be allowed to telephone Malaga. I spoke to the British consul there, asking him to contact Gibraltar.

"Tell the admiral in command," I said, "that Mr. John Churchill requires a destroyer in Malaga harbor at once to take off as many refugees as possible."

What's in a name? I dislike cashing in on family connections, but this, I felt, was a justifiable occasion.

It turned out that summoning a destroyer of the Royal Navy was much easier than ringing for a taxicab in central London. The magic of the name worked instantly. A message came through to say that a destroyer would report next morning. I then gibbered away in Churchillian Spanish to the commune, reminding them how essential it was to get all the foreigners out of the town at once to save precious food. They had no idea what they were doing and agreed with me easily. In the evening a gang of toughs called to collect the miller and take him off to the quarry. I did a sketch of his departure which I still have.

Early the following day I was cheered by the grand sight of a destroyer steaming past our house on its way to Malaga. A bus was commandeered and crammed with every foreigner we could find. Then an amazing assortment of fiercely armed Spaniards perched themselves on the bonnet, running board, and roof to "offer protection" in case any of their fellow countrymen opened fire on us.

The British consul in Malaga, who merited the highest possible award for his service but who probably received nothing, as is often the case on such occasions, managed the superhuman task of rounding up some two hundred local foreigners of British and other nationalities for a rendezvous on the quay. We sailed at once for Gibraltar, where those of us going to England were transferred to a P. & O. liner. My German nurse became ill on the voyage and I had to look after Sally myself. By the time we reached London I was expert at mixing Cow and Gate baby food in the right proportions, changing and washing nappies.

Newspaper reporters kept chasing me for lurid stories, but I assured them I had none to offer. The correspondents' reports in the British press seemed to me to be much too exaggerated, and I sent the editor of the *Daily Telegraph* a letter, which was published. *I have not seen any bloodshed,* I wrote, *and as for the stories of nuns being murdered, they are simply not true; at least in Malaga.*

As a matter of fact, appalling atrocities were later committed by both sides during the course of the Civil War, but my letter looked as if I were sticking up for the Communist régime — a declaration which brought forth a rebuke from my uncle. I was summoned to Chartwell, where he looked at me sternly over the tops of his spectacles.

"Why did you write that letter?"

"It is what I saw, Uncle Winston, I said, "and I considered I ought to put the situation in correct perspective."

He then made it very clear that the opinions I had éxpressed did not coincide with his own on the matter, and almost hinted that I would be well advised to mind my own business, namely painting. Both of us were to change our views later, but at that time, August 1936, it seemed to me that if either the Communists or the Fascists were to gain power in Spain, the Communists would be the lesser of the two evils; they were such a long way from their Russian homeland.

Spain was Russia's first serious effort at distant colonization. It failed, and for that Russia has never forgiven Spain. My own feelings are that any foreigners, of whatever side, who interfered individually in the Spanish Civil War deserved what they got. The only people acting with sense and caution were the British Government, who stood aloof and watched.

Recently I had occasion to talk with one of the secretaries at the Spanish Embassy in London and remarked to him that although Spain has received attentions from a large number of foreign countries, the Spaniard is astonishingly like the Irishman. "He is superstitious, proud, and very Catholic," I said.

"Not at all," smiled the secretary. "Actually the Spaniard is more like the Englishman. When you go to Spain you will find the Spaniard very kind and sympathetic towards you. You do not know why. But the reason is that he is sorry for you because you are not a Spaniard."

I saw his point. And the Spaniard is further like the Englishman in that he detests foreign interference, Communist or Fascist.

VII

The Sword and the Scabbard

WHEN I WAS VERY YOUNG indeed I had a strange dream about my birth. I dreamed that my mother went out to a store and bought my limbs, one by one, from the different departments. Then she came home and put them together, on the top floor of the house in which I was born — No. 10, Talbot Square, Paddington, W.2. The odd thing is that my parents moved to Cromwell Road when I was about two, and therefore I could not possibly have remembered Talbot Square, yet because of the dream I always had a vivid picture of the nursery quarters in my mind.

When I arrived in London from Spain in 1936, my parents had moved to a new house overlooking the sea at Ringstead Bay near Weymouth, Dorset, and I had nowhere to go in London. So, with a kind of basic homing instinct I suppose, I made my way to Talbot Square, an area which I knew had numerous flats and apartment houses. The front door of No. 10 was still painted red as I hoped it would be, and by luck the top floor was vacant. It was exactly as I had seen it in my dream. I moved in with Sally and the German nurse.

The nurse was still not well after the voyage, and I had to arrange for her embassy to send her back to Germany. A Danish girl took over temporarily, and then I went with Sally down to Dorset to see my parents. I planned on getting them to look after her while I re-established my contacts. My bank balance had vanished and I was in urgent need of commissions.

It was one of those occasions when an offspring, especially a rebellious one such as myself, can be so selfish, and so insensitive towards his parents. I blithely assumed that my mother and father would be more than pleased to take on, at least for the time being, the responsibility of their grandchild. But I had underestimated the degree to which they disapproved of my marriage, and nothing could have been further from their minds. I was greeted with: "I told you so," and "What are you going to do now?" and "How are you going to eat?"

There were other reasons for this attitude which I had not realized, or even known about. My parents were beset by worries of their own. My mother was not very strong and had to be cared for by my father, who, without telling a soul, had developed an aneurysm — a cracked main artery — in the intestines, and doctors had given him only two years to live. In addition, my sister Clarissa was going through a complicated teen-ager phase, and it was difficult to organize her education.

I solved my problem myself, with confidence and determination. Much to everyone's amazement, I packed my bags and announced that I was returning to London.

"If you will please have Sally for just a very short

while," I said, "I will collect her at the earliest possible moment and relieve you of any trouble. I admit that the situation is entirely my fault, and therefore it is up to me to do something about it."

Being very independent by nature, I cannot say that I regret my action, but I am sorry that as a result of this discord my relationship with my parents became strained from then on. Had not my mother been so abnormally engrossed in my sister, she might have spared some affection for little Sally; after all, she adored girls. I was never to know what she really thought or felt about my private life in the years immediately to come.

In London I started to look up my friends and was greatly surprised to find that Jim Lees Milne had been converted to Catholicism. He made an observation which I thought most interesting. "The most difficult aspect of religion," he said, "is to control one's mind into believing that something exists when it does not." The task is easier perhaps for an artist, particularly in my branch of the profession, because we create and live in a world of the imagination.

The friend who was able to help me in my plight was the journalist Patrick Balfour, now Lord Kinross. "I know of a rather extraordinary family," he said, "where the mother is mad on children and animals. I would almost say she collects them. She might be pleased to give Sally a home for a bit."

I went to a party in Patrick's flat in order to meet this lady. She was attractive and elegant, and chain-smoked the whole time. Her name was the Marchioness of Tweed-

dale, but she was known to everyone as Midge, I suppose
because she was so small. Patrick told her my story, whereupon she invited him to bring me and my daughter down
to lunch the next Sunday at Fairlawne, the Kentish home
of Victor Cazelet, which she was renting.

"If I like the child," she promised, "I will be very
pleased to look after her for a time."

This was the beginning of a friendship with a family of
benefactors to whom I owe a great deal, not only because
of Sally but because of my career. The setup at Fairlawne
consisted of the Marquess, the Marchioness and their four
daughters, the eldest of whom was a little younger than I
and married, and the youngest only a few years older than
Sally. A distant cousin of mine, Lady Kathleen Curzon-
Herrick, was a co-hostess. The entertaining was nonstop.
The house had a constant ebb and flow of ambassadors,
journalists, artists, zoologists like Professor Zuckerman,
and literary men like Shane Leslie, who would arrive for
lunch in a kilt, having walked the thirty-four miles from
London. In the middle of it all were governesses, nurses,
babies, and children of all ages, some visiting and some
staying on like Sally. And surrounding the human activity
were monkeys, geese, tortoises, snakes, horses, dogs, lion
cubs, and cats.

Sally thrived in this astonishing household. She grew up
alongside George, a chimpanzee of about her own age.
Afternoon tea, for which all the children and all the animals capable of eating at table foregathered, was one of
the occasions when we could judge whether Sally or
George was making the most progress. George was clearly

ahead up to the age of about two. He could handle a spoon and eat cake and behave himself with considerable control. He always wore a pair of pants just in case, but I had successfully house-trained him by demonstration. (Monkeys can be trained in this way because they are born mimics.) However, he was madly jealous of men when women were around, and this particularly applied to me and his friend Sally. I never let him take her hand unless I had hold of him as well; I knew he would try to drag her away. After the age of two, Sally developed much more quickly and passed him. For the war he was sent to Manchester Zoo, where he died.

There had not been much time or opportunity to have Sally christened, and she was two and a half when I took her to Westminster Cathedral. I had made an appointment for the ceremony beforehand, but when we walked in the main door with her godmother, Lady Eleanor Smith, the place seemed empty. I happened to see a rope hanging near the door, so I pulled it. The result was a sharp, reverberating *clang-clang* in the vast upper darkness of the roof, and priests started running around in confusion, thinking they had missed a service. I had accidentally rung the communion bell.

Angela appeared in England at about this time to see Sally, and the Tweeddales most kindly arranged for her to come down to Fairlawne, enabling me to make one more attempt at a reconciliation. I asked Patrick Balfour to bring her. She made it clear that she wanted a divorce in order to marry the Comte de Chatellus. I decided to insti-tute proceedings against her, as I wished to be the innocent party, and she accepted gladly. But on returning to France, Angela found that the count had tired of her. She came back to England and married Patrick Balfour — a startling turn of events, to put it mildly. Eventually she divorced him, and fifteen years later, after the war, she found a three-year-old letter addressed to her from the count. It said that if she was still free, he would be delighted to marry her. She agreed. But the wanderlust took hold of her again and they were divorced.

In the three years of peace that remained before the war, I was to execute fifteen murals in addition to numerous paintings and portraits. I was also to learn that sometimes there are snags to having a well-known name such as Churchill. People are apt to think that the entire family is individually rich, or kept in luxury by their "fairy godfather" Winston.

I can only suppose that this was the case with Lady Sysonby. She sat next to me at a dinner party given by the Tweeddales at their London home where, in consideration of the hospitality and generosity shown to me by the Marquess and Marchioness, I had executed some large murals. Lady Sysonby complimented me on my work and asked if I would like to do something very special for her. I replied that of course I would, for so charming a lady.

"The problem," she said, "is that it is not for me. It is for two very old ladies I know in Bath. Can you do them a mural which is simple and cheap?"

"Delighted," I replied. "What does it involve? Perhaps I can reduce my fee."

"They have a dining room about fifteen feet by twelve

feet," she said. "They are extremely hard up and in very weak health, and it would be wonderful for them to have a beautiful room to gaze at in the twilight of their lives. How much would it cost?"

I did some rapid mental calculation and told her that normally my fee would be approximately two hundred pounds, but in view of the circumstances I would take on the commission for one hundred.

"Good gracious," she exclaimed, "they cannot possibly afford as much as that!"

I failed to see how I could do it for much less, but I offered: "Make it seventy-five pounds."

"Couldn't you do it for fifty?" she asked.

"The traveling to Bath, the canvas and paints," I pointed out, "might cost fifty pounds, not to mention the time needed, and my skill and experience."

Her ladyship looked crestfallen. "Is there absolutely no hope of your doing it for thirty?"

"No," I told her. "I will do it for thirty-five, and the old ladies must try and help me buy the canvas if necessary."

At this she brightened up and smiled. "That is very sweet of you, Mr. Churchill," she said. "I must now let you into a secret. I was teasing when I said that the mural is for two old ladies. In fact, it is for my daughter, the Duchess of Westminster!"

Having been beaten down to a ridiculously low price which would probably show a loss on the job, I was rather shattered, but felt I had committed myself. I went to the Duchess's home at 8 Little College Street, Westminster, and executed the work in six tones of gray in ten days. Today the property belongs to the Crown Agents, but my mural is still there. You can see it from the street by looking through the ground-floor windows.

Sir Michael Duff then commissioned me to paint the stair well at Vaynol, his house near Bangor. The subject, the Welsh castles surrounding his estate, had to be finished in a fortnight; he needed the house for a shoot at the end of that time. It was a prodigious task. There were nine panels, each four feet wide and eight feet high. But I did my paintings in sepia in a Chinese transparent technique — to schedule. Across the straits at Plas Newydd, my friend Rex Whistler was executing for Lord Anglesey an enormous and exquisite mural which must have taken him six months or longer.

While I was busy at Vaynol, Michael Duff had one of the most extraordinary romances of all time. He did not sleep very well and often used to ring up a friend for a gossip in the middle of the night. On one occasion, he tried to ring a friend at about three o'clock in the morning and got a wrong number. He apologized profusely for causing unpardonable inconvenience, but before he could put down the receiver the lady at the other end said: "Oh, please don't apologize. It does not matter at all. I cannot sleep either. Let's have a chat." Intrigued, Michael started an animated conversation about nothing in particular. When he said he would have to say good night, she replied "You do not know who I am, and I do not know who you are, but I like your conversation. So please, if you want to talk in the night, ring this number again." He did. After many nocturnal conversations, embracing every possible topic from politics, sex and love to racing, Michael asked her to tell him her identity in order that they could meet. But she refused. Then one night, years later, he rang her number again. The maid answered and told him that alas, Madam had just died. Michael never found out for certain who the lady was, though he scanned the obituary columns of *The Times* and made a guess.

In addition to the panels at Vaynol, I painted an over-mantel at Hackwood Park, Basingstoke, the home of Lord Camrose. Lord Birkenhead was giving it to his father-in-law as a birthday present. Most of the Berry family were there. One evening when Lord Camrose was away, I came down to dinner wearing a false mustache. Lady Camrose was so frightened she was only just prevented from calling the police to evict a gate-crasher. Neville Ford was also a guest that evening. Freddie Birkenhead persuaded us to do one of our famous Birkenhead-Churchill after-dinner conversations.

I often went down to Chartwell for short visits to see how the Marlborough Pavilion was getting on and to repair damage caused by the weather. Usually I went alone or with a relative. It is a family rule never to take strangers. Such an enormous number of people want to go to Chartwell merely to be able to say they have met my uncle and aunt that it has become necessary to draw the line. His own family is large enough. If nephews started bringing visitors just to see the great man, the situation would get out of hand. Therefore the rule is: No introductions. The only exception I have ever made was Ella Maillart the traveler, who before the war had recently come back from Tibet. I asked for permission to take her to Chartwell, and to my delight my uncle agreed. The old boy liked her very much. They got along famously.

At Chartwell it never ceases to amaze me how my aunt copes with the running of the place. Her role is that of an A.D.C. Extraordinary and Super Quartermaster to the greatest of Captain-Generals. For Chartwell, and indeed any other house my uncle occupies, is not only a kind of military headquarters but also a large factory filled with high-powered executives. To see that this factory runs smoothly, with meals at odd hours for visiting experts and the relays of secretaries working through the night, calls for tremendously detailed organization. How my aunt has been able to do it is a secret which perhaps she herself will tell one day; it would be fascinating to know. In addition to bringing up a large family, she has been present to act as a gracious hostess to every conceivable sort of guest. Even when she is not feeling well, she never allows anyone to know it.

The hospitality which my uncle and aunt offer at table is quite out of this world. In addition to special dishes to suit the idiosyncrasies of guests — the Prof, for instance, was a vegetarian, which meant arranging two menus — there is always champagne, superb port and brandy for lunch, followed by more port, brandy and cigars when the ladies have withdrawn.

I had a bit of trouble with the cigars once. The box which the butler hands round is usually filled with a mixture of cigars of different lengths and qualities. Liking cigars very much, I take care to choose a good one; in fact, my uncle sees to it that I do. But during one period there was a special brand of extra-large cigar which he preferred above all others. The butler made sure that one of them was placed in the box. Unfortunately, when the box was presented to me, I inadvertently took *the* cigar, with the result that when the box arrived at my uncle, he looked at the contents, saw that his favorite was missing, and gave me a black look. Another cigar had to be fetched from the main stock in the cupboard, but I succeeded in mitigating my offense by replacing the special and asking the butler to bring me a smaller one.

Lunch at Chartwell has always been an event. Something inevitably happens which provides a memorable experience. One day before the war, I entered the dining room with my uncle, Randolph and Bill Deakin, and discovered a parrot in the corner, clutching at a perch affair. This was a new and exciting innovation, and Mr. Parrot, who had been given by Daisy Fellowes, was making great progress in endearing himself to his new master. Alas, the friendship did not last long. At the port stage of that very lunch my uncle rose and went to the parrot, holding out a thumb.

"Pretty Polly!" he said. "Pretty Poll!" Whereupon the ungrateful bird snapped its beak over my uncle's thumb and refused to let go. My uncle unleashed a tremendous vocabulary until the parrot released its grip. As soon as he left the room, having become bored with our conversation, I amused Randolph and Bill by imitating the whole scene over again: the friendly advance to the parrot, the sticking out of the stubby thumb, the lightning attack, attempted withdrawal and violent outburst of words. To my dismay, the door opened and my uncle suddenly came back.

"Taking me off, I see," he observed with great displeasure, and left.

Mr. Parrot was banished forthwith, and we never saw him again.

At another Chartwell lunch around this time, there were only three of us — my uncle, William Nicholson and myself — at the table when in walked Mr. Cat. My uncle ignored the animal's entrance, but Nicholson and I stared at each other in horror and amazement. Mr. Cat was now a Manx. He had a mere stump for a tail.

"Uncle Winston," I said, "whatever has happened to Mr. Cat?"

"Oh," he said, lowering his voice, "I forgot to tell you. But will both of you please convince yourselves that you have seen nothing unusual? Mr. Cat is very, very self-conscious about his tail."

"What happened?" I repeated.

"You know," my uncle began, "that the trout in the upper lake have been making progress. They have caused no one any harm; they just cruise about their own waters, unmolested by foreign bodies. Looking out of the window at this moment, you must admit that there could be no greater peace anywhere."

I began to think that Mr. Cat had done something terrible to the trout, but no. With a sad glance at Mr. Cat, my uncle continued: "Not long ago I was sitting here, just like this, and saw a hostile bird, a cormorant, appear over the lake. It then began to dive on the trout, eating them. I ordered the gardener to shoot this monstrous invader. He did, but some of the pellets hit Mr. Cat's tail.

"Poor Mr. Cat wouldn't come home for some time because his tail was broken. He was too shy to present himself for inspection. Eventually he did come in and we sent him to Maidstone Hospital to have it amputated. After that, we decided he must never think we have noticed the absence of his tail or care about it."

My uncle's love of animals, birds, fish, and so on is one of the most remarkable and charming sides of his character. He told me that if Mr. Cat happened to be sleeping on his bed, he would climb in and curl himself in such a way as not to disturb his pet's slumber. And if at five o'clock in the morning even, Mr. Cat should scratch on the bedroom door, my uncle gets up to let him in.

A mysterious figure whose visits to Chartwell became more and more frequent around this time was Major Morton, subsequently Sir Desmond Morton, a typical-looking English major with a mustache. Wounded in the First World War by a bullet which lodged in his heart, he had been expecting to die ever since and thought he might as well take on work with an element of risk. Being a brilliant linguist, he accordingly often became my uncle's "private spy" as it were, traveling round the Continent and gathering confidential information on the war machines of the various countries. Morton may have been the secret of how it was possible for my uncle to rise in the House of Commons armed with sensational facts which did not appear to be known even to the Prime Minister. Baldwin and Chamberlain must have found this one-up-manship extremely aggravating.

After my hard work on the commissions for Sir Michael Duff, Lord Birkenhead, and other patrons, I felt in need of a holiday. I chased a delightful lady down to the French Riviera, using an assumed name and wearing a false mustache and beard which Nathan's the costumiers had taught me how to put on each day. Everything went well until I rashly showed off with a high dive at the Eden Rock. I surfaced minus my disguise, which followed later. Most embarrassing.

Another diversion was joining a traveling circus. I went with Eleanor Smith to the West Country, near Bournemouth, where as usual she was in touch with the nearest Big Top. When she heard that an equestrian rider had fallen ill, she at once offered to take her place. Not to be outdone, I asked to be allowed to do some comedy acrobatics. I suggested running across the ring at a galloping horse and jumping as if I were going to land on its back in a handstand. The trick would be carefully timed so that I missed the horse and landed in the sawdust with a full somersault. But the ringmaster was shocked.

"Too dangerous," he said. "You might get hurt and we are not insured."

I had to content myself with being a clown for one performance. In between Eleanor's appearances as a rider, I tumbled into the ring dressed in a floppy coat and baggy trousers, and wearing a clown's surrealistic make-up. I kept on the move, doing double somersaults.

It was a wonderful experience. What went on behind

the scenes at that circus was unbelievable. The lovers' quarrels were tempestuous, and the amount of alcohol — port, chiefly — drunk after the show was fantastic, yet everyone was absolutely clearheaded for the performance next day. Apart from the bad feeling caused by the arrogance of a few German acrobats, the brotherhood of the sawdust ring was immensely heartwarming. Priscilla the Woman Lion Tamer was a most endearing creature, but as strong as a lioness herself. I kept my distance.

My number of commissions increased enough for me to rent a shop in Ebury Street. The idea was that the front of the premises would be my exhibition showroom, while at the rear I would work hard at new canvases. As events turned out, I did a lot of showing at the front and not much work behind. People came in for a look round, but it was shortly before the war and a bad time for the art business. I sold so few of my paintings that after a while my savings were gone and I had to pawn my godmother's christening present, a gold watch, to buy bacon and eggs for the following morning's breakfast. (When I went back to redeem the watch in 1949 it had been sold the week before.)

I decided that showmanship was needed. I put an ordinary mirror in a decorative picture frame and captioned it: "Why not have your portrait painted just like this?"

Another idea was to fill the window with pictures that would compel passers-by to pause and look. I had noticed that when an ambulance drew up outside St. George's Hospital at Hyde Park Corner a curious crowd collected, peering in at the door and eagerly waiting for the stretcher to come out. What did they hope to see? An accident victim in high spirits, greeting them cheerfully with thumbs up? Not at all; secretly, and against their will, they were hoping for a gory, mangled mess. I accordingly painted and put on display several pictures which were deliberately horrific. They showed animals suffering in vivisection experiments and atrocities committed in the Spanish Civil War. Covering a gap in the curtain at the back of the window I fixed a one-way mirror which enabled me to observe passers-by without being seen. Public reaction to these awful paintings was most remarkable. Quite a number of people actually crossed the road to get a closer glimpse; then they spent minutes studying the canvases. I took a delight in photographing their expressions. Among the many faces I recorded was Hore-Belisha's.

When I was bored with "shockers" I decided to try my luck with another unfailingly successful eye-catcher: nudes. The girl who forgets to draw her curtains while undressing has always had men watching and gloating in the expectation of seeing her naked — at least, that has been the case in the Western world. I therefore planned some extremely interesting paintings showing beautiful girls reclining in serene surroundings in delicious states of undress. Done masterfully, and with artistry, I felt sure they would be widely acceptable. The style of execution would not really matter. Years ago the Italian painter Annigoni, whose work is realistic, held up traffic in Bond Street with a picture of a girl whose breast was hanging out of her dress. He was made at once; people went inside the gallery to learn more. The Spanish painter Picasso, on the

other hand, has produced in the French review *Verve* a
series of no less than a hundred and eighty drawings
which could be described as variations of this theme. They
were not realistic by any means, but equally successful.

Unhappily these plans of mine never materialized. The
war intervened.

Immediately after the Munich crisis, my uncle had
warned Randolph and me to organize ourselves for the
coming storm. "It is much better in every way to be a
commissioned officer in war," he said.

A department of the Army which appealed to me was
the Royal Engineers and Signals Board. Staffed by Royal
Engineers, it was a law unto itself. It had a president, Brigadier Sayer, and the various sections worked on aspects of
mines, signals, bridges, and any subject which was new
to the Army in general. Such a subject was camouflage,
which seemed to be right up my street. The previous year
the War Office had thought it a good idea to open a department for studying camouflage, because they planned
to build some new ordnance factories and ammunition
dumps which they wanted to hide. They called in Major
Simmons, a Regular soldier who had been doing this sort
of thing in the First World War, but he was deaf. Then
they summoned Joseph Gray, an artist who had been in
the war as a private in the Black Watch and had written a
remarkable account of the strategic possibilities of the
subject, which was promptly thrust into a secret safe and
forgotten. He was deaf too. I happened to be extraordinarily lucky when applying for work in this department,
because in walked a very important gentleman from Ord-

nance who wanted advice about concealing his factory. He was deaf as well, and his deaf-aid machines would not work. Thus my first unofficial military job was shouting out and then writing down secret information about his factory, while Simmons and Grey "Whatted?" their heads off with hands cupped to their ears.

There being no vacancy for me on the board at that time, I enlisted with Pebin as a Territorial in our father's regiment, the Queen's Own Oxfordshire Hussars, as it was known in his Army days. Originally, it was a cavalry regiment, and at the beginning of the century, when my father, my uncle, Lord Birkenhead, the Duke of Marlborough and their friends had horses, they used to camp with it at Blenheim Palace. When Pebin and I joined we met the sons of our parents' friends, most of whom I already knew, such as Freddie Birkenhead and Rodney Berry, a son of Lord Camrose. After 1918 the regiment had changed its name from Hussars to Yeomanry and was equipped with howitzers. It was extremely proficient in these weapons and expected several more guns for practice purposes. However, directly I signed on, hoping for a commission, the War Office decided to alter the situation and make it a two-pounder antitank gun regiment. Everyone had to start from the beginning again.

I shall never forget the first time we all assembled at Banbury for a lecture on the characteristics of this weapon given by the brigade major, a Regular who had come to pep us Territorials to the hilt. In a precise military staccato he explained:

"Gentlemen, the two-pounder antitank gun which has

been allotted to our regiment has a very different role from that of the howitzer. Your duty with this weapon will be to destroy any attack by enemy tanks. You will anticipate an onslaught of about seven hundred German Panzer tanks against the three or four batteries of antitank guns deployed on the divisional front; that is to say, twelve or sixteen guns. The method you will use to achieve this object will be to aim at the first one you see. If you miss him you will rapidly endeavor to hit the second and third one, and so on."

This seemed to be fairly sensible. The major continued:

"According to our latest Intelligence reports, nevertheless, I have to tell you that the two-pounder shell you will be firing is unable to penetrate the armor of the new German Panzer tanks. Actually, it bounces off. I have to add that there will be absolutely no question of retreat."

Our jaws dropped in unison, and I felt a bit green. I noticed an expression of consternation on Freddie Birkenhead's face. But imperturbably the major went on:

"Finally, I regret I have to say to you, gentlemen, that in these circumstances and under these conditions, it would appear that the entire regiment may very well be annihilated at the opening of hostilities. We will now repair to the sand table to learn about the deployment of this weapon."

The speech ended with a gust of laughter from Freddie and me and a disapproving glare from the major.

Not long afterward I went to Chartwell and related this story to my uncle, who received it with gloom and despondency. It exactly fitted what he had been saying in the House of Commons for years. I was also worried by a personal problem. The regiment was about to hold a camp which I had to attend. It was essential that I possess enough money to keep my place among my brother officers, but my funds were low. On occasions my father had sent me handsome presents of money, but because I regarded my misfortunes as my own responsibility, I had resolved never to ask him for help. I confided in my uncle; he had always been sympathetic about my leaving the City, and I felt he would understand. I was not mistaken. He wrote me a sizable check — a typically generous gesture. My uncle can always be relied upon to assist in times of crisis, though with one reservation. There is one thing he will not do and has never done to my knowledge, and that is pull strings for members of his family in the field of public life. Unlike Napoleon, who seemed to share out important posts among his relatives, my uncle refuses to make use of his position to feather the nest of a Churchill. Whatever job I had in the war, I often overhead in the mess: "Oh, that's Churchill. His uncle put him here." But it was always completely untrue.

The brigade major's talk having made me feel I had joined a suicide squad, I tried to cheer myself up by taking a lady friend to the cinema. Strangely enough, it was an outing which changed my entire war career. The newsreel included several shots of Hitler, and whenever he appeared a fellow sitting on the far side of my lady friend annoyed her by clapping loudly. I leaned over to this man.

"Would you be so good as not to clap?" I asked. "We don't particularly like it."

I had hardly finished when he swung me a straight right on the chin which dazed me for a second. But when I had recovered I slammed I don't know how many punches into his face and stomach. My lady friend sank to the floor in the fight. Then attendants came and dragged the man out by his collar.

Randolph was working on the London *Evening Standard* at the time, and when I told him this story he mentioned it in the "Londoner's Diary" feature. Immediately afterward I had a message telling me to report to the Royal Engineers and Signals Board. Simmons and Gray interviewed me.

"Are you the chap who beat up the Nazi in the cinema?" they asked.

"Yes!" I shouted, remembering that both of them were deaf.

"You are the very person we want. There will shortly be a vacancy here in camouflage."

I was delighted. The work was really suited to my talents, and there was the comforting thought that if a battle became really desperate, retreat would surely be permissible. I at once went down to Chartwell and asked my uncle if he approved of my prospective job. He did, so I wrote him a check returning in full the money he had given me for the Oxfordshire Yeomanry's camp which I no longer needed. He tore it up.

The summer of 1939 was the time of a most significant happening at Chartwell. Three Emden geese flew in and landed on the lake. Where they came from, and why they came at all, no one has ever found out. Now the Emden goose has one very Germanic characteristic. When he is alone he is a reasonably quiet bird, perfectly harmless and almost friendly. But when he gangs up with another he turns ferocious and arrogant. These three geese became positively hostile and started to provoke my uncle's famous black swans and their cygnets. We were nearing the end of lunch one day when the geese launched an attack at the edge of the lake near the swans' headquarters. The whole scene was clearly visible from the low arched windows of the dining room. My uncle was furious.

"Oh!" he said indignantly. "Look at those frightful Nazi geese molesting the peace of the swans! This must be stopped at once. Come on."

With that, he leaped from the table, grabbed a walking stick, and ran out across the rough stubbly grass of the field that slopes down to the lake. "You horrible Nazis, get out!" he shouted. "Fetch the gardener, Johnny, and tell him to make a concentration camp for them." The swans meanwhile were holding their own and paddling towards the middle of the lake, hissing and pecking. The Emden geese followed. They had no alternative; my uncle was thrashing at them with his stick. The sequel to the encounter was that the geese were rounded up and put in a strong wire enclosure, rather like a concentration camp, where they sat and glowered at the triumphant swans.

Years later the incident struck me as a foretaste of future events: Nazi invaders disturbing the peace, rescue by my uncle, and the invaders' defeat. The full-scale version of the story was to occur very soon.

I joined the Royal Engineers and Signals Board about a

week after war was declared. Officially, I was a civil servant with a salary of thirty pounds a month. It was the first
time I had received a pay packet since my job on the Stock
Exchange and marked a temporary end to my "playing
the ass in the gutter." After a month, by which time Major
Simmons had gone to France, the president of the board,
Brigadier Sayer, invited me to lunch at the Senior, the
club opposite the Athenaeum. Joseph Gray warned me
beforehand what to expect. "You will be asked whether
you would like to join the expeditionary force in France as
a camouflage officer with the rank of second lieutenant,"
he said. "Asking whether you would like to go is the
Army way of ordering you to go."

At the end of lunch, when we were having coffee in the
huge lounge, surrounded by senior generals and admirals
who made me feel very insignificant, the brigadier put the
question. Being very honest with myself, I replied: "Yes,
of course I wish to go. But I can hardly promise that my
knowledge of the subject will enable me to work with the
Army in the field with the efficiency I consider necessary."

"Oh, that's fine," he said, rather inconsequently. "I will
have you posted to the Royal Engineers at once."

I relied on two people to tell me how to behave in war.
The first was my uncle. I went to lunch at the Admiralty
with him and my aunt. My mother and father were there
too, together with Randolph, who was already in the uniform of his father's regiment, the Fourth Hussars, much to
my annoyance; I was in civvies still. When the interesting
"Twenty-five Years On" photograph, which I mentioned in
Chapter II, had been taken, my uncle gave me advice

which was concise and to the point — though I noticed he chose to ignore it himself during the blitz.

"Remember," he said, "if you think you hear buzzing which might be a shell or a bomb, waste no time; duck. It is quite pointless to rush around and expose yourself unnecessarily when you think a big explosion is imminent. Take cover."

My other advice came from Joseph Gray, who knew all about the wisdom of taking cover. In the First World War he had the classic experience of "going over the top." He threw himself down in such an unhappy manner that his Black Watch kilt folded itself over the top half of his body, exposing a very white and fleshy backside. The target was apparently too tempting for a German sniper, who promptly dispatched a bullet through both gluteus maximus muscles without doing any other damage. Joe's advice to me was: "Be natural, especially with generals, because we will be dealing with high-ranking officers. Furthermore, be able to drink but also hold it. Our work will meet with opposition and indifference, and often the most difficult issues — the fixing of permission to do this and that — will be settled in the mess."

Joe was undoubtedly right. Our job was indeed uphill. It took nearly four years to convince the War Office of the full potentialities of camouflage; that its proper title within the Royal Engineers and Signals Board should have been "Counterintelligence." In Europe, not until the offensive for crossing the Rhine in 1945 were we able to persuade the General Staff that to ensure success it was necessary to make a dummy attack, involving bogus wireless messages and cannon fire, in addition to concealing the positions of the tanks and guns which were to achieve the crossing.

At the beginning of 1940 I became a staff officer with the rank of captain attached to 1st Corps Headquarters at Douai. I worked under the chief engineer, Brigadier Bond, and had a lieutenant with a car, plus driver. Despite my deplorable lack of experience, I had to supervise the construction of a secret operational corps headquarters at Roost-Warendin, near Raches, conceal all the pillboxes along the front line facing Belgium, build a lot of dummy ones and instruct sixty thousand men how to behave so that they would not be seen by the enemy on the ground or from the air.

One of my first assignments was to go forward to the little village of Orchies and lecture to some troops of the Norfolk Regiment. I knew the staff blokes from headquarters were looked down on by the fighting men of the front line, but I felt sure I could handle them. When I arrived in my car with my lieutenant and all my paraphernalia, the company commander and his officers met me with a certain amount of correct pomp and saluting. I did not look carefully at the commander until quite suddenly the whole of Orchies seemed to shake under the loudest and longest guffaw I have ever heard. The commander had doubled up. "Man," he shouted, "what in the name of heaven are *you* doing here?" It was then that I saw it was my roommate at Harrow, Captain Peter Barclay, who had just won his M.C., the first of the war.

"How did you manage to win it?" I asked.

Casually he replied: "Oh, it was just like one of our escapades at Harrow."

To mark the Sunday before St. George's Day, the corps commander, General Dill, asked me to do a special decoration of St. George and the Dragon for the altar of the military chapel in Douai. Other senior officers too, I found, were capable of the unexpected. My visit to the commander of the 1st Division, Major General Alexander, became an artistic survey of the landscape under his control; he was very keen on painting. And the 2nd Division commander, Major General Lloyd, caused consternation when his staff car was seen to speed through Douai with the glamorous blonde actress Frances Day sitting beside him in the back seat.

I contrived to get an airplane for myself from the 13th Squadron of the Army Co-operation Unit. It was a Lysander. I reasoned that if I happened to be air-borne when the German attack started, the plane flew so slowly and could turn so sharply that no German fighter would be able to hit it — a supposition which was not quite accurate, for many Lysanders were shot down. On May 9, 1940, I was making a reconnaissance in the late evening along the Belgian frontier over the two forward divisional fronts to see how they looked from the air, when suddenly my pilot turned swiftly, losing height. "There's a fast plane coming over the frontier," he explained. "I don't like the look of it."

Six hours later the German attack began. At midnight Douai was bombed and the whole headquarters prepared to move forward to the secret operational headquarters at Roost-Warendin. We never got there because events moved fast and we went forward to Brussels. It occurred to me that my duties as a Counterintelligence officer were rather mythical, because I had no power to operate any counterintelligence. Furthermore, although I was independent in that I had a car and a driver, I was herded about with the Engineers. When, as often happened, I shared quarters with Major Paine, the staff officer of the Royal Engineers, he seemed to do nothing but sit and read.

"What on earth are you reading so calmly?" I once asked him.

"Schopenhauer," he replied. "You see, R.E.s are either mad, married or Methodist. An old Sapper saying."

Brussels was a free city, and our headquarters was a large château in Uccle, the southern suburb. My friend Major Geoffrey Ingham, the assistant provost marshal, who looked somewhat forbidding but had great charm, appreciated good food and wine. He saw to it that our mess was always situated in a house with a good cellar. The one in Brussels was a luxurious flat. The owner and his wife had decided to flee west, and they threw open their cellar to us. An excellent one it was too. Ingham was having a fairly difficult time, because apart from his ordinary jobs of security and traffic control there began to appear loads of enemy paratroopers, four of whom landed with wireless sets, machine guns and civilian clothes right in the grounds of headquarters. We rounded them up. Local Belgians who had been caught spying were an added problem. Therefore, on May 15, with the permission of the chief engineer, who had little use for me except as a messenger, I was attached to the staff of the provost marshal to help with some of his security work.

A withdrawal was ordered for the next day, to defend the Scheldt as a result of a breakthrough along the French sector at Sedan. So my first job in my new capacity as policeman was to rush forward with the Military Police and "Q" officers responsible for reconnoitering the new headquarters in the Château Mayberg, about eight miles west of Brussels. Everything went well. I earmarked concealed spots in the nearby countryside for all the many branches of a corps headquarters. Next day, May 16, I climbed with two M.P.s onto an upturned box which we had put in the middle of the road, and rather like one of those astoundingly gymnastic point-duty policemen in Rome, I conducted the vehicles of corps headquarters to their appointed places by waving my arms in all directions. The trouble was that it was early in the morning and a large batch of men decided to walk out onto the lawns for a strip-wash and shave. At exactly that moment, a Lysander appeared at not much more than treetop height and started to peer at corners of the estate in a most suspicious manner. Nobody fired because it was English — or was it? Of course it wasn't; it was a captured one being used by the Germans. I cursed and swore at everyone because I could see that the château would now be listed for bombing.

Before the raid came though, as indeed it did, Ingham ordered me to take six important Luftwaffe prisoners back to the prison cages in France and return quickly. The

Nazis were terrifying baboonlike types who clearly would stop at nothing. I gave a piece of my mind to the one who understood English and bundled the lot into the back of a lorry with two husky M.P.s. It occurred to me that my prisoners might knock out the guards, attack me, and make a dash for it, so I kept my ears open. The villages through which we passed were in flames. Refugees poured out of them. At Tournai the main road was blocked by a gigantic crater. The whole place was alight and silent except for one terrible wail from a cellar. There was no alternative but to make a detour round the town over the fields. My orders were to hand over my prisoners to the French at the frontier. When we got there, six tough-looking poilus emerged from their hut. I said: "I have been told to deliver these prisoners to you. Presumably you know where to put them and what to do with them."

"Do with them?" they said. "Of course we know what to do with them!" With that, they booted the six Huns into a hut. God knows what they did do with them; I hesitate to imagine. But I was glad to be rid of them myself.

We made our way back to the Château Mayberg through roads choked with refugees driving cars, pulling handcarts, or simply trudging along in despair, carrying enormous bundles. The headquarters had moved; already the Germans had embraced Brussels. We turned round and after some confusion discovered our headquarters in the village of Flaubecq. Next morning I had the unique experience of strolling past the tent of the corps commander, General Barker, while he was washing. It was the largest stark-naked form I have ever seen.

Our next destination was Capelle, a village some two miles inside the French frontier. *En route* I was to see one of those ghastly incidents of which there were so many: the strafing of refugees on the road. We had just passed through Renaix when two captured Hurricanes suddenly appeared and dived on the road, raking it with machine-gun fire. But we had to press on and leave the screaming injured and dying to their fate. I did a sketch of the scene and wondered whether the Official War Artists and Photographers were doing the same sort of thing else-where. As a matter of fact they were not, for all the artists and photographers were being evacuated home as redundant and noncombatant, and just so many more mouths to feed. The result of the bombing at the Château Mayberg was that the General Staff issued orders for all positions to be carefully concealed in future, but the Germans were firmly on our tail and our arrival at Capelle was an occasion for a vigorous bombardment and low strafing. Our Bofors guns brought down six planes in an hour, and those pilots who were not burned alive in their machines were scattered over the countryside. It was the duty of the Military Police to clear up the mess and dispose of it in a proper manner. I had to inspect the situation for the Assistant Provost Marshal and saw a French liaison officer cutting off a dead pilot's finger in order to pull off a gold ring. But I have heard of worse. I did some more drawings of frightful subjects.

When the officer commanding 102 Provost Company left us, Ingham asked me whether I would like to take over. "I know that in the Army a remark such as that is

an order," I replied, "but really I've had no experience
commanding troops."

"Do it," was all Ingham said. "And hurry up."

"Right, sir" — and with a smart salute I became Temporary Officer Commanding 102 Provost Company. For
an ex-Bohemian such as myself, no change could have
been more drastic. Geoffrey Ingham was a disciplinarian
of the first order, and his 102 Company, many of whom
had been policemen in peacetime, was like a brigade of
Guards. He was absolutely ruthless, which meant that his
men discharged their difficult duties with remarkable efficiency in appallingly adverse conditions.

On May 19 we moved to Ascq, a few miles south of
Lille. The General Staff was getting so windy about the
speed with which the Germans were tracing our where-
abouts that the whole headquarters was dispersed in shops
and houses instead of a large château. Next day we
reached Armentières, where by great misfortune 2nd
Corps Headquarters arrived at the same time. We were
sitting targets for any reconnaissance plane, and the consequent bombing was terrific. Ammunition convoys were
passing through the whole time, and I and my M.P.s
struggled to keep them moving. An extra-large convoy
halted right in the middle of the town at the precise moment that a squadron of Heinkels swooped. The chaos was
nightmarish, not least because the walls of the local lunatic
asylum were breached, and crowds of patients wandered
around the streets, leaning against lamp posts and sitting
on the pavements, wondering what the fuss was about.
The prisoners and spies whom we caught we locked in the

school cellars. My second-in-command, Lieutenant Dibben, a typical policeman, utterly reliable, did a most wonderful job supervising the bombed convoy when the heat of fires made the shells start to explode. His bravery deserved the highest of awards but he received nothing because of the system of distributing medals, about which I have something to say later.

In Armentières I came across some odd sides of the human character under duress. A brigadier was in such a tizzy that he had to have jazz music blaring loudly on the radio in his office all the time. Mind you, he was grappling with very large headaches. I myself was in a state of perpetual terror, though Ingham told me that the *sang-froid* with which I held a pay parade in the middle of a bombing raid was absolutely up to his standard of discipline. I don't believe it.

While waiting for encouraging news confirming the holding of the Scheldt, I had time to draw pictures of Armentières in its agony: the refugees, the homeless monks and nuns, the lunatics, and other scenes. No such news came. Ever since reaching Armentières the corps headquarters staff had been apprehensive. Holland had capitulated and large formations of Belgian troops were moving across our path at Renaix. It has always astounded me how Intelligence manages to transmit information, especially amidst the confusion of battle, yet on May 21 we had news that we might have to evacuate through Dunkirk. This was most disheartening; it stank of defeat. But there was little chance to think about it, because on May 22 we moved to Ryveld, a tiny village about two miles east of Cassel. From my dugout I sketched the fantastic scene of bombers attacking Cassel. The whole scene, with the bombers flying over and guns belching up towards them, resembled a duck shoot. Not so far away I could see the oil tanks of Dunkirk burning.

On May 23, when a battery of German field guns had sited themselves just behind us, and German tanks were reported only a few miles away, we were ordered to burn all documents and man the guns for a heroic, last-ditch stand. For some inexplicable reason we were never put to this test, because the enemy tanks halted where they were. On May 24, therefore, we made for the outskirts of the Dunkirk perimeter. The bombing and machine-gunning of roads had become very intense, so before setting off in my open car, followed by the whole company on motorcycles, I acted on my uncle's advice and announced that if I were to stand up and fire my pistol into the air it would mean that everyone had to stop, draw in to the side of the road, and take cover. The effectiveness of this was proved when we were speeding down towards Bergues, near Dunkirk, and a German plane came straight towards us along the road at hedgetop height, guns blazing. I signaled, and my hundred men vanished. Immediately the plane had gone we were off again. No one had been hit.

When we drove into Warham, Brigadier Bond appeared. "Hullo, Churchill," he said. "What has happened to 'A' Mess? Would you mind running over to Poperinge and seeing if you can collect the plate and silver, and so on?"

I knew that Poperinge was in German hands, or would be by the time I got there, but I was not in a position to argue. "Certainly, sir," I said, and climbed back into my car.

"Wait a minute!" called the brigadier. "I think the commander is coming."

I waited. That order petered out, but another came up. Ingham told me to position three M.P.s at a major road junction nearby to usher the B.E.F. through Dunkirk onto the beaches. I did this and returned to our headquarters. Then there was an almighty storm. Ingham demanded: "What the hell do you mean by not putting your men on point duty?"

"But I have, sir," I told him.

We set off for the junction, but none of my men was there. All three had deserted and gone to the beaches for a quick trip home. I have never dared ask what Ingham did about them, or to them, when he got back to the Provost Headquarters at Aldershot.

On Saturday, May 25, we were ordered to abandon all equipment except transport, weapons and ammunition, and go to a farmhouse headquarters within the Dunkirk perimeter. The 3rd Corps, who were inside the perimeter between Dunkirk and Bray Dunes, were to be evacuated meanwhile, followed by the 2nd Corps. This would leave the 1st Corps holding a beachhead rectangle from Bergues to the coast at Dunkirk and east to the frontier two miles away. The first thing Ingham did on arrival at our farmhouse was to order an inspection.

"The company will be inspected at 6 A.M. tomorrow morning, fully armed for battle," he snapped.

"Right, sir," I snapped back. I drew up the company

along one side of a field and with my second-in-command
went to receive Ingham, who approached through a gap
in the hedge as coolly and calmly as if it were the main
entrance of Wellington Barracks in London. The inspection was rather a barrack parade-ground affair anyway.
Although my men desperately needed sleep, every uniform was properly creased, every boot shone, and every
button was polished to perfection. Ingham had a sound
reason for his order, nevertheless. A mood of alarm and
hysteria was developing among the troops of the B.E.F.
The feeling of "Let's run for it!" had to be checked, and
discipline enforced.

The 1st Corps headquarters was set up on the Dunkirk
beaches on May 29 in a sort of glorified bathing hut.
Major Ransome, now Lieutenant General Ransome, took
over control of us Military Police. Our job was to keep
order and prevent panic. Together with my M.P. batman,
Corporal Jenkins, I walked up the beach towards Dunkirk
as far as the hospital at Zuydcoote, calming chaps as best
I could.

General Alexander then mounted a bleak, empty band-
stand that had known happier days and began to address
the troops under his command. Immediately a gigantic
formation of Stukas dive-bombed the boats offshore.
There was nothing for me to do, so I ventured to the top
of a high sand dune and observed the whole dramatic
scene. I was remembering what Augustus John had once
told me — that war offers an artist unique scope — when
two captured Hurricanes detached themselves from the
German bomber formation and headed straight towards

me at the same height as the dunes. Orange flame erupted from their wings. *Christ,* I thought, *my number's up. I've had it.* But my acrobatic training saved me. I hurled myself over the top of the dune with a lively somersault and escaped harm, except for an uncomfortable landing. Before leaving London I had asked Wilkinson's, the sword specialists of Pall Mall, to make a special metal protector for my private parts. Understandably, Wilkinson's had not expected me to go leaping over dunes, and the protector was dislodged by the somersault.

Shortly before dusk the Stukas mounted another savage attack. A paddle steamer full of wounded was hit and had to be beached. The Stukas came over in sevens and dropped three bombs each on their sitting targets. Further out to sea, destroyers of the Royal Navy steamed up and down quickly and escaped serious harm. A strange, absolutely incredible moment was when a squadron of French cavalry suddenly appeared and galloped silently across the soft sand towards Dunkirk. They were like phantoms, going whither no one knew, or why.

The tide was quite a way out, and the main difficulty was getting the men from the beach to the boats, which had to wait some distance offshore. The only solution was somehow or other to obtain a fleet of small craft which could cross the shallows and come much closer to the water's edge. Major Ransome, with the approval of the G.O.C.-in-C., therefore entrusted me with an historic mission: to report the situation direct to my uncle and tell him what was needed.

At 9 P.M. on the 29th I waded out to a large rowboat.

Twenty men were already aboard it, their combined weight making it so low in the water that it would not move. I suppose they feared that if they got out they would lose their places. Their getting out was the only means of floating the boat, however. I ordered them off, and when this had no effect I brandished my revolver. On seeing that I meant business, they all leaped overboard with commendable speed. We then pushed the boat into deeper water. I accompanied the men back in again and we reached a trawler. It was packed with badly burned and injured survivors from the paddle steamer.

Still soaking wet, and in full battle kit, I got on a train at Dover and traveled up to London. I noticed two staff officers in the same railway coach. They were General Pownall and Captain Lord Munster, A.D.C. to General Lord Gort, who looked very smartly dressed and "staff." I felt terribly unkempt by comparison, especially considering that my mission was to the Prime Minister. Not knowing Lord Munster very well, I did not talk to him on the journey. On arrival at Victoria Station, I went straight to the adjoining Grosvenor Hotel and shaved. Then, without wasting further time, I took a taxi to the Admiralty. I arrived and stepped into the lift for the Prime Minister's apartments at the same moment as Lord Munster, who, it turned out, had been sent over by Lord Gort on a similar mission.

Our reception at 8 A.M. by my uncle and aunt, both of whom were in dressing gowns, was a moment never to be forgotten. The contrast between Lord Munster's uniform and mine was rather acute; he, I recollect, was in jack-boots and staff dress appropriate to his function as A.D.C. to the Commander-in-Chief of the B.E.F., and dry, having been put aboard a special boat, I suppose. I was in ordinary battle dress, absolutely sodden and thoroughly shaken by my ordeals.

"Johnny!" exclaimed my uncle delightedly. "I see you have come straight from battle!"

Preferring to give way to my fellow emissary, whom I considered to be far more important, I replied: "I think Lord Munster has also come . . ."

But my uncle was determined to hear my story first. "Who sent you and what have you got to say about the situation?" he asked. "I believe we have taken off about eighty thousand men and still have another two hundred and fifty thousand."

"I have been sent by General Alexander, 1st Corps Commander," I said, "to say that in his opinion the most urgent need is for small boats to get the troops off the beaches out to the bigger ships."

My uncle next wanted to know why I was so wet. "Have you come straight out of the sea?" he asked.

"Yes," I told him. "And I will be pleased to go back again in a fast motorboat to give everyone encouragement."

At long last Lord Munster was able to get a word in edgeways. "I have exactly the same message to report," he said. "The C.-in-C. thinks that the small boats can be our salvation."

For some odd reason, my arrival at the Admiralty that morning has always stuck in my uncle's mind. When,

exactly ten years later, I had finished my painting of the
Dunkirk beaches, he insisted on having it in his house,
where he studied it for long periods at a time, I am told.
It now hangs in the Institute of Army Education.

My mission from Dunkirk concluded, I went straight
to the Royal Engineers and Signals Board, where I was
greeted enthusiastically by Brigadier Sayer and Joseph
Gray. When I retired to the latter's office, I was handed
a sandwich for breakfast and some large sheets of drawing
paper. A bottle of kümmel was produced and two glasses
were poured out. I was so tired that I practically collapsed
across the desk.

"Let me sleep for a couple of hours and I'll be all right,"
I murmured.

"Rot," said Gray firmly, and whacked me on the head
with a roll of paper. "You will now use your sketch notes
and draw at once what you have seen, before it goes from
your mind."

I slumped again. Bang went the roll of paper and a
glass of kümmel was tipped down my throat. Thank
heaven it was not tea, or I would have slumped again.
Within two hours I had executed my two famous pen-and-
wash drawings of the evacuation of Dunkirk. Every time
I began to doze off, Gray hit me on the head with his roll
of paper. In the absence of official artists and photographers on the beaches, these two drawings are probably the
only authentic ones in existence. They were published in
the *Illustrated London News* of June 8, 1940. I offered
them to the War Museum, but everyone was too busy to

take much notice. One was sold to America the following year and Lord Chesham bought the other.

I had a few days' leave to visit Sally, whom the Tweeddales had taken up to Yester, their superb Adam house near Haddington, East Lothian, for the war. One item in the house, an old-fashioned water closet, was most unusual. It was flushed by pulling up a handle which was level with the seat. Railway trains used to have contraptions of this kind, but the Tweeddales' was different — the whole seating area, including the handle, was covered with deep red plush velvet. It was luxuriously comfortable. On asking about the history of this remarkable piece of furniture, I learned that it was specially installed for Her Majesty Queen Victoria when she visited the mansion towards the end of her reign.

After my leave I was appointed General Staff Officer, 2nd Grade, with the rank of major, at Anti-Aircraft Command, Stanmore, Middlesex, under General Pile. Within this command were eventually three corps and twelve Divisions, their business being to defend England from air attack. We shared a vast mess with Fighter Command, which was exhilarating. The first thing I did was to commandeer an old Anson bomber and find a pilot, Wing Commander Cundall. He was a brilliant aviator but had won his wings during the First World War and was not exactly *au fait* in the latest techniques of navigation. In poor weather we had some strange experiences trying to find out where we were. My job was to examine and photograph A.A. positions in Britain to discover how much the Germans could see. The answer was that they could easily see much more than anyone thought.

To assist me in my duties I had a staff captain, twelve other captains, and a lieutenant. My staff officer was Captain Coldstream, later Sir William Coldstream, Warden of the Slade School of University College. He made an excellent brain behind the scenes. And scenes we had, for we dealt directly with various departments of the War Office, where so many people seemed to have never been on operations of any sort, still less heard about camouflage. I would storm at them; then Captain Coldstream would take over and explain what I meant. Our two-pronged attacks worked well, on the whole. But we never succeeded in making any headway with the inhabitants of the Fortifications and Works Department. Everything seemed to be of concrete there, including their heads!

I was with A.A. Command for three years. Meanwhile, in 1941, several major personal events were to take place. In May I married for the second time. In June my wife's R.A.F. brother was killed in a Spitfire sortie. And in July my mother died.

VIII

George Spencer, Interior Decorator

MY SECOND WIFE was Mary Cookson, who came from a mining family in Newcastle. When I met her she was with Anti-Aircraft Command as a driver in the Field Auxiliary Nursing Yeomanry. Since the outbreak of war a large number of girls had been working voluntarily in the F.A.N.Y., using their own cars. When the War Office decided to abolish the organization officially and amalgamate it with the Regular women's service, the A.T.S., the Fannies, as they were called — to the amusement of American friends — had the choice of either conforming to the amalgamation or resigning. I strongly urged Mary to give up her steering wheel and take me in hand instead.

She looked exceedingly attractive in her khaki uniform. I have always had a passion for women in uniforms, perhaps the most beautiful of them all being the waitresses in the Imperial Hotel, Tokyo, at dinnertime. Their costume at that hour is a kimono, and how they shuffle along in their wooden shoes and keep their balance is a mystery. My father once had a Greek parlormaid named Anastasia who was ravishingly lovely. When we were living in Cromwell Road she used to call me in the morning and press my clothes. Her rich peerless skin and dark eyes were admirably suited to her black and white uniform with the usual frilly white cap on her head. I was young. Putting our women into khaki for the Second World War was going rather too far, I thought. Khaki is not an attractive color, and when garments which were not even on display, such as bloomers, had to be khaki as well, it became obvious that the war machine was losing its grip.

Mary was twenty-four. My parents were displeased with the match, taking a snooty view of what appeared to them to be her humble lineage, yet actually her mother's family (Butler) descends directly from the Earls of Ormonde, a very ancient Irish ancestry. Her own parents, meanwhile, were upset for religious reasons. They were Irish Protestants, who can be more Protestant than their English counterparts, and the idea of a daughter marrying someone who had been involved in divorce, though innocently, was quite unacceptable to them. Mary was happy at the prospect of getting married but very understandably insisted that the ceremony had to be in church. On the face of it, this presented no difficulty: my previous marriage had been a civil one, and I was the innocent party in the divorce. So we went to our local vicar and asked him to put up the banns. He was pleased to help us until I told him my past history. Then he tut-tutted and said most regretfully that he could do nothing for us.

This was an unexpected setback. If, as I have already

suggested, religious faith can be likened to a hospital, with ministers as its doctors and surgeons, then the vicar's refusal was a deep, wounding incision into Mary's soul. We applied to another vicar, and another, without success, until eventually we reached the Bishop of London. His reply emanated from his secretary, the Reverend Mr. Synge, and was a monstrous and double-sided document. It said, in essence, that we were free to marry but not in church. Nevertheless, if we behaved ourselves, after a time it would be possible for us to take Holy Communion together.

Where were we, then? How could we possibly take Communion if, in the eyes of the Church, we were not married at all and living in sin?

I was perplexed by the whole affair and asked my uncle what he thought.

"In my personal view," he said, "the Church is wrong, because it is an Established and State Church. If the State recognizes your divorce, then the Church should do so as well. Similarly, if the State is prepared to remarry you, the Church should be willing to do the same, particularly in your case."

Unfortunately, unlike the Church in Spain and certain other Catholic countries, the Church of England is too weak to fight the State and lay down rulings on common problems. In 1941, when Mary and I wanted to marry, there was but one minister in the whole of the English Established Protestant Church ready to be true to his conscience and perform the ceremony — the Reverend Giekie Cobb of St. Ethelburga's, in the City of London.

He had given hope, contentment, and salvation to other couples in similar dilemmas, but his superiors did not bother to stop him because he was old and likely to die. He gladly agreed to marry us.

For our entry, the organist played a slow-measured choral march in D major which I had written just before the war. It was suitably solemn for a solemn occasion. My aunt came, and her presence was comforting, but the service was held one morning between air raids, and the proceedings in the bleak, empty church had a touch of unreality. This feeling persisted after our reception at the Savoy. Although our marriage had been in church, was it really valid, since Cobb was openly defying the Archbishop of Canterbury? The answer of course was no, it was not. And thus did poor Mary's spiritual hurt get worse while the "doctors" who ought to have been able to render aid were powerless to do anything.

Two tragedies followed in heartbreaking succession. Barely a month after our wedding my wife was stunned to learn that her brother Christopher had been shot down and killed in his Spitfire. Then, in July, when my mother was staying with her half sister and brother-in-law Viscount FitzAlan at Windsor, she caught a cold in the park. Serious complications developed, and on July 5 I was granted compassionate leave to see her. I kissed her, knowing somehow it was the last time I would see her alive. She was only fifty-six, but at one time had suffered from cancer, and this may have aggravated her illness. Two days later, greatly against her will, she died. My father asked me if I would like to see her in death. I did, and in one way regret it. When she was living her face was life itself, and that is how I remember her; in death it was just as beautiful, but a mask.

She was buried in the little convent churchyard of the nuns of Begbrook, about three miles from Blenheim Palace.

My father was a mortally sick man but contributed to the war effort by running a mess in the Foreign Office for the secretaries and senior staff such as Lord Cherwell, enabling them to snatch quick meals and get back to work quickly. I believe it functioned during most of the war, and I often had a meal there myself. After dinner we would go through to my uncle's apartments, where he and my aunt would be relaxing with a game of six-pack bezique.

During October, 1941, my inspection of Anti-Aircraft defenses took me near Chequers, and my uncle invited me to lunch. As usual he cross-examined me about my work and how it was going. I was very outspoken about the War Office's inefficiency with regard to counterintelligence.

"It has given no direction on the subject, either for the concealment of installations or for deception with dummy wireless messages, signals and so on," I said.

My uncle was listening to me attentively when we were interrupted by the arrival of details of the merchant shipping losses which had been published in the papers. My uncle studied the information and turned to me sadly. "It is most extraordinary," he commented. "Even when I implore admirals not to publish these figures, they go and do it. They seem to be a law unto themselves." It occurred to me that although people may have thought his handling of the war machine almost dictatorial, they little knew how difficult it was to keep control.

We returned to the matter under discussion. My uncle really understood the strategic power of counterintelligence and was perturbed because no one else did.

"Now look here," he said. "Go next door and write all that you have to say in a few lines on one side of a piece of paper — and mind that it's on only one side."

This seemed a tall order but I did as I was told. On the biggest piece of Chequers note paper I could find, I framed the following document.

CHEQUERS

BUTLER'S CROSS, AYLESBURY

BUCKS

October, 1941.

1. There is not one person in the War Office with power who is disposed to understand the use of passive or aggressive military concealment. The War Office therefore *does not* implement a policy or, where necessary, put a case to the Treasury for financial authority, because it *cannot.*

2. For the Army in the field, the Director of Staff Duties should have a Deputy with the rank of Brigadier who is a technical expert. His branch would be S.D.12.

3. For static camouflage, decoys, etc., the Director of Anti-Aircraft and Coast Defence should have a similar Deputy. His branch would be A.A.6.

J.S.C.

I must have taken my uncle aback a bit, particularly with regard to the actual branches involved. But paragraph 1 was the situation and paragraphs 2 and 3 the method of dealing with it. I forgot about the memo and was getting on with my work when my uncle surprised me with quick action. In a matter of days General Pile of A. A. Command recalled me from an assignment and told me to report to the War Office on November 2 for a conference on Military Concealment, Recent Developments and Possibilities.

I managed to pull in my brother Pebin, who was a civilian expert with the Air Ministry. Major General Loch, the director of A.A. and C.D., War Office, presided, and his deputy was my old friend Brigadier Sayer. The atmosphere was very cordial, the meeting ending with the director's conclusion that concealment was a strategic weapon, depending on the labor and materials available.

It has always seemed odd to me that such a great brain was needed to arrive at this. And even when it had been agreed, a long time was required to educate the General Staff in the field, and Chiefs of Staff had to work hard to obtain the wherewithal for any sizable double-crossing of enemy Intelligence. I know that General Montgomery, for one, was alive to it, and a successful effort was made at El Alamein. But even so, the War Office never got around to setting up a Counterintelligence Department as such — the reason, I suspect, being that the head would have had to possess lively imagination, a type of mind which is apt to seem haywire and unmilitary. The outcome was that the whole affair lapsed permanently under the vague overall heading of Camouflage and was carried out by a corps of more than a hundred conscripted artists, dress designers and others with no co-ordinated direction from the War Office.

In 1941 it was still quite possible that the Germans would cross the Channel and invade England. Large batches of children were being evacuated abroad for safety, and towards the end of the year Lady Tweeddale arranged for her youngest daughter, Frances, to stay in Canada until the end of the war. She fixed up for Sally to go too. Sally came down to London from Scotland, and I had special compassionate leave to say farewell. But just as she was about to board the train for the docks, a message came through from my uncle to say that on no account could she go. It might, he said, give propaganda to Goebbels, and anyway it was a bad example to set. I think he was right, but I was acutely disappointed for Sally's sake. Life in Canada would have been a wonderful experience.

The following year Lady Tweeddale died, and when Lord Tweeddale remarried he asked Mary and me to look after Sally. The bombing in London was so bad that we at once organized her into a boarding school on the far side of England, in Herefordshire.

Everyone, I suppose, has a favorite air raid story. Mine is of the evening when Major Joseph Gray and I had a drink with Pebin at a place in Bruton Mews which was next door to the Florida — a night club. When we left, my brother decided to make a telephone call from a box in the Mews. I strolled ahead with Gray, and we had reached Bruton Street when I heard a terrible, slippery rushing

noise. Gray being deaf heard nothing, so I yelled: "Bombs
— duck!" and pushed him up against a wall. A stick landed
right across us and wiped out the Florida. We ran back
and found Pebin still in the phone box, which was upside
down in the roadway. By a miracle he was unharmed, but
as we pulled him out of the wreckage he protested calmly:
"Wait a minute. I haven't pressed Button B."

In 1943 I was offered the post of General Staff Officer
(1) in Italy, with the rank of lieutenant colonel, but I hon-
estly did not feel cut out for such an exalted sinecure. Although I knew it would cost me loss of rank, I applied for
a transfer to an associated and active branch of the war
machine: Air Photographic Interpretation, to which I was
posted as a captain. Foolish? Yes, but sincere.

Air Photographic Interpretation also had teething troubles at the beginning of the war, but because it came so
logically under the heading of Intelligence and yielded
spectacular results, it was developed with energy and became one of the Allies' most reliable sources of information. Curiously, our opposite numbers in Germany, whose
setup I was fascinated to examine after the war, were in-
efficient by comparison. Their counterintelligence was en-
viably thorough, but not above mistakes. Take, for example, the siting of the V – 1 ramps along the Channel
coast. A lack of co-ordination between the various departments concerned led to a classic blunder which enabled us
to frustrate Hitler's dreams of annihilating London. Having taken the most elaborate care to hide each ramp
within a little farm enclosure surrounded by trees, the
Germans laid a conspicuously thick power cable from the

nearest road. In nearly every case they let it run straight across a field. I cannot remember a single instance of their taking the trouble to conceal it under a hedge. If only they had done so, we might have been very much slower in spotting the precise locations of the sites.

At the end of 1943 the first medals were issued. To my astonishment there was none for the B.E.F. operation. I found myself awarded a 1943 Star, which seemed to be distributed to masses of people who had never heard a gun fired. I was rather indignant. I thought of the thousands of Regular soldiers who had been captured at Dunkirk and Calais and to whom medals meant a great deal. On one of my leaves, I stayed at Chequers for a day or two and raised the subject with my uncle.

"The British Expeditionary Force in France," I argued, "was a complete campaign. It began and it ended, and went on for several months, involving a lot of fighting. It ought to have a campaign medal of its own."

My uncle sighed. "I have been into all that and am inclined to agree with you," he said, "though it is very difficult to know where to begin and end in such a vast war. The view of the Army Chiefs is that Dunkirk was a retreat, and they could not recommend a campaign medal for a retreat. Apart from this, there are raids or expeditions such as Narvik to be considered for medals."

I suggested that a way round the difficulty would be to use the same system as in the Boer War — a campaign medal with bars or stars — but the policy had been laid down, whatever my uncle thought. Indeed, the final result was a medal called the 1939-45 Star which covered the whole five and a half years of war in Europe. A fine recognition for those who went through Dunkirk!

In 1944 I was posted to 21 Army Group Headquarters in Süchteln, Germany, as Inter-Service Liaison Officer with Air Photographic Headquarters in England. Our living accommodations at Süchteln were in tents pitched on a hill outside the town. Lunatics from the local asylum worked in the fields, and wherever we went or whatever we did, they stared at us incredulously as though we were the ones who were off our heads.

My duties were varied. One of our department's jobs was to rush to captured airdromes and rescue any German photographic intelligence from destruction. What with the Germans themselves smashing everything, not to mention our own paratroopers, this was difficult.

Sometimes I was entrusted with fetching and carrying top-secret papier-mâché models of enemy territory which were used in briefing forward area troops. On these missions I usually traveled in worn-out freight Dakotas crewed by very exhausted airmen. One trip was outstandingly alarming. I boarded the machine at Gloucester, clutching my precious cargo, and was the only passenger. I went up to the front of the plane to chat with the crew. By this time I was accustomed to aircraft that seemed on the point of falling to bits, but when we were approaching Redhill I noticed a stream of oil pouring from the engine nearest me. Not wishing to seem windy, I nudged the pilot and said casually, "I suppose you know about it," at which he cast a bleary eye at the engine, practically leaped out of his seat with fright, and shouted, "Hell, no! Thanks for the tip-off. That's dangerous!" We made an emergency landing and had to wait for another machine to bring us a spare part. Then, when we touched down in France, we overshot the runway and smashed the wheels. Perhaps it was as well that I am not unduly superstitious. The date was Friday the 13th.

My father became very ill in 1945, and my aunt and uncle kindly had him down to stay at Chequers in order to recuperate. I took compassionate leave from time to time to see him. With the end of the war in Europe in May of that year, my leave was extended. At 9:15 P.M. on June 4 my uncle made a forceful election speech on the B.B.C. Immediately afterward I found myself drifting with two of his secretaries back to their office. My uncle came with us. He at once sat down and began to read State papers. He gave me a rather disapproving look, for this was a holy of holies, filled with secrets, and had he wanted to mention, say, the atomic bomb, he would have had to turn me out. So I slipped away of my own accord, but not before I had made a rapid sketch. I went straight upstairs and completed a very small but characteristic, intimate painting of this moment, which is now in the possession of the American ambassador. The two secretaries on duty that evening were Leslie Rowan and Jock Colville. Of the six secretaries my uncle had at one period of the war, John Peck perhaps excelled in having the most Boswell-like memory. I recall one evening he told me that when de Gaulle had been expounding on the military situation and my uncle wished to say that evidently the French general had the roots of the matter, my uncle was heard to tell one of de Gaulle's aides: *"Je crois qu'il avait les racines de la matière."*

It was during a lunch at Chequers that my uncle asked me what I thought of the idea of his accepting a knighthood.

"If I were you," I said, "I would not take anything less than a dukedom. Knighthoods are bestowed on so many lesser people." But I think he must have meant a K G — Knight of the Garter — which is different and which he eventually accepted.

My remarks were received with a lapse into cogitation. Personally I have doubts about the whole business of distributing honors and titles. Sometimes the achievements of those who receive them are slight compared to what is done by people who remain unrecognized in the shareout. The awards become even more meaningless if they are automatic. When one has reached the C.B.E. grade, for instance, one gets a K.C.B.E. or some such honor, merely providing one has not tripped up socially or done anything wrong. I can accept existing titles, but in modern times I find new ones rather like handing round caps and colors at school. Certainly with regard to artists, who rarely get singled out for distinction anyway, I think that honors bear little relation to deeds and probably ought to be refused. I have always thought it rather fatuous that Reynolds should have been Sir Joshua, and I wonder whether T. E. Lawrence of Arabia held views similar to mine when he publicly refused to accept an honor which was about to be conferred on him by the King.

My demobilization imminent, Mary and I took a house

on Campden Hill. We moved in, with her beloved little poodle Paula, and Sally joined us in school holidays. My wife refused to play the rôle of stepmother, and it became my responsibility to see to Sally's upbringing.

I had agreed with Mary that we would not start a family until the end of the war, but when the time came we discovered to our great disappointment that she was unable to have a baby. This situation presented various problems: a substitute for a family had to be provided.

We decided to open a shop. It was an idea which, in addition to creating the necessary interest, had the distinct advantage that Mary's charm and intelligence would earn some badly needed funds. Wearing my uniform, I sat in a bare, bleak room in West London somewhere, queueing for permission to trade. The democratic law at the time was that no one was allowed to start a shop unless he had had one in 1939. After waiting miserably for hours, I was granted a license on the strength of my modest efforts in Ebury Street. Mary and I toured Knightsbridge and found excellent vacant premises in Sloane Street. We collected four other people who were willing to put up money, and with fifteen hundred pounds capital opened for business as interior decorators, calling the venture by my two middle names: George Spencer.

One of our chief helpers was a tall, attractive and talented woman, Peggy Hancock. I immediately set about teaching her and Mary certain architectural and proportional musts, and helped them to create special designs for clients. As interior decorators, we did everything from painting bathrooms to putting up wallpaper and installing chandeliers. New furniture of any quality did not exist. We combed secondhand shops and junk yards for pieces suited to the rather chi-chi tastes of the Sloane Street area. Then we cleaned and painted them. The girls learned quickly, showing tremendous talent and business acumen. I confess they were the ones who did the really hard work; my contribution was the designing. Many London homes must still be equipped with original Churchillian pelmets. I designed hundreds.

A fascinating aspect of our activities was the extraordinary people we came across. One afternoon a man strolled in and demanded: "Why is this place called George Spencer?"

We explained. Then he protested indignantly: "But *my* name is George Spencer!"

We repeated our explanations, after which it transpired that our caller was none other than Lord George Spencer, who happened to be passing and saw our name board. His family owns the main relics of the first Duke of Marlborough. The first duchess, having no son, bequeathed them to the Spencer family.

Perhaps the most fantastic character we met in those raw, early days was a well-known West End actress who asked us to redecorate her bedroom. When our representative arrived one morning for the preliminary measuring, he was directed to the bedroom and discovered, to his embarrassment, the dear lady flat out on the bed with a man. Our representative offered profound apologies and said he would return at a more convenient moment, but the actress was not in the least upset.

"Don't mind us," she said cheerfully. "Carry on!"

So the room was duly taped while she indulged in her pleasures. She never paid her bill, incidentally.

In addition to working in the shop, which I regarded as a stopgap measure, I had to tackle the difficulty of resuming my career as a painter. I was thirty-six when the war ended, and had lost six important and formative years. I had created nothing worthwhile and had not even touched a piano. There was a lot of time to catch up, and I threw myself into my work. For Mrs. Ghislaine Alexander in Hill Street, Mayfair, I did *grisailles* in six tones of gray depicting Athens and Olympia in classical times. I used to ride to Hill Street on my bicycle with an outsize basket loaded with paints, sounding a most unusual horn. When my Army unit had reached the Munster-Unterlüss artillery range in the advance on Hanover during the war, I thought it was time I collected a souvenir, so I took the horn — a curved affair about two feet long which was blown to give warning of firing. Equipped with a rubber bulb and fixed to my handle bars, it could stop the traffic in Piccadilly with one toot.

Composers are lucky, because whatever attempt is made to destroy their labors, they can always keep exact replicas of their creations in their minds. A mural artist is not as fortunate. I painted a small dining room at this time and decorated the furniture and door panels with minute reproductions of very old musical instruments. I devoted an enormous amount of time and thought to the detail and arrangement of these designs, but recently the house was sold and redecorated and my work vanished — hours of labor obliterated.

In 1946 I was delighted to receive one of my biggest commissions. Mrs. Drexel Biddle invited me to design a vast mural for the private cinema in her new home at Sainthill, Sussex. The subject was to be a *singerie* — a monkey decoration. The work had to be done on canvas to cover three walls, and when stretched out measured one hundred feet long and ten feet high. My studio at Campden Hill was by no means large enough; I explored Essex, renting the studio at Dedham used by Sir Alfred Munnings for his horse paintings.

I made numerous visits to the London Zoo and spent hours sketching all the monkey species, after which I returned to Dedham and started placing them in an Arcadian landscape. Much as I tried to prevent its happening, the monkeys resembled human beings; the Brazzar monkey, for instance, is very like Sir Thomas Beecham. Some of my figures were portraits of actual monkeys, such as Jim, the pig-tailed monkey in the zoo, who did not like me much, and Audrey, the green monkey, who did. Then I included that terrible long-nosed ring-tailed lemur which belonged to Maxine Elliot, the actress, and was kept at her Château l'Horizon in the South of France. She (the monkey) had a predilection for gin and used to get extremely drunk. Apart from rude behavior all through lunch, she would explore under the table and take a deep nip into any bare foot available. The ensuing shriek made Maxine burst into laughter, but it was not my idea of humor.

The Sainthill *singerie* took six months to execute. Munnings lived next door to the studio at Dedham, and used to fortify me with some of his very special 1908 port. I think he talked as much nonsense about Art with a capital A as he painted horses magnificently. At dusk I used to cycle along the country roads with our poodle Paula in the front basket. She loved it. I was allowed to have her as company because Mary was hard at work in London. When Sainthill had been decorated and my mural put in position, Mrs. Biddle took up residence. Exactly one month later she left for Paris and sold the house — not, I believe, on account of my work, which she said she liked very much.

In contrast to the substantial commission of the *singerie,* I was asked to execute a small panel for Lady d'Abernon. Lord and Lady d'Abernon had been lifelong friends of my mother and father, and when she asked me if I could do a humble *"au dessus de la porte,"* as she called it, meaning an overdoor, I could not refuse. I had to travel down to Stoke d'Abernon from London every day and take infinite care to get exactly the right representation of a garden sundial erected in memory of her husband.

"I can afford only eighteen pounds," she said, which was somewhat strange, because while I was actually working she sold an El Greco for several thousand. In all, the commission cost me about thirty-six pounds from my own pocket, but it was a pleasure. When I was busy up the ladder, she came and chatted, telling stories of my own family and of her husband, who was the British Ambassador in Berlin before the First World War and was painted by Augustus John.

My father's health grew worse, and he came to live with us at Campden Hill. Poor Mary, who already had enough complications looking after me and Sally while not wishing to be a stepmother at all, had to be armed with a hypodermic with which to inject morphia into him when the pain became unbearable. We thought he might die. My brother called and announced that he had found a will made by my mother. It was an interesting document because she had left me all her books, a Greek torso, and various other things specially chosen because I was her artist son. But nobody had heard about it, and when it was shown to my father he tore it up.

My father recovered and immediately frightened us by insisting on going to the City again — by tube. He might have fallen dead at any moment. We decided he would be happier in a place of his own, surrounded by his books and possessions, so we found him a delightful flat which we decorated ourselves. It was next door to Katie, an early girl-friend of his, one of the five beautiful Trefusis sisters, who was now Mrs. Arthur Crichton. I have come across several of these famous sisters, but Katie was and still is the loveliest of them all.

It was during these last few months of life which remained to him that he realized what was probably his third greatest ambition. His first had been to join the Royal Navy — he had a passion for the sea, and whenever he got near it he donned a yachting cap, blue in winter and white in summer. However, he was nearly blind in one eye and this ruled out a naval career, though it enabled him to wear a monocle. His second ambition had been to join a cavalry regiment in the Army, but it was too expensive and he had to make do with the Oxfordshire Yeomanry. The third aspiration was to join the Turf Club in Piccadilly. His original application for membership had been refused, the official reason being that he was a stockbroker. The Turf was strictly the preserve of aristocracy who did not need to work for a living. (It was whispered, though, that the club had got more than it bargained for by accepting his brother Winston, and did not want any more Churchills.) Anyway, my father was now elected, and with intense joy and pride he took me to lunch there, introducing me to everyone.

In the icy February of 1947 he became ill again, this time fatally. His medical adviser was Lord Horder, that well-known theoretical physician. In practical matters Horder had not impressed me as exceptionally brilliant. When, in 1921, he had amputated the leg of my grandmother, Lady Randolph Churchill, she died of septicemia. He was very old now at seventy-six, but my father seemed to have faith in him. The illness had reached an advanced stage and there was little Horder could do except direct the situation, and he made it quite plain to me, in so many words, that he despised the lot of us because we had not taken proper care of our father. The truth, of course, is that we did not even know he had been gravely unwell for more than twelve years, nor did my uncle.

Two nights before my father died, Lord Horder spoke to us in an adjoining room. He told us what an aneurysm was, and said that once after giving a lecture on some diseased part of a cadaver laid before him, he had asked the students if there were any questions. "One student," he said, "wanted to know why the subject did not die sooner. I answered that it was a stupid question. He should have asked me why the subject lived so long. It is extraordinary how so many people do in fact go on living with diseases all over their anatomies."

I was in constant touch with my uncle by telephone. He wished to have bulletins on his brother's condition at almost hourly intervals. Normally, as head of the family, I would have taken the advice of the general practitioner we had handling the case and made decisions on the spot, but in the circumstances I felt obliged to consult my uncle. The final crisis came on a Sunday night. Lord Horder had left London for the country and was unobtainable. I sent for my uncle and we went into the bedroom together. My father said farewell. Both of us cried. When he began the death agony, I left my uncle alone with him in meditation.

After making the preliminary funeral arrangements, I went round to my uncle to ask his opinion on the choice of prayers, hymns, psalms, and incidental music. He has always been most interested in these matters at funerals. He began listing a large number of hymns and psalms which had been sung at various funerals, and by listing I mean that he quoted long passages from memory and gave names and dates connected with the services. His knowledge of the Hymn Book Ancient and Modern and the psalms was quite extraordinary. When we came to agree on the incidental music which I wanted after the service, I suggested

the opening of Part Three of Handel's *Messiah*, No. 45, the
air "I know that my Redeemer liveth."

"Why have you chosen that?" he asked.

"Because my father liked it so much," I said.

"How do you know that he did?"

"I played it for him many times shortly before he died,
and he expressed his appreciation."

For the anthem I chose the music, again without voices,
of one of the variations of the famous chorale from Bach's
St. Matthew Passion, No. 63: "O sacred head surrounded."
I had to explain my reason for this choice too. We were
both feeling rather emotional, and my uncle told me
about the death of his own father, how he had been so
affected by the event that he was prostrate for a whole day
and night. Quite suddenly, seeing my distress, my uncle
said impulsively: "Johnny, I will take your father's place.
Come to me if you are in trouble. I will be your father."

Then, by way of soothing me, if not himself as well, he
went to a bookcase and pulled out a copy of his book *The
River War* and started to read from it aloud. We were
alone and I think he must have read for a full half-hour, at
the end of which he remarked: "That is pretty good writing, you know. I wish I could write like that today." All
the same, I thought it an unusual book to choose in the
circumstances.

The weather was so cold that my uncle's doctors would
not allow him to attend the funeral service in Bladon
churchyard, near Blenheim, where my father was buried
next to his mother. I arranged for a memorial service to be

held in London at the same time, and it was attended by my uncle and my father's friends.

In the spring I took Mary to Florence and Venice and did many paintings as a result of the journey. In Venice I made a special effort to visit the Palazzo Vendramin on the Grand Canal, where Wagner died, but was refused entry. On our return home Mary underwent an operation in order to have a baby. It was a comparatively simple one, but the acute appendicitis she had in childhood had caused adhesions and she became very ill. To add to these domestic complications, she began to brood on the religious inadequacies of our marriage. And her continued insistence on not being the "traditional hated stepmother" meant I had to deal with Sally myself on aspects of discipline. Peggy Hancock took over the running of George Spencer, and for a whole year I did practically no work in order to look after Mary. I became known to our friends as the State Registered Nurse. Actually I am disposed that way and can discharge almost any sickroom duties, but I am told that I tend to fuss too much. By degrees Mary made a slow recovery, leaving me free for work again. This was just as well; our money was getting very low.

One of the few jobs I managed to do in 1948 was a mural commissioned by Smith's Clocks for their stand at the *Daily Mail* Ideal Home Exhibition at Olympia. I mention it because I came up against the trade union movement. As an artist I am naturally opposed to the trade unionism of today, especially when it interferes with high-skilled craftmanship and the arts. As an armchair politician my view, purely my own, is that it is one of the worst features of inefficiency in almost every trade. Some fifty years ago it had its point and usefully discharged its function of protecting underpaid labor. But like so many good ideas, when its function was completed the wise men of politics stepped in to use it as a weapon. Today, in my opinion, it is just a tool for reaching political ends.

For the mural at the exhibition my theme, appropriately for a clockmaking firm, was The River of Time. It was an imaginary scene; the river flowed from right to left, from a mediaeval setting through a Georgian one to the present day. On a hill in the foreground I had a pub, the Hourglass, and a customer was being thrown out because it was Time, Gentlemen, Please. Done in semi-Dutch style, the picture measured seventeen feet by about ten.

In order to complete the finishing touches in time for the exhibition's opening ceremony next morning, I had to work all the night before. At 5 P.M. I was busy with my ladders, brushes and paints when a union official strode up.

"Where is your card?" he asked.

I thought this a ridiculous interruption. "Not only have I not got one," I told him, "but I have no intention of ever having one."

"Then we will have to organize a strike of painters," he said.

"Don't be so puerile," I told him. "This is not a school for children. This is life. If you had any guts you would work hard yourself instead of drinking tea and doing only about five hours' work a day. Anyhow, I am an artist and above such juvenile rubbish."

The house painters around me were rather impressed

by this outburst, and like all painters they agreed with me. They liked to get work done, make a good job of it and be proud. But they had to belong to a union, and the union ruling was: Knock off at 5 P.M. sharp. A conference was summoned, and at eleven o'clock head stewards came round to inspect me. An eccentric animal, they maintained.

"You ought to be ashamed of yourselves," I said, "belonging to an organization used by the Communists as a means to cause disruption in our country. I am not interested in your rules and regulations. I propose continuing my work all night because I have to in order to get it done. My efforts will make me much richer than you, but as far as I am concerned you are at liberty to sink to the lowest level of moronic human development and stew in your muddled, meaningless quagmire of indolent mush for the rest of your negative lives."

Strong words. I did not truthfully know if the reference to Communism was justified, but I meant what I said. I suppose that if my mural had brought Olympia out on strike, the whole of the rest of the union would have struck. Other unions would have come out in sympathy, and in no time I would have been accused of bringing the nation to its knees. Honor was satisfied, however, in a somewhat farcical manner when the Society of Mural Painters, of which I am a member, was asked to equip me with a membership card. This they did, and everyone was happy.

I do not think my uncle agrees with my opinions on trade unionism, perhaps for political reasons. He is a member of the Bricklayers' Union and in his more active days

enjoyed the quiet satisfaction of wielding a trowel. I remember one morning around 1948 going down to Chartwell before lunch. My uncle was enlarging the outer wall
which borders the road when our friend Paul Maze, the
French painter, arrived on the scene. Without meaning to
be rude in the least, Paul declared that my uncle's work
was not really level and that he thought he could lay the
bricks better himself. My uncle was most put out.

"I do not know why you say that," he grumbled. "It is
very easy to find fault. The difficulty is to praise — yet it is
simple really, if you try."

Another time I reached Chartwell just as a disaster occurred. Bill Deakin and my uncle had decided to try some
boating on the lake. The object of the exercise was to row
from the bank out to the small island. The distance was
short, but the boat was old and the oars were as useless as
sticks. My uncle got rather impatient with Bill's lack of
headway. "Here, let me take over," he said, rising from his
seat at the stern and trying to change places. My uncle is
quite a weight, and the boat was never intended for people who wanted to walk about. There was a flurry of arms,
a lot of holding on, balancing, and shouts of "Steady!" —
after which the boat capsized and my uncle and Bill fell
into the water. My uncle surfaced nobly. His cigar, still
firmly clamped in his mouth, came to the surface first, followed by his head.

In the autumn I went to Chartwell to stay for a while.
Since the war, my aunt had rearranged the house, turning
it upside down, as it were, to simplify the day-to-day organization. The old dining room from which we had

watched the Emden geese chase the swans had become a cinema, and the kitchen had been moved right to the top of the building. The new dining room, formerly the Elizabethan bedroom, was on the floor below. The drawing room had been changed temporarily into my uncle's working studio, saving him the trouble of going down to the studio in the garden.

One day after lunch we both went into his studio, where he was busy painting a picture of Mont St. Victoire, a subject chiefly of interest to him I think because Cézanne painted it so often. He wanted to show me his new collection of Swiss tempera paints, and as he settled down at his easel he said: "Try them. Paint something with them." It was a wonderful opportunity — but what subject should I choose? I decided that a perfect one was right in front of me. In forty minutes I did what can only be described as a portrait, though it is a back view of my uncle at work on his picture. Ten years later I gave it to him for his eighty-fourth birthday, when it was studied intently.

It is a canvas of some historical interest because it shows on each side of the window the two alcoves filled with his books about Napoleon. I doubt very much if there is any book on Napoleon which my uncle does not possess. I remember how before the war we used to have discussions — or rather, hear discussions — about Napoleon, and I used to wonder how much my uncle's destiny had been influenced by the great French leader. After the war, when my uncle had equaled and surpassed Napoleon's achievements, the Napoleonic influence waned. In 1954 I found a beautiful head and shoulders of Napoleon painted by

David, which was either a copy from or a sketch for the famous full-length portrait sold to America for thousands of pounds. I offered it to my uncle for a fraction of its value, but he was not interested any more.

During my stay at Chartwell we both concentrated on creative pursuits. My uncle at this time was going through the galley proofs of Volume II of his history, the *Second World War*, and recalling once again my dramatic visit to him at the Admiralty on that morning in May, 1940, he gave me his account of the Dunkirk evacuation to read. I corrected one date — with trepidation! When I showed him my album of about thirty-five photographs of the murals, landscapes and townscape paintings I had executed since turning professional, I believe he was duly impressed. Then we both set about painting the swans. Nicholson had done two pictures of them years previously, one of which was bought by my aunt and the other by my father. My aunt now had both canvases as a result of my father's will, but I hoped I might be able to give her my own version of the swans. My uncle moved too quickly for me and gave her his version first. I still have *my* swans. I did, however, give my aunt a tiny sketch in profile of my uncle at work painting. I am flattered how much she treasures it and that she has it hanging in her apartments.

Early in 1949 my aunt mentioned to me that the Marlborough Pavilion was in a sad state of disrepair due to neglect during the war. She asked me to repaint it as her gift to my uncle for his seventy-fifth birthday on November 30. The weather had caused such damage that the whole job had to be tackled again from the start. I did not like the idea of merely painting exactly what I had done fifteen years previously, so I suggested re-creating the design in a different and more durable medium. My aunt readily agreed. The problem was to find a good medium suited to a pavilion which was so openly exposed to the elements. I liked the idea of executing the work in plaster, incising it as the Spanish do or embossing it in the manner of the East Anglians in their pargetry work, but plaster was obviously far from suitable. Should I use stone, I wondered?

I went and consulted my old wartime colleague Sir William Coldstream, head of the Slade School of Art in University College. I also had a word with Professor Gerrard, his assistant in sculpture. The main feature of the new design I had conceived was to be a magnificent frieze round the pavilion, where the lunettes of the four battles had been. A visit to the British Museum had enabled me to study two techniques: the carving away of the background to reveal the figures, as in the Parthenon Frieze, and the making of incisions to release the figures from within the stone, as in the hieroglyphic reliefs on Egyptian tombs. I decided on the latter. Professor Gerrard made an invaluable suggestion.

"Why not try slate?" he said. "It is nonabsorbent. Therefore the damp in the sandstone walls of the pavilion will not cause the paint to peel off."

I accepted the idea at once. Bill Coldstream offered me the use of the school's sculpture rooms during the summer vacation, and Gerrard promised to find me some postgraduates to help with the work. For the next four or five

months I did elaborate research. I spent hours behind the
scenes at Bertram Mills's Circus watching and sketching
the Liberty Horses, which are the nearest equivalent to
the horses used in Queen Anne's day. Also I studied contemporary prints and illustrations for details of uniforms,
hats, boots, weapons and so on. Everything had to be absolutely accurate in a gift for a man who was already an
eminent authority on the subject.

I decided to concentrate solely on the battle of Blenheim and to work the whole scene into a frieze on a "flat"
basis without much perspective, yet keeping it moving.
This required a tremendous amount of designing, and the
degree of elimination had to be drastic. Under the four
sections of the frieze, in the alcoves at each of the corners
of the pavilion, were to be cast concrete busts in low relief of the four principal characters as before: the Duke of
Marlborough, the Duchess, Prince Eugene of Savoy and
Queen Anne. There were also terra-cotta plaques in high
relief representing the four rivers — the Danube, Rhine,
Meuse and Moselle — and two large slate-carved plaques:
one a colorful trophy of drums, bugles, flags and pistols,
and the other the Marlborough arms incorporating the
Spanish motto *Fiel Pero Desdichado* — "Faithful but Unfortunate."

I tend to be absent-minded when traveling, and I lost
the designs for the pavilion twice. The first occasion was in
a train at Paddington Station. The train was shunted into
the sidings. My designs were put in an incinerator and I
had to start all over again. The second time I lost them

was in a bus, but I managed to get them back from the Lost Property Office.

When I took the finished designs to Chartwell, they were well received, though I think my uncle was apprehensive about the treatment of the battle of Blenheim. When I said I proposed to carve it in slate, he did not believe me.

"In what?" he asked. "Really?"

I described the advantages, especially with regard to repairs.

"Extraordinary idea," he mumbled.

The whole grand conception was something he had not bargained for, nor had my aunt. Still less did they realize what carving some thirty feet of frieze in slate involved. I had misjudged the schedule myself, because in the four months remaining until November 30 I planned to execute the frieze, plaques and busts, paint them and erect them in the pavilion.

I started work at the Slade on July 25. Professor Gerrard had assembled four volunteers to help me. They were Pascoe, the head of the Sculpture Department at Bristol University; Currie, a postgraduate at the Slade; and two Poles, Blasiak and Brackachi. We had twelve black Welsh slates, each three feet long, two feet six inches high, and about half an inch thick. We fixed them to the wall so that they would not crack while being carved. It took roughly ten days to carve one slate, so I estimated that if all went well the entire frieze would be done in six weeks. It was, in spite of a major difficulty which I had not foreseen and which strained my tact and ingenuity. Although my de-

sign was clear enough to understand, all five of us were
highly skilled, mature and individual artists. My helpers
were not students who wanted to learn, as I expected
them to be, but artists in their own right. This led to variations in style.

Where I gained was in the knowledge and experience
of these men. Blasiak had been in the Polish Artillery. A
man of about forty, he had been a carver and stonemason
in Warsaw. There was absolutely nothing he did not know
about artillery horses. Also he knew about death, for he
had shot his way out of German prison camps to come to
England via Spain. Brackachi was a poetic youngster. At
night he slept secretly on a mattress under the tables in
the school, which accounted for his always being first on
the job in the morning. Pascoe, a youthful professor from
Cornwall, was amazing. His self-confidence was equaled
only by his skill. Currie, though, was still struggling with
himself and inclined to experiment, sometimes without
logic, which meant I had difficulty in rectifying his mistakes.

We completed the twelve panels on September 7, and
then I had the problem of knitting my helpers' efforts together to make the frieze appear to be the work of a single
sculptor. This was not easy. The autumn term was about
to start, and I was obliged to spend a fortnight on the
frieze by myself in another room lent to me by Bill Coldstream. Following this, the slates had to be cut and sheared
to fit so that they tilted correctly at an angle of thirty degrees and were joined when placed against the pavilion's
vaulted roof. Meanwhile, in my studio, I carved the coat

of arms and the trophy; also I modeled the plaques of the rivers and busts.

My uncle was most intrigued when he happened to find the clay model for the bust of Prince Eugene of Savoy, which I based on the portrait by Jacob van Schuppen in the Rijksmuseum, Amsterdam. The Prince was an extraordinary man. Born in Paris in 1663, he had a passion for war. When he was denied a commission in the French Army because of his father's exile, he migrated to Vienna and entered the Austrian service, swearing a kind of vengeance against France. He became a commander in chief ten years before Marlborough and was still a commander in chief twenty years after Marlborough had finished the War of the Spanish Succession, in which the two great generals worked together. These astonishing achievements fascinated my uncle. After insisting that I had not made the Prince's snub nose turn up enough, he commented on the rumor that the Prince had been a homosexual.

"He was very ugly," said my uncle, "and so were his habits."

I confess I found myself pressing my own snub nose down as far as I could, while concealing a broad smile under my palm.

Time was getting extremely short, but the slates and busts were in position by November 30. The painting had yet to be done, however, and my uncle protested that he could not see the frieze, which was magnificent in its natural slate color, if rather dark. I had to point out that it was going to be painted, though my aunt agreed with me it was a pity.

To finish the frieze I followed the same strict routine of work I adopted fifteen years before, but at night I strapped an electric blanket round my waist to keep me warm. On one occasion I arrived at Chartwell with a copy of Guy de Maupassant's *Bel Ami*. My uncle noticed, and observed: "It is a good thing to read French literature in French sometimes. It clears one's brain and broadens one's approach to reading. But Guy de Maupassant was one thing and Flaubert another. Get *Madame Bovary* of Flaubert and you will see from where the inspiration and technique of Guy de Maupassant springs!"

I was most interested to hear him say this, because his verbal French is very Churchillian, whereas my Father's was flawless. I acquired *Madame Bovary* at once, but my reading in French is very slow.

My uncle at this time had reached Volume III of the *Second World War*, and Bill Deakin was again at Chartwell helping him. The usual inspection of my labors took place at 11 A.M., en route for the elaborate feeding of the golden orf. He was not quite sure about the frieze medium.

"I must say I have never seen a battle like that," he commented. When I explained the principles of presenting a story in frieze, he seemed resigned to the result. In fact he thoroughly appreciated that it was a fine example of art — with the reservation that it was not his idea of the battle of Blenheim.

Nevertheless, as the work blossomed in reds and blues, and the black of the Welsh slate contrasted with the yellow ocher and white (I did not use green at all), he became enthusiastic. He could see much more clearly what it was about. Then my troubles began. One morning he strode across the lawn to me in lively critical form.

"That French officer is not sitting on his horse properly," he said. "The near side of his bottom should be more this way or he will fall off."

When a frieze has been carved it cannot be altered as if it were a painting. And the alarming factor in this instance was that the slates were fixed in position. If I started to carve them they might crack. I told my uncle this.

"What you say is very interesting," he replied stubbornly. "But the officer's right cheek will have to be changed."

Luckily, with a delicate widening of the line in question, I managed to do it.

On the completion of the pavilion in the spring of 1950, my uncle was most complimentary. "It is assured a place in history," he said — a reference to the purchase of Chartwell by a group of his friends to preserve it as a national monument.

He had reached the age of seventy-five and I was forty. Often I was entirely alone with him for lunch, and because I was one of the family I was free of the obligation to make conversation. On such occasions he would always excuse himself because he wanted to study newspaper articles or read official documents. One day after glancing at a sheet of typescript, he handed it to me to read. It was a list of headings — Politicians, Scientists, Trade Unions, Charities, Lawyers, Diplomats, etc. — and against each was a number. One heading caught my eye.

"What," I asked, "is meant by 'Lunatics, Four'?"

"Exactly what it says," snapped my uncle. "You are holding an analysis of the correspondence I received this morning. I have a constant correspondence from lunatics. Today it was only four letters. For some unknown reason the lunatics usually want to kill me. That is why I have a detective sergeant hanging around."

If there was any possibility of creative work being done at the lunch table, his secretary, Miss Jo Sturdee, would have her meal with us. I remember that once when this happened my uncle did not trouble to pick up any documents. He just sat in contemplation, munching away.

"You must chew the more you grow older," he said.

In undertones I chatted with Jo Sturdee about the swans and the fish, while outside in the road, at the tall wooden gates across the drive to the house, a crowd of eager spectators watched us. The dining table was quite visible from the road, and a mass of people always collected at meal-time. I felt rather like an animal in a zoo, but my uncle paid not the slightest attention to the stares. Everything was going according to plan at this particular lunch when the sweet course appeared. Then suddenly my uncle without any warning and regardless of the fact that Miss Sturdee and I were talking, raised his head and interrupted: "Take this down."

Instantly her full concentration was switched to my uncle. She took up her pencil and shorthand book. Carefully, and in measured tones, my uncle dictated sentence after sentence, now and again asking for passages to be repeated; then he approved them or made amendments.

When he had dictated about four hundred words he said: "Bring that to me right away." Miss Sturdee was gone. Lunch, for her, was over.

On more ceremonial occasions at Chartwell, of course, agreeable conversation is an important part of the hospitality which my uncle and aunt offer to guests. In this connection something awful happened to me at a dinner party one evening. Sarah had asked a friend of hers named Pussy Waring. Now Pussy was a rather large young girl of a naturally quiet disposition. I found myself sitting next to her at table. The table was large and round, and Sarah, being opposite me, was unable to say much to her friend. I started off by talking to Pussy but made absolutely no headway. Probably because of shyness, she said nothing beyond a murmured yes or no. I turned to my neighbor on my right and then made another attempt at Pussy, but it was no good. I could not draw her out at all. So when I was not talking to my other neighbor, I lapsed into a sad silence.

Suddenly I became aware of my uncle. He was sitting on the far side of Pussy and gazing at me intently. It was definitely a meaningful, disapproving stare and I wondered what I had done wrong. I grew so worried I froze, incapable of conversation with Pussy or anyone else. For the rest of the meal I nervously fingered my shirt front, the studs and my collar. All the time my uncle's glare became more and more hostile. Eventually he took the unusual step of saying: "Clemmie, we will join you later," at which the table rose and the men were left behind. He came across to me angrily.

"How dare you make no attempt to talk to your neighbor!" he fumed. "Don't you know it is manners to make some kind of effort?"

I was speechless and wilted under this unfair bombardment. I could only say: "But I did my best, Uncle Winston . . ."

Shortly after the finishing of the Marlborough Pavilion I arranged to take my wife on a trip to Madrid, where we were to meet my aunt and her youngest daughter Mary, who were going to Spain on a short holiday. My brother Pebin happened to be motoring to Spain, and knowing how people like driving their own cars, we thought he might want to give us a lift. That was indeed his wish, although he got so exhausted that Mary had to take over for a while. I do not drive and never will, because I am inclined to start thinking of something else and forget which way I am supposed to be going. Besides, so many people seem to be willing to drive me about.

The plan was to go to Madrid via France and visit Barcelona on the way back. Pebin's car was my father's old 1938 Buick. It had been heavily bombed in the war but was specially overhauled for the trip. Furthermore, my brother describes himself as C.E., which I always thought stood for Church of England but which he assures me means Civil Engineer. So we felt fairly safe. But at Perigeux the engine conked out. While Mary and I indulged in *pâté de fois gras*, poor Pebin had to wrangle with the French mechanics in his Harrow French. They began to dismantle the car. I somehow felt that things were not going quite right, so I went to interfere. We might be stuck in Perigeux for weeks, I thought. The difficulty was how to translate English motorcar language into French. Such perfectly ordinary engineering expressions as "Are you sure the male part is fitting into the female properly?" are apt to be misunderstood. I made them put the bits together again and it worked. What we did not know, and were not to know for a long time, was the real cause of the trouble. Despite the special overhaul, the rubber flange between the two cones of the carburetor had not been inspected and was deteriorating rapidly.

On our way to the Pyrenees, we saw the fantastic Lascaux Cave paintings, twenty-five thousand years old, which had recently been discovered in the Dordogne Valley as a result of a boy's falling down a hole hidden in the scrub on the hills. Then, halfway up the Pyrenees, the engine gasped to a stop again. While Mary made herself comfortable on the back seat with a book, I blew as hard as I could into the petrol tank and Pebin sucked at the carburetor end of the fuel pipe. This seemed to work. The car went and we reached Madrid, where Pebin gave up driving because the police prosecuted him for not going fast enough in the Alcala, the main street. Quite a change from London.

When my aunt arrived by air with my cousin Mary, she became fascinated by the tragic story of the Princess Eboli, who had a black patch over one eye and was condemned to lifelong imprisonment by the King of Spain because of a love affair with Antonio Perez, his Foreign Minister. We all made an excursion to see the prison, which is in Pastrana.

Owing to General Franco's neutral attitude towards Britain in the war, my uncle was aloof from Spain, politically speaking, and therefore my aunt's visit was unofficial and informal. This, however, did not prevent some interesting semiofficial invitations being extended to her. One of these was a visit to the farm of the famous bullfighting family, the Dominguens, west of Madrid. Papa Dominguen was getting on in years but could still hold a cape effectively. His son had reached the top of the bullfighting profession. Our invitation was to a *tienta*, a small-scale, teasing fight without killing or blood, in which various cows were to be tried out in order to choose ferocious ones for breeding. My aunt was pleased to go, but on condition that there would be no publicity and no photographs.

Everyone else of note in the locality contrived to get invited too, and the event became like a race meeting. Huge glinting Cadillacs swept along the roads at a hundred kilometers an hour, enveloping poor starving peasants in hurricanes of dust. The dust was probably their only meal that day, such is the contrast of riches and poverty in Spain.

The ring had a central box in which all the ladies sat, my aunt occupying the place of honor. With my indifferent Spanish, I walked around trying to overhear what the male spectators were saying, and discovered that the *tienta* was regarded as highly important. Then to my horror I saw a cine-camera being focused on my aunt. Press photographers' flashbulbs exploded. The Spaniards had not kept their promise. My aunt's serene expression changed in a second to the glare of a tigress. That night she complained to the Spanish authorities, and all the newspapers withdrew their pictures of our outing.

My aunt and cousin returned to England.

Pebin, Mary and I started out for Barcelona in Pebin's car. On the way, Mary was at the wheel, and had slowed down to cross a railway line, when the unbelievable happened. The car stopped, and refused to budge, just at the moment it straddled the track. A train could be heard approaching in the distance. Panic-stricken, Pebin and I leaped out and starting blowing and sucking, while Mary pleaded: "Hurry! Hurry!"

When the train appeared, it was a goods engine clanking along at a couple of miles an hour. The driver spotted us and stopped amid shouts, gesticulations, and clouds of steam. A Buick is a heavy car, but we managed to push it off the railway line onto the road again, where more blowing and sucking enabled us to reach Barcelona. We sped up the mountainside through a cloud to the hotel on the Tibidabo. The management for some reason thought we were my aunt and party, and showed us to the royal suite. We did not think it worth disillusioning them.

In Barcelona I had an introduction to a brother artist and textile magnate, José Porta. Surprisingly, he was on very familiar terms with gypsies, and in consequence we were able to visit some of them who were living under the arches of the main road near his country house at Llavanares, north of the city. I did many sketches of these amazing people dancing. The best was a girl about thirteen years old. When I visited Barcelona again about five years later, José found the same girl and her family for me.

But although she was only eighteen, she could dance no more, or had lost the inspiration. Amongst very wild gypsies, the dancers reach their top performance between the ages of twelve and fifteen.

Around 1950, the year that Mary and I went to Spain with Pebin, a film company asked the wife of Aurelio Valls, a friend of mine in the Spanish Embassy in London, to recommend a Spanish location for *The Flying Dutchman*. She said: "Try Tossa del Mar on the Costa Brava." An outcome of this was that when we got to Tossa, the film-struck locals were talking more about Ava Gardner than Ave Maria. In every other respect, nevertheless, the town remained primitive and our hotel on the beach was only half-built. When Mary and I began to wash we noticed that the water had a strange yellow tinge. It smelt, too, rather unpleasantly, so we did not wash. We asked the manager about it and he was apologetic, explaining that unfortunately when boring for water the engineers had struck the main drain.

Peggy Hancock arrived from London to join us at the hotel and came down to dinner that evening all smiles. "How nice to have had a bath at last!" she told us.

To stop her repeating her experience, we decided to tell her the nature of her bath water.

"Oh, well, that's Spain," was all she said. A most sensible attitude to take.

We were twenty-one kilometers from Chateauroux on our way back home through France when the car stopped again. No amount of blowing and sucking would start it, so with great difficulty I managed to thumb a lift into the town. It was eleven o'clock on Sunday night, and the only mechanic I could find was a woefully thin, bony Frenchman who looked the image of Death. Reluctantly he agreed to help us, and in silence he drove me along the dark roads back to the scene of the trouble. When we arrived he produced a dim flashlight and sadly investigated the engine. At last he came to the carburetor. I shall never forget this amazing apparition suddenly pronouncing in a voice of doom: *"Il est mort."*

He towed us into the town and fitted the carburetor with a new rubber band, but it was now Monday morning. We had no money, and all French banks are closed on Monday except in Paris. Our boat train was due to leave soon, so with immense difficulty and use of the name of Churchill, we managed to persuade the town clerk, a local lawyer and our hotel proprietor to entrust us with enough ready cash to return to England. How different, I thought, from 1930, when I wanted to borrow money in Assisi, Italy. No one there had ever heard of Winston Churchill, still less of his nephew John. Yet the hotel manager cashed me a check for ten pounds on the basis that an Englishman's word was always a guarantee of good faith.

No sooner had we returned to London than my Spanish Embassy friend Aurelio Valls mentioned that his country's Ministry of Fine Arts was sponsoring a cultural visit to Segovia. As guests of the Spanish Government, artists were given twenty-five pounds, plus board and lodging for six weeks. The offer was very tempting. Many internationally known people had already accepted invitations, and this would be a unique chance to meet them. I raised the matter with Mary, emphasizing that the trip would help my career, and she promised she had no objections to my going.

I grew to love Segovia best of all the Spanish towns I know. Our party consisted of about ten Spaniards of both sexes from all parts of Spain, an American girl, a Dutchman who could speak no language except Dutch, two Indians, a French girl, an Italian girl named Elena Lacava, who was extremely advanced and has since had great success in Italy, and two or three Spanish art masters taking a cultural holiday. Distinguished Spanish painters and poets visited us, and the atmosphere was very cordial.

Elena Lacava and I discovered that for sketching purposes the most remarkable view of the town was from the cemetery. We bribed the caretakers with cigarettes and they allowed us to clamber along the walls. We reached a square, chimneylike structure about twenty feet high, built into the exterior of the walls and filled with earth, and had settled down comfortably on top of it with our sketchbooks when Elena pulled something white from the earth.

"Look what I have found, Giovanni," she exclaimed. "It looks like a thighbone." Indeed it was, and we found that we had perched ourselves on top of a filled-up paupers' grave. All the same, we continued to make use of the spot. Then I climbed up a high wall to our right, thinking it might offer a better view. I came across a similar hollow square extension. In a heap at the bottom of it were the latest pauper corpses, which had been burnt. This sur-

prised me; I had thought Catholics did not accept crema-
tion.

Our work schedule at Segovia was free and easy. We
rose at 5 A.M. and without food or drink went out to
sketch what we wished. Breakfast of coffee with bread
dipped in it was served at 8:30 A.M. and lunch with wine
came at 3 P.M. Dinner with wine was not until 10:30,
though of course at about six o'clock I stopped work and,
accompanied by Elena and Fernando Weyler (the Marques de Teneriffe incognito) went to the various taverns. I
managed to sample every known *tapas* and *tapitas* (titbit),
such as cows' lips, newborn birds, and most special of all,
bulls' testicles. Often on these excursions we were joined
by the nephew of the famous Spanish painter Zuluaga. He
was a violent young man who ran the local pottery and
kiln, which had been set up in a church. In the evenings
we sang innumerable songs of our various countries, and I
can still play some of the Spanish ones from memory.

Segovia was for me a delightful and instructive interlude. I did about sixty sketches and made many friends.
But at home, meanwhile, unhappy developments were
taking place. Although Mary had willingly agreed to my
six weeks in Spain, the separation had given her opportunity to reflect in solitude on the nature of our spiritual
relationship. The outcome was that she was very disillu-
sioned.

Our little poodle Paula died at Christmas. Paula was
our talisman, and I felt her death keenly.

Early the following year Mary decided to make a three-
month visit to her parents, who had emigrated to South

Africa. I did not interfere with this idea. Her spiritual worries had affected her whole attitude towards me, and her departure seemed the ideal opportunity for doing what so many ordinary married men do: lead a double life. As a Gemini I thought myself eminently capable of keeping up the grand deception without anyone's knowing. I was mistaken.

IX

Adam and Eve Mews

LONDON IN THE SPRING, 1951. A lady crossed my path, and her power and influence over me can only be described as passion.

I happened to meet her on going for a drink at the Pheasantry Club in Chelsea. She was Kathlyn Tandy, a tall, extremely attractive brunette, the daughter of a Regular Army officer, Major General W. S. Beddall, Director of Army Education at the War Office. Kitty, as her friends called her, was a rebellious, possessive character, and an artist. Before the war I had made her acquaintance in Chelsea on several occasions in artistic circles. She was the sort of strong personality one either took to at once or did not.

I liked her very much.

Her marriage had been wrecked by unhappiness. At the beginning of the war she had married Edward Tandy, an erudite, witty and amusing Wykhamist who was a relative of the famous "Napper" Tandy. He was studying medicine at that time, and although because of this he was under no obligation to join the services, he became an R.A.F. pilot and flew bombers over Berlin. At that extraordinary stage of the war, bombs were not allowed, lest they hurt somebody. Instead, the planes carried beer bottles, which were dropped overboard as a kind of sporting gesture to show the Germans that their capital's defenses could be breached. Edward Tandy discharged his full quota of bombing sorties. He saw many of his friends killed but always came back. He received no recognition of his experiences and would have considered it shooting a line, as they say in the R.A.F., to have even mentioned them. His ordeals took their toll, nevertheless. Piloting bombers imposed on him an immense mental strain which showed itself in his home life, as indeed it did with many other airmen. Eventually he and Kitty were divorced.

When I met Kitty in the club we talked over old times. We had much in common — both of us were artists; both our marriages had not worked out properly — and our friendship came as a refreshing diversion in a period of painful sadness. When Mary returned from visiting her parents in South Africa, I decided that the only solution to the problem was to be a true Gemini and lead two lives, an "official" one and a private one. I tried; I tried really hard, but could not keep up the deception. The truth is that I am a monogamist by nature, definitely a one-person person. Only a short while elapsed before I let the cat out of the bag, and Mary, who must have had her suspicions, knew for certain what was going on. Thus disruption of the mutual trust between us was added to the growing spiritual discord. Of course, any normal husband, and especially a Gemini, would have kept the situation under control. After all, a secret does not exist until a third person shares it.

For six months I endured a conflict between Passion and Duty. At the end, Duty won. Kitty went abroad, and I resolved to convince myself that the affair was nothing more than a brief encounter.

I made changes in our way of life. I bought a large airy studio, formerly a stable, in Adam and Eve Mews, South Kensington, and Mary's improved state of health enabled me to buy her a shop in Walton Street to set her up in business as an interior decorator again. We lived in a little mews house in Devonshire Street. For a long time Mary had criticized my style in painting, which she considered too eclectic for a contemporary artist, despite my powers of invention and original design. While in Spain I had made a start in breaking away from this strong traditional training and influence, and we decided to go further and live in surroundings that were so-called contemporary. The drawing room was large and stark. We covered the entire floor with a buff-colored composition material. When finished and dry, it looked exactly like sand, and the place resembled a beach. Then, most appropriately, the ground-floor lavatory overflowed, and the tide, as it were, came in over the virgin sand. When a state of low tide had been restored, we furnished the room with just a table with a rubber plant on it, a bright scarlet sofa, and a new acquisition: a boudoir grand Steinway piano. Mary gave me this magnificent instrument as a birthday present. As a result of our family's long association with Steinways and my consequent friendship with

Mr. Horwood, the head of the London branch at Steinway Hall in George Street, we were able to choose a particularly special piano. I have never liked Bluthners, but Steinways and Bechsteins I find more or less the same to play. To my surprise, I discovered in Steinway Hall a beautiful Bechstein, which I thought irresistible. But, keeping loyal to Steinway, I chose one of theirs made in Hamburg in 1911. The old Steinway Welte-Mignon upright was already in my studio in Adam and Eve Mews; now, with the boudoir grand, I was able to play to Mary at home as well. As a further change I took Sally away from her school, which was rather snobby, and sent her to a tough bourgeois one in Cannes. She hated it, so then I attached her to the university at Aix-en-Provence and allowed her to meet Angela, her mother, for the first time since the war. I agreed to this now that she had completed her basic education and my paternal responsibilities had been achieved. The pair of them got on very well together, but Angela financed her for a ride on horseback from Aix-en-Provence to St. Tropez, which she did, all by herself, at the age of sixteen. It was just after the Drummond family had been murdered, and I was not pleased.

Meanwhile, Mary and I made strong efforts to start our marriage anew. We went to Holland; we went to Spain. Then she suggested I go to Italy to adjust myself. But the situation remained exactly the same, and when she came out to Rome to join me for a few days, she decided that spiritually we were treading different paths.

"And anyway," as she kept pointing out, "according to the Church we are not married."

I demonstrated my fighting spirit, and my anxiety to find an end to my troubles, by growing a beard. Short and triangular, it gave me a formidable, distinguished air. An extraordinary Italian sculptress named Fiore Henriques took such a liking to it that she made me pose for a bust. Yet, although it was a perfectly acceptable thing for an artist to wear, it was not me. It felt like a mask. People who met me for the first time approved of it, but my existing friends protested: "No, no, dear chap. It will have to come off."

The final word on the subject came from my uncle. "Your beard," he said sadly, "reminds me of my father in his last days."

I cut it off immediately.

The frequent visits to Chartwell were a solace amidst my personal worries. It was always a pleasure to arrive at about 12:30 P.M., in time to accompany my aunt on the short walk round the garden which she liked before lunch. It was a remarkable experience to come out through the garden door and hear "wows" and "meows" ringing across the valley. It is a family idiosyncrasy to greet one another with the noises made by pets. As soon as my uncle and aunt started their wowing and meowing, my cousin Mary Soames would appear from her farmhouse, which is next to the oast houses down towards the lake, and add her own noises; then the animals began theirs. I think it all started with my uncle's trying to talk to his swans, answering their greeting when he arrived to feed them.

A great annual feature around this time was my uncle's birthday party. To begin with, it was an intimate family affair, including a small number of distinguished guests such as Lord Beaverbrook, Brendan Bracken and Lord Cherwell. As in the days when I used to be a small boy, choosing a birthday present worthy of my uncle became quite a problem, especially when well-wishers like Brendan Bracken produced four magnums of special brandy and cases of supervintage Pol Roger, and others arrived with boxes and boxes of cigars, or priceless pieces of Ming.

One year I gave my uncle three silk handkerchiefs with his initials inscribed on them. I have also given him his portrait, specially inscribed, a little sketch of my father, and a sketch of the view from Chartwell, all of which he unwrapped and examined with obvious pleasure. For the occasion of his being invested with the Knighthood of the Garter, my present was my Coronation March in E Major, with five verses written in my own script. He said he liked it enormously, and I presume the Prof must have played it to him.

Lord Beaverbrook, I remember, when I met him at one of my uncle's birthday parties, made a lasting impression on me. It was when Mary and I were running the shop George Spencer. He questioned me with a speed and penetrating clarity which I found rather frightening. In a matter of minutes he obtained facts and figures on our turnover, the money coming in, the money going out, stock held, our methods of operation, and so on.

"That's good," he nodded, and "That's interesting," and "That's right." His grasp of the subject was phenomenal.

I soon realized he understood it well enough to run the shop himself.

On my uncle's return to power, his birthday celebrations became much bigger affairs, with a larger dinner party and a gathering of friends coming in afterward. Then, shortly before he retired, there was no dinner but a gigantic reception. For me it was the event of the year, because I was able to see again in one place many of my old friends. When I saw Lord Camrose at one of the parties, it was the first time we had met since the war. He had changed somewhat in the intervening fifteen years, and I was not absolutely positive it was he. He came across the room to me.

"I bet you don't know who I am," he said.

I hesitated before replying: "Lord Camrose, surely," which I thought a bit rude. Next day I sent him a line of apology for my hesitation and a signed sketch of my uncle done in 1945. The following day a colossal Rolls-Royce drew up outside my tiny house, and the chauffeur handed me a brace of pheasant with Lord Camrose's best wishes.

When Kitty suddenly reappeared in England to wind up her marital affairs, I sought her company and sympathy. The emotional conflict started again. Kitty insisted on bringing matters to a head and having the whole thing out, as a result of which Mary asked for a divorce.

In the middle of this upset my sister Clarissa was married to Anthony Eden. She asked me to give her away because Father was no longer alive, but when we got to the registry office at Caxton Hall, Westminster, it was difficult to discharge my duties properly. Such a large number of people were surging about to get in on the occasion and be photographed with my uncle that I found myself as usual relegated to the background. As regards signing the register, a vast number of well-known guests seemed eligible for this and I was forgotten altogether. When someone remembered me I had to squeeze my signature in a corner in my smallest handwriting.

Immediately after the wedding I told my aunt and uncle of my domestic catastrophe. They commended me on the dignified way I had handled it, but were very displeased because they liked Mary. Of course they had no idea of the dreadful heartaches and complications which lay behind it, but then, who does know these intimate details of other peoples' lives?

In March, 1953, I married for the third time. Kitty and I became man and wife at Kensington Registry Office. And although the Church did not come into our wedding at all, we were to attain the highest pinnacles of extra-religious spiritual understanding. In fact, had Kitty been a less sincere woman, I think she might have become a Catholic. But she considered such a move hypocritical.

I asked Mary to look after Sally while I finished enlarging my studio in Adam and Eve Mews to turn it into a home. Strangely, and in contrast to her attitudes to Sally during our marriage, Mary suddenly became more and more possessive of the girl. When finally I asked her to hand my daughter back, she had acquired such a hold that Sally herself was unwilling to come to me. This caused me untold pain, and many upheavals were to take place as a result.

Exactly twenty years to the day after the Spanish Revolution, I took Kitty to Torremolinos to see my house there. The village had become very touristic, but the mill house, the tower, and my house, El Rosario, were untouched. Then a figure came out of the mill house. He looked astonishingly like the miller whom I had seen being taken to the quarry and thought was shot. I asked my hostess to ask him if he remembered a person named John Churchill who lived next door in 1936. He looked at me, and with a wonderful smile of dawning recognition said: "Man, it is you — who telephoned for the boat!" There was quite a confusion of embraces, in which he explained that the quarry incident was merely a little misunderstanding.

We went to Barcelona, Majorca and Corsica, where we stayed in Calvi. In the bishop's palace on the Citadel there was a sort of night club run by a fabulous Russian character called Tao. He claimed to be a brother officer of the famous Prince Yussupov who murdered the priest Rasputin, though I suspected that actually he was the prince's batman. Anyway, he was a Cossack of the old school, and we at once became brothers. His club was prohibitively expensive except for people he liked. He must have liked me a lot, for I drank a great deal and never paid him anything. He invited us to lunch just before we were going, and as a surprise arranged for the mayor, the chief of police and several other dignitaries to come up and have a drink to meet us. I thought it just as well to be on the right side of these people.

In Venice I tried to visit the Palazzo Labia to see the

famous Tiepolo frescoes again, but was refused permission on the orders of M. Bestuigi, an Argentine millionaire who owned the place. Only after a terrific Churchillian blitz was I allowed in.

Shortly before my uncle retired, Kitty and I had lunch at Downing Street with him and my aunt. My uncle was silent and pensive, and in one of his staring moods; taking in Kitty, I suppose. My aunt carried the conversation, which got around to Spain, where we had been recently. She told us she had become involved in an awkward situation. The Spanish Foreign Minister, Señor Suñer (pronounced "Soonyaire"), who was regarded as pro-Nazi during the war, had asked her if she could place his niece in a good convent school in England.

"I have managed it," she said, "but I hope I haven't done anything diplomatically wrong."

My uncle appeared to be very far away in his thoughts but was nothing of the kind. After a few moments he commented: "Well, we will know Suñer or later."

Always in my travels abroad I had marveled at the cheapness of wines in their native countries and their expensiveness by the time they reached the table in England. Surely, I thought, somebody somewhere is making too much profit and sending up the retail prices. A splendid opening must exist for an importer who was prepared to take a smaller cut. Accordingly, with hopes of establishing an income that would supplement my earnings as an artist, I started importing wine. I bought a couple of dozen casks of three types: a very good 1952 claret, an excellent white burgundy of the same year, and a Beaujolais. But I quickly ran into difficulties, discovering that other traders could not be such profiteers after all. By the time I had paid the purchase price (which turned out to be rather higher than I thought it would be), transport costs, and duty, the charge for bottling, labeling and distributing would have made the wine more expensive than its rivals.

From the outset, I hoped it would be possible to sidetrack a few bottles into my own cellar. What happened was that I was landed with the whole lot, the consolation being that I did so at cost price.

Building operations in Adam and Eve Mews continued with success, and I had a number of major commissions to take my mind off my personal worries. I did a mural for the Star Restaurant in Jersey, a huge screen for the British Embassy in Lisbon, and a series of transparent murals, painted on glass, for the first-class dining room of the new P. & O. liner *Arcadia*. This last commission was especially interesting. I happened to come across the basic idea for the technique some years before the war. I was in Bruges and visited the Hospital of St. John to study the famous masterpieces of Memlinc. After absorbing the pleasure of these great paintings, I went up to the roof of the building, where, inserted in the dormer windows on the top floor, I found a very different and fascinating spectacle: a gallery of fairy "stage sets," each about eighteen inches long and twelve high, the wings and back cloths of which were painted on five or six panes of glass placed one behind the other. They were beautifully executed in delicate eighteenth-century manner with a transparent pigment, so that they were mysteriously illuminated by the daylight outside, producing a three-dimensional effect.

As I came down the stairs, it occurred to me that here was a most original form of decoration which could be used nowadays. For quality, I have not seen anything like the Bruges examples before or since, though contemporary work of this kind, usually inferior, does exist in England and France and is known among decorators and connoisseurs as "bathroom nonsense."

Appropriately enough for the *Arcadia,* I concentrated on Arcadian-type scenes. I painted them in classical style, though one of the workmen thought differently. Beholding a centaur, he exclaimed to his mate: "Cor, this is a real modern bit of work. Here's a man with a horse's bottom!"

My *Hermes Arriving at Megalopolis* was designed to be lit by a 150-watt fluorescent light concealed above the back pane. An unexpected technical problem arose because the liner's electrical circuit could allow me only forty watts, which was not enough to counteract the reflection on the glass from the many powerful lights in the dining room. We solved this difficulty by tilting the whole "box" of panes forward. The unwanted reflections were then directed out of sight, towards the floor.

It was a most unhappy trait of Kitty's that even a book I was reading, or my work, could make her jealous. Life in such conditions can be rather tempestuous. I like to be possessed and am very possessive, but I cannot stand jealousy. I find it a thoroughly uncivilized and disruptive quality.

Kitty was jealous of the existence of Sally, but made a supreme effort to control her feelings, and eventually Sally arrived to live with us for good — or so we thought. I was building her a cottage which was not quite finished; in the meantime she stayed in a small attic room. But the cottage remained unoccupied, because she walked out one evening never to return. She was eighteen.

I was appalled to learn that she had gone to my uncle and aunt for protection, which they offered, having been primed by various tongue-waggers who had taken sides against me in my marriage. This was the only occasion on which I have ever had an unpleasant session with my uncle and aunt. I took great exception to what appeared to me an interference in my private affairs. I went along to Downing Street to discuss the matter. It was 9:30 A.M., and my uncle was in bed.

"Children," he said, handing me an enormous cigar, "very often like their nurses more than their parents. My own nurse, Mrs. Everest, was my closest and dearest friend. Mary is the same to Sally. She has looked after her all this time."

I was standing very near to him indeed, and with all the pent-up anger and frustration within me I was glad I had already made up my mind not to upset him, but to give in to him. Here was this great man, benign and fatherly as always, ready to help everyone to the best of his ability — and it was Sally he wanted to help. I thought to myself: Yes, you are indeed a most generous and won-

derful person, and even though you do not know the
terrible tensions, jealousies, and perhaps revenges which
are behind the situation, it is better for you to think you
have been advised correctly and be content, rather than
know the truth. So I said: "Perhaps you are right, Uncle
Winston," and left.

Everything was smoothed over by early September,
1955, when an unfortunate incident took place. As a result
of it we were able to see very clearly who were our friends
and who were not.

What would you do if you had occasion at 8 P.M. one
evening to complain to your neighbors in a house opposite
of the noise and inconvenience caused by their servant's
wife and children? Supposing the servant suddenly appears in the street and hits you in the face, and then, when
you have summoned the police to arrest him for assault,
they inadvertently arrest you, drag your wife from your
own house and arrest her as well. Further, let us suppose
you are marched through the streets to the police station,
where you are prevented from explaining to the sergeant
that the wrong person has been arrested. Instead, you
are searched and kicked unconscious into a cell. After
about twenty minutes you are brought before the sergeant, who, to your amazement, charges you with being
both drunk and disorderly (even though you have had
only three drinks since 3 P.M.) and tells you to appear at
the magistrates' court at 10 A.M. the following morning.
Next, still without having said anything, you are advised
to plead guilty and told that if you wish, the court will be
cleared to avoid publicity. Then you are ordered to sign

for one pound bail because you have no ready money, the alternative being a night in the cells.

All this happened to me and Kitty, and I wonder what you would have done at this juncture (a) if you were guilty and (b) if you were innocent.

With regard to (a), the answer of course is that if you were guilty and did not admit it, you would thoroughly deserve whatever penalty was demanded. But I was not guilty, and finding a solution to situation (b) was far from simple. The curious fact is that under English law it is much easier to prove an innocent man guilty than a guilty man innocent. It is entirely a matter of evidence, and anyone unsure of his strength in this direction is tempted to save a lot of bother by pretending to be guilty. Now the Churchills have one terrible characteristic. If they think they are in the wrong about a matter, they deal with it, forget it, and move on. But if they are in the right, they fight like lions to prove themselves. Well, I was in the right. I tackled my predicament with tenacity and vigor, telling the police that I would fight the case and sue them for wrongful arrest and at the same time bring an action against the servant.

The first thing I did was to ring my cousin Randolph and ask him about breaking the news to my uncle and my brother-in-law, Anthony Eden, who was Prime Minister.

"Leave it all to me," said Randolph loyally. "I will tell Papa and deal with Anthony and Clarissa. Did you say anything frightful to anyone?"

"No," I promised.

"Have you any witnesses?"

"At least one; perhaps more."

"Have *they* got any witnesses?"

"Lots."

"Hm. Doesn't sound too good."

Next day I received a charming letter from my uncle: *My dear Johnny, I am so sorry to hear of your misfortune. I hope everything will be all right. Yours affectionately, W.* But there was no communication from my sister, and except on formal occasions I have not spoken to her or my brother-in-law since! My father-in-law, Major General Beddall, came along at once. Otherwise, no one offered help. It was frightening.

After the preliminaries in the magistrate's court, two months and ten days elapsed before our case was actually finished. During this period my wife's health suffered so much that I took her to Rome for a short holiday to recover. We were on bail, of course. While we were away the police brought a third charge against me, that of using insulting language in a public highway, and I can only assume it was done to make sure of securing some kind of conviction.

By this time the story of our idiotic case — at least the police version of it — had been printed in papers all over the world in fifteen or more languages. Reluctantly I decided to stop it all by offering to plead guilty, if the police would clear my wife on lack of evidence. However, the case had gone too far and had to come up for hearing.

The affair had humorous moments, nevertheless. When I recovered in my cell on that dreadful first evening, I found a colossal red bell push by the door. It looked rather like a fire alarm, and I presumed it was for calling the warder in an emergency. I thought I would have a go at trying to make the sergeant see reason. (After all, I had had experience with the police; had I not been Officer Commanding 102 Provost Company in the retreat to Dunkirk, handling mass hysteria, criminals, spies, German prisoners, and even escaped lunatics?) So I pressed the bell push. To my astonishment, all it did was to flush a concealed water closet at the other end of the cell. In anticlimax and desolation I sat down and sang the whole of the *Mastersingers* overture (fifteen minutes) to myself and the beginning of the second act of Beethoven's *Fidelio* (eight minutes), which seemed most appropriate because it is about wrongfully imprisoned people.

The result of the case? Fined 5s. each for being drunk and disorderly, plus £10 10s. costs each and an extra 5s. fine for me for the alleged insulting language. I was supposed to have called the servant a "poof," so he said, which I am told is an obscure Welsh word for a thief. Rarely has the Churchill motto, *Faithful but Unfortunate*, been more apt.

I tell this story only to clear Kitty's name. I myself bear no ill will towards the police, and have only sympathy and friendship for them; indeed, they look after me very well to this day, and I am always anxious to assist them in their difficult work. But it was a pity I did not elect to go for trial, because I have been assured that no jury would have convicted on such slender evidence. And it was a pity I did not win.

I might add that among the more painful aspects of our

disastrous miscarriage of justice were the accusations by total strangers of my having let down my uncle and the name of Churchill. My wife and I were plagued by telephone calls. By keeping one of these cranks talking, and contacting the police on another line, we nearly caught him, in a telephone booth in Shepherds Bush. One wonders how many madmen move freely in our midst. We were also subjected to an avalanche of letters. Some of the writers were pathetically illiterate, but a great many were educated. The postmarks included places in France and America. It baffles me why such people should want to remain anonymous and therefore prevent any chance of learning the true facts of the situation. One man in the north of Scotland deigned to sign himself, though, and since his letter was a witty one, with a quotation from *As You Like It*, I thought it merited a witty reply, which I sent.

To be considered drunk when one is sober is very humiliating, but to be considered sober when in fact one is drunk is quite a different matter. Shortly after this episode we stayed for a week end with some friends in the country. It was very cold, and on the Sunday morning we went to a lovely village for a drink in one of the old taverns. We then had a date to call on an earl and his wife for a drink before lunch. As we sped through the lanes in our hostess's enormous car she said: "We really must keep the date because the poor fellow is paralytic."

Being a rather kind and sympathetic character, I agreed it would be dreadfully rude not to go to someone who was handicapped. We arrived, and indeed the noble earl was on the doorstep with his wife to greet us. I noticed he was standing on one foot and I felt genuinely sorry for him. He even appeared to limp as he escorted us into the drawing room. There was a step to the upper part of the room where the drinks were prepared. I noticed he could not manage it with only one foot and hurriedly offered to help by arranging his drinks for him. It was just as well, for he slumped into a chair and the countess took us round the house.

"You see," she explained, "he has been absolutely paralytic since nine o'clock this morning — as usual."

It was then I suddenly remembered a tip I was given during the war. When under the influence of drink and in doubt about your balance, stand on one foot.

The closing months of 1955 brought a happy commission. I returned to my old Stock Exchange firm of brokers, Vickers da Costa, to decorate their new boardroom. Then the Duke and Duchess of Marlborough invited me to do some work at Blenheim. Each duke likes to make personal contributions to the general splendor of the palace. The ninth duke, for example, built at gigantic cost the enormous Italian terraces and pools down to the lake (though I rather preferred the old rambling lawn myself). Then he devised the most extraordinary of embellishments. He had the six gigantic coffers of the ceiling of the main portico filled with huge paintings of eyes, three green and three blue, which stare down as one approaches the main door. The green ones represent those of his second wife and the blue ones are his. The present duke, who created a very fine rock garden, commissioned me to decorate one of the three temples in the grounds and paint two overdoors, each about five feet square, in the duchess's private sitting room.

To avoid causing inconvenience I worked at times when the duke and his family were away. Kitty often came as well to keep me company, and we enjoyed a superb lunch served by the Italian footmen who have long been a feature of the palace. The duke does not drink port, but for lunch one day he put at my disposal a bottle from his magnificent cellar. Afterward I decided to take Kitty on a tour of the state rooms. We had reached the Grand Cabinet, which adjoins the duchess's sitting room, when the time came for the palace to be opened to the public. One of the stewards, whose job is to protect the private quarters, therefore locked the door to the Grand Cabinet and we agreed to go back to work through the door to the duchess's apartments. But when I had finished pointing out the pictures, one of which is of my mother by Orpen, which I do not like much, I found the duchess's door locked as well. The palace is so vast that to have made oneself heard in such circumstances would have needed a foghorn. We were marooned. So I climbed out onto the window ledge and jumped. One of the hazards of living in palaces is that the extra-large doors, windows, fireplaces, and even furniture begin to seem of normal size. What I took to be an ordinary ground-floor window sill proved to be ten feet off the ground. I leaped out and landed on the stone on my back. Perhaps it was the port.

In 1957, building operations at my house and studio in Adam and Eve Mews were completed, and I executed various internal and external mural decorations, particularly in the garden, which has high walls and catches the sun. Soon after Christmas my favorite kitten was born. It was Kitty, who looked somewhat like a kitten and had very feline ways, who introduced me to the world of cats. When we married she moved in with four of them. There was the "Queen Mum," called Princess Natasha Louise Tania of Imperial Russia; a harlequin tortoise shell and her son Pompey, a ginger tom, by whom she very wickedly, but permissibly in the cat world, had another tom born the year before, on my birthday. He was named Prince John of Mindelheim in Swabia, a Marlborough title from Blenheim days. Pompey had a look round the place for about two hours and vanished. He reappeared four days later in Kitty's house in Chelsea and stayed there until he died. He had gall bladder trouble.

The kitten born that Christmas is jet-black and called the Lady Arabella. She is the ideal artist's cat. She sits with me when I work, smiles, and talks to me a great deal. She is now almost four. Prince John, who is seven, is very highly strung and a latent queer. He has a passion for music, and when ladies are singing he lies on his back with paws outstretched. All our cats are members of the Dustbin Club. But only Natasha, who died in 1958, was a D.D. — Dame of the Dustbins.

These were happy and industrious days with much painting. Kitty gave me her piano for my birthday. She did not play herself and the instrument was purely ornamental. It was a Stodart Oblong Grand, dated about 1795, I believe, and it did not work. At once I took it to Mr.

Horwood at Steinway's to be restored to action — a major operation. Kitty had bought it in the King's Road, Chelsea, for five pounds; Steinway's made it work for fifty pounds. They only did it out of love for our family. Both Mr. Spring and Mr. Sharp, and I believe Mr. Flat, got on to the job, and one complete room became a mass of bits and pieces, hammers and wires. After this experience I began to collect pianos. I bought an 1820 Oblong Grand at an auction for £3 10s., and my patron Ralph Vickers produced one from the country, made in 1775, which cost £6 10s. But it proved to be too difficult to mend these instruments.

When Dr. Simpson, the owner of the important store in Piccadilly which bears his name, commissioned me to paint a mural for its Clover Room restaurant, he gave me *carte blanche*. The space to be filled was rather disconcerting, because it was twenty-one feet long and four feet high; in other words, more than five times its own height. I chose a view of London from the South Bank as my subject and did a very rough cartoon, which was immediately accepted. This was an ideal thing to happen. Imagination is needed to visualize from a cartoon what the full-scale version is going to look like, but luckily Dr. Simpson possesses that imagination. Furthermore, he did not bother me during the preparation or execution. He is a perfect patron; but then, he paints very well himself.

Kitty and I set aside two months for the research work on details of the design. We walked from Tower Bridge right down to the west side of Battersea Bridge, both making copious notes of the various architectural sky lines of the North Bank. I was anxious to view the whole scene from

the Shot Tower, on the site of the 1951 Festival of Britain
Exhibition, but the London County Council refused permission. They pointed out that they were not insured for
accidents. This seemed incredibly stupid of them, but the
tower has no balcony (which I did not realize at the time
of making my application), and I suppose they thought I
was planning a dramatic suicide. However, I managed to
obtain a mass of information from the Council's architectural, survey and photographic departments. Finally I was
allowed to go up on the roofs of the County Hall and the
Festival Hall.

When we completed our research, a specially made piece
of canvas twenty-one feet long was stretched out in my
studio, and I drew the general design. Then began the difficult process of elimination, deciding which details to put
in and which to leave out. The date for finishing and displaying the mural in the restaurant was fixed for July 2. By
the first week in June it was nearly ready. The style was
very free and the result is most satisfying, so I am told. We
got very excited. Then, quite suddenly and without warning, something terrible happened that was to change my
life again. A tragedy descended.

Kitty never liked the idea of children, though I dare say
that if she'd had one she would have adored it. Many
years previously, during her first marriage, she had complicated septic trouble which she and her medical advisers
thought debarred her from any possibility of having a
child. In view of her adverse feelings towards children,
this did not worry her. She was inclined to be scornful of
doctors and hospitals, and being of a tough and healthy

physique, it was difficult for anybody, including herself, to tell if anything was wrong with her. So when she felt rather ill in the beginning of June, no one suspected she was pregnant; still less did anyone guess that it was an ectopic pregnancy, in the Fallopian tubes. A condition such as this is dangerous after six weeks. Normally it is diagnosed quite easily and operated on at once. Kitty, in fact, was nine weeks pregnant.

On Sunday, June 23, I painted her portrait. She was in great discomfort some of the time, and with difficulty I persuaded her to enter a nursing home to be properly examined under anaesthesia.

The examination, on the following Tuesday, June 25, caused a hemorrhage. Kitty died that afternoon, without regaining consciousness.

The shock was so tremendously deep that when I went in and kissed her, I turned to the nun by my side and asked: "Is she really dead? Are you sure it is not a relapse — can't we massage her heart?"

"Yes, she is dead," the nun replied quietly. "We have tried everything we can. She is very, very beautiful."

Kitty was buried in the family churchyard at Bladon, near Blenheim Palace. I arranged for a memorial service to be held at the same time in the famous Old Chelsea Church, next to which she lived for most of her life, and of which she had done many paintings. Leslie Woodgate of the British Broadcasting Corporation kindly loaned me the B.B.C. Choral Singers, who sang Bach's *St. Matthew Passion* chorale, No. 72: "Be near me, Lord, when dying."

I began to participate in the spiritual life and prayer for which I had been training myself for so long. And the memory of Kitty gave me strength in my deep solitude and sadness.

X

Today and Tomorrow

IN MY DISTRESSED STATE I wished to see absolutely
no one. I am not much good at looking after myself,
and it soon became a matter of either eating something or
dying of starvation. Kitty, who was a first-class Provençal
cook, had left a small notebook. It was the beginning of a
collection of special recipes and contained several dishes I
had watched her prepare. So I threw myself into cooking,
using her little book. When I started I could not boil an
egg, but I soon mastered the recipes and they kept me
alive during this sorrowful time.

In the autumn I arranged to meet Sally in Venice. It
was a happy and consoling reunion for me because she
was sweet and understanding. When we returned to London I had to apply myself to finishing the Simpson mural.
This was difficult. But at last the thrilling moment came
when the end was in sight. Usually about ten days beforehand I can name the exact hour when a work will be completed. In this way I have always finished my commissions
on schedule.

The opening day had been postponed to October. My

mural was safely in position on time, and the large crowd
which duly assembled included several critics. I will di-
gress here about critics, and about art dealers, because I
have never depended on, or paid attention to, any of
them. In fact, I have never had an exhibition in a gallery,
even in nearly thirty years' painting. Officially speaking,
therefore, nobody has ever heard of me, and one might
wonder in the circumstances how I have achieved anything at all. However, I have executed no less than sixty-
two murals of different kinds, and this has not been due to
either critics or dealers. Furthermore, it has enabled me
to live, because the latter usually take 33 per cent and
sometimes as much as 50 per cent of an artist's commission. It was my master William Nicholson who gave me
some important advice.

"Critics," he said, "are dangerous because they rarely do
good, yet can cause much harm. They are often unsuc-
cessful and frustrated artists, frustrated would-be artists,
or just queer artists with a sour disposition. Very few have
any profound knowledge, and still less the ability to write
constructive criticism of art."

The really classic example of the frustrated critic was
the hate and loathing that the music critic Hanslick directed at Wagner. He tried his damnedest to destroy the
great composer. But Wagner, whose powerful music easily
withstood the onslaught, had the extreme pleasure of seeing Hanslick writhing in ridicule in the rôle of Beckmesser in *The Mastersingers*.

Then come the dealers, and first let me expose the experts on so-called "old masters." A great friend of mine

was one of the best picture restorers in England, and he let me into quite a few secrets which I feel had better be kept. I have found that experts do know their stuff and their scholarship usually enables them to say, for example, if a painting is genuine. The iniquitous side of the business arises when the expert on such-and-such a painter holds the monopoly and has the power to lay down the ruling on whether a canvas is by that painter. His verdict can depend on what is convenient for him financially. I know of a case where a genuine picture is not by the master simply because *the* expert says it is not. It would weaken the value of certain other paintings by the same artist.

With regard to living painters, the situation is even more alarming. Painters may be good or they may be indifferent; they may be sincere artists or charlatans. None of this affects the dealer. He, naturally enough, is interested in eating, and to eat one must have money. So he will examine a picture with a view to selling it in the same way that a theatrical producer judges a script — and there have been some pretty moronic scripts which have made producers money on the stage.

As far as charlatan painters are concerned, their vicissitudes can influence the tastes of the unintelligent but wealthy buying public. A scruffy individual whose name has ten consonants and one vowel, and who has lived on rats while trekking across Europe to London, has a very good chance of being able to hold an exhibition. If his style of painting consists of throwing a handful of matches at an adhesive board, setting fire to it and putting out the blaze with an extinguisher, so much the better. He is a dead cert from the selling point of view. Everyone is happy. Eccentric ladies with faces like horses will come and sip the dealer's vodka and buy the painter's efforts, and the critics, having been fixed, will acclaim the new wonder boy.

What can easily happen next is unfortunate for the dealer because the wonder boy becomes the protégé of one of the female horses, and from then on the dealer, who has taken the risks, receives no more commission. As a safeguard against this contingency, astute dealers put promising artists under contract. I know of a case where a very good painter with an individual style was signed up by a dealer to place all his work through him in return for a steady income. The dealer then made the artist fashionable, and promptly reaped the rewards. The artist meanwhile battles along on his modest allowance, creating lovely paintings for next to nothing. The French dealers have done a marvelous job with popularizing Picasso and Matisse, but rightly so; they are both good artists. A good time has been had by all.

What the critics said about my Simpson mural, Opus 86: *London from the South Bank,* or whether they said anything at all, I have not the slightest idea. I am very lucky not to have to care, because, being highly self-critical, I move on without being influenced by schools, isms, movements, and what have you. My only aim is to fulfill my artistic aspirations and produce the best work I can at the time. That was the advice of William Nicholson. Sticking to it has brought me not only great artistic satisfaction, but also an ever-widening circle of friends and patrons. Men and women famous in all walks of life come to my studio. The occasion of the first sitting for a portrait is always an event, and I find the sizing up by both parties — me studying the sitter, and the sitter studying me — an intriguing challenge. If a sitter is ill at ease in the unaccustomed business of posing, I play relaxing gramophone records. To hold my daughter Sally's attention I used an American record about the Kinsey Report. Her expression at once became very intense. When a sitter has left the studio, I never use models for filling in details as some artists do, the great water-colorist Russell Flint in particular. In my opinion there is no substitute for the real thing. The knowledge that when the sitter has gone nothing more can be obtained concentrates one's mind wonderfully, and one omits unessentials.

In November, 1957, Sally married Colin Crewe, a Lloyd's broker whose half sister, Mary O'Neil, was one of the girls accompanying me on my first visit to Rome twenty-eight years previously. One gets so bored with Mendelssohn at weddings that I set about writing down the Wedding March in A Major which I composed in Austria before the war. It was played at the ceremony in Grosvenor Chapel. I gave Sally a huge reception-dance at the Swedish Embassy. About four hundred friends were invited, but over a hundred gate crashers arrived too. Her mother Angela came, and we got on very well together. The past was the past, we found.

Soon after this I had a spiritual message from Kitty. A

mutual friend of ours had a dream so vivid that she rang me up specially.

"I saw Kitty," she said. "She was very happy, and in a flat with a tall, fair-haired woman who I think was a journalist."

Psychic matters make me a little wary. I am not at all psychic myself, though I am prepared to accept the possibility of another existence different from ours. I thought no more of the mysterious "message."

The following spring I held a party at my studio, and one of my guests was a Swedish lady, Lullan Boston, whom Kitty and I had met in 1957, and whom Kitty liked. By chance she had come round to our house about ten days before Kitty died. She had mentioned that her husband was ill. What I did not know when I invited her to my party was that he had recently died in tragic circumstances. Being in the same state of distress myself, I found her company very consoling. I also discovered that she already knew Mary, my second wife, and I introduced her to Angela, my first wife.

Lullan and I were married at Kensington Registry Office on August 27. Her vitality and controlling influence enabled me to begin creative work again. I composed a Wedding March in E Major, but had no time to write it down, and it could not be played. In fact, the entire ceremony was a rush. Ten minutes before it was due to begin, I suddenly realized I had been so busy preparing the celebration lunch that I had forgotten to shave. We got to the registry office just in time.

Lullan does not play any instrument, but she is as inter-

ested in music as she is in painting. She at once produced
a whole collection of records of Scandinavian music, including of course Sibelius. When we went for our first
holiday in France, we naturally had to have a piano. So
for my birthday I received an upright Parisian Playl in
rosewood, which we take to wherever we move to in
France. This is my sixth piano. I love them all.

My wife has a son, Charles Sands, by her first husband,
and the three of us were invited down to Chartwell for my
uncle's birthday in 1958. It was an intimate little family
party, in delightful contrast to the vast Downing Street
affairs. Randolph was there, and towards the end of lunch
he began to tell me a story in an undertone. This did not
please my uncle, who was deep in conversation with
Charlie.

"What are you saying," he asked, "and why the undertone?"

"I am only telling Johnny a silly story I told you yester-
day," Randolph explained. "I didn't want to bore you
with it."

"Well, don't bore Johnny with it!" said my uncle.

But Randolph got his own back, for at the same lunch
my uncle ticked off the butler for filling his glass with so
much hock that he could not finish it.

"Why not use proper hock glasses instead of tumblers,"
Randolph suggested. "Then there would be no possibility
of a glass holding too much."

"Mind your own business," snapped my uncle.

Randolph pointed out: "I am only trying to help you
mind yours!"

The truth is that Randolph and I have always been regarded by our parents as children. If my father were alive today, my painting would still be termed "playing the ass in the gutter," and talking to a lady would be "playing the ass in the bulrushes." In my uncle's formidable presence, of course, I have always felt very much a junior. I remember a lunch at Chartwell many years ago when I put to him the theory that sound waves have a surprising affinity to light rays. "Take the twelve notes, including the sharps, of the central octave on a piano keyboard," I said, "and place on them the rainbow divided into primary, secondary and tertiary colors. Take middle C, for example, and put vermilion on it. C major is red-orange; D is orange; D major yellow-orange; E yellow; F yellow-green; F major green, and G blue-green. Strike the chord of C major and you will find you have a major chord in color — red, yellow and blue-green. This was the color theme of almost all of Raphael's Madonnas and children."

My uncle digested this in silence, and then, failing to believe that a *child* could produce such a theory — it was not a new one by any means — he turned and asked the opinion of the Prof, who was lunching with us that day. The Prof, being opposed to any scientific knowledge reaching my uncle except through himself, vetoed it at once.

"The analogy is impossible because of the difference in the speeds of sound and light," he said.

And so I was back again where I started, just Johnny the child.

It so happens that my uncle and my stepson share the same birth date, November 30. When we attended the

1958 birthday celebrations at Chartwell, the discovery of this caused quite a situation. Immediately a complete set of volumes of my uncle's *History of the English-Speaking Peoples* was produced and inscribed for Charlie. Randolph and I looked on in wonderment. It was a rare occasion. Neither of us ever get such V.I.P. treatment.

In the private cinema in the evening we saw a rather racy film starring my uncle's daughter Sarah. The opening shots were of a couple with bicycles getting up from a ditch in semi-undress. To miss the point of that shot was to miss the point of the entire film. But my uncle missed it, and we had to explain it all to him afterward. As a matter of fact he often has difficulty in following the quick sequence of a film presentation. We both have one thing in common, though — in cinemas and theaters we pour tears at the slightest provocation.

Having for many years observed enormous stacks of cigars of all kinds in his study at Chartwell, I once decided on a cursory investigation into what he proposed to do with them. I wondered if perhaps he might sidetrack a box to his nephew. At the end of the meal, having chosen a Partagas and lit it, I remarked that I preferred Partagas, Romeo and Juliet, and Punch. "Have you any preference, Uncle Winston?" I asked.

"No," he said. "I have all these cigars sent by a friend in Havana and find them very nice. Do you know, I have three thousand of them upstairs."

"Three thousand!" I exclaimed. "What are you going to do with them?"

"Well," he said, "I am smoking them as fast as I can."

That was 1959.

During the summer of that year, Jo Mattli, the dress designer, looked at the vine I had planted in our garden and recognized it as a Brandt, an ideal variety for wine making. It was bearing two hundred bunches of grapes. The previous year we had thrown the grapes away because they tasted so dreadful, but acting on Jo's advice we picked the latest crop and put them in a barrel. Then I stamped on them with naked feet in the traditional manner, added a bottle of brandy, and bottled the wine, which is like a vin rosé and cannot be drunk for about two years. We call it *Chateau Adam and Eve 1959*, and eventually it will take an honored place in my drinking schedule. We made fifteen bottles.

I keep to a fairly strict routine for drink. I enjoy it as much as I do my daily sessions of listening to music, and vary it from time to time, just as in music one moves from Bach to Sibelius and then to Mozart.

On rising at 7 A.M., I have a lemon juice and hot water, but with no sugar. The citric acid becomes an alkali on reaching the stomach; also the juice has vitamin C. I then drink a considerable amount of tea, China and Indian mixed, followed by a lot of coffee. In view of the tannic acid and caffeine in these respective beverages, I confine my enjoyment of them to this early hour. For elevenses I have a glass of ruby port from the wood and a digestive biscuit if it is very cold; alternatively, a glass of stout or beer. Abroad it is a glass of vin rosé. For the midday apéritif I have a pink gin, Bols gin or a schnapps of some sort. In France I prefer a Pastis, Pernod or Ricard; in

Spain a dopla of Manzanilla. I might even vary this with Japanese sake. At lunchtime I have half a bottle of claret or a pint of beer, and for liqueurs a kümmel, calvados or brandy, but not always. "Teatime" is the occasion for a whisky and soda or two, followed by some sort of gin drink. Dry sherry or Manzanilla is my evening apéritif, and at dinner I open another half bottle of claret. When entertaining, this is preceded by a dry white wine and champagne, and followed by port and brandy. At about 10 P.M. I start whiskies and sodas at approximately half-hourly intervals until about 3 A.M. or 4 A.M. if I am working late, when I go on to lemon juice and water. At midnight, if I have guests, I might follow my mother's example and have Russian tea.

The result of this program is that I feel half my age and very healthy.

In every way, 1959 was a great year for us. There were two new arrivals. The first was a very small person in the form of the Princess Sophie Louise of Sweden, a long-haired tabby kitten of immense distinction. This led to a special Fiftieth Birthday Honors List being made. The black kitten Lady Arabella was raised to the rank of Duchess of Catalunia and Countess of Barcelona in her own right. Prince John was made a K.D. — Knight of the Dustbins. Next, after a happy birthday party for my wife Lullan on July 11, my daughter Sally went home and gave birth to a son, Peregrine John Crewe, the next morning. This important event culminated my half-century. I like being a grandfather.

What is in store for tomorrow?

The first Duke of Marlborough was fifty-two when he fought the battle of Blenheim. My uncle was sixty-four when he attained his greatest rôle.

I still have time for the uplands of greater achievement.